The Gender Question
in Education

The Gender Question in Education

Theory, Pedagogy, and Politics

ANN DILLER, BARBARA HOUSTON,

KATHRYN PAULY MORGAN,

& MARYANN AYIM

with a Foreword by Jane Roland Martin

WestviewPress

A Division of HarperCollins*Publishers*

Portions of Chapter 6 were first published as "Theorizing Gender: How Much of It Do We Need?" in *Educational Philosophy and Theory*. Copyright ©1991 *Educational Philosophy and Theory*.

Copyright © 1996 by Westview Press, Inc., A Division of HarperCollins Publishers, Inc.

Published in 1996 in the United States of America by Westview Press, Inc., 5500 Central Avenue, Boulder, Colorado 80301-2877, and in the United Kingdom by Westview Press, 12 Hid's Copse Road, Cumnor Hill, Oxford OX2 9JJ

Library of Congress Cataloging-in-Publication Data
The gender question in education : theory, pedagogy, and politics /
    Ann Diller . . . [et al.].
      p.   cm.
    Includes bibliographical references and index.
    ISBN 0-8133-2562-5 (hardcover) — ISBN 0-8133-2563-3 (pbk.)
    1. Sex differences in education. 2. Sex discrimination in
education. 3. Sexism in education. 4. Politics and education.
I. Diller, Ann.
LC212.9.G45   1996
370.19'345—dc20   95-41944
                                                                                    CIP

The paper used in this publication meets the requirements of the American National Standard for Permanence of Paper for Printed Library Materials Z39.48-1984.

10   9   8   7   6   5   4   3   2   1

For our Mothers,
Grace Ella Hamilton Snelbaker
Ellen Houston
Estelle Sophia Kummer Pauly
Anne Mercy Cassidy Neely

Contents

Foreword, JANE ROLAND MARTIN   ix
Acknowledgments   xi

Introduction
ANN DILLER   1

Part One: Theory

1 A Conceptual Analysis of Sexism and Sexist Education
   MARYANN AYIM & BARBARA HOUSTON   9

   SUBPART ONE: SHOULD PUBLIC EDUCATION
   BE GENDER FREE?

2 Genderized Education: Tradition Reconsidered
   MARYANN AYIM   32

3 Freeing the Children: The Abolition of Gender
   KATHRYN PAULY MORGAN   41

4 Gender Freedom and the Subtleties of Sexist Education
   BARBARA HOUSTON   50

5 The Androgynous Classroom: Liberation or Tyranny?
   KATHRYN PAULY MORGAN   64

6 Theorizing Gender: How Much of It Do We Need?
   BARBARA HOUSTON   75

Part Two: Pedagogy

7 The Ethics of Care and Education: A New Paradigm,
   Its Critics, and Its Educational Significance
   ANN DILLER   89

8   Describing the Emperor's New Clothes: Three Myths of
    Educational (In-)Equity
    KATHRYN PAULY MORGAN   105

        SUBPART TWO: FEMINIST PEDAGOGY AND
              THE ETHICS OF CARE

9   The Perils and Paradoxes of the Bearded Mothers
    KATHRYN PAULY MORGAN   124

10 Is Rapprochement Possible Between Educational Criticism
    and Nurturance?
    ANN DILLER   135

11 Role Models: Help or Hindrance in the Pursuit of Autonomy?
    BARBARA HOUSTON   144

Part Three: Politics

12 An Ethics of Care Takes On Pluralism
    ANN DILLER   161

13 The Moral Politics of Sex Education
    KATHRYN PAULY MORGAN   170

14 Women's Physical Education: A Gender-Sensitive Perspective
    ANN DILLER & BARBARA HOUSTON   179

15 Political Correctness: The Debate Continues
    MARYANN AYIM   199

References   215
About the Book and Authors   239
Index   241

Foreword

What with the poverty question, the illiteracy question, the math and science question, and the question of multiculturalism, it is only too easy for teachers, school administrators, and even parents to forget just how important the gender question in education really is. The authors of this wonderful volume of essays not only remind us of gender's centrality in education but also provide us with immensely helpful ways in which to think and talk about gender and education.

For more than 2,000 years—indeed, ever since Plato wrote in the *Republic* that sex is a difference that makes no difference—philosophical discussions of gender and education have swung back and forth between two extreme positions. The parties to the historical conversation about gender and education have either denied the relevance of gender to education or insisted that gender is the difference that makes all the difference. Neither answer to the gender question in education is satisfactory.

Those who opt for gender *freedom* or *neutrality* appear to be on the side of the angels. Starting from the valid premise that both males and females are human beings, they correctly conclude that both sexes are entitled to the full rights of citizenship. Unfortunately, from the simple fact of universal citizenship, nothing whatsoever follows about gender's bearing on education. As it happens, study after study of education has revealed that gender does make a difference to education, and an enormous one at that.[1]

It should come as no surprise that gender is relevant to education. Having projected it not just onto our own species but also onto our social and natural worlds, we humans could scarcely have been expected to create a gender-free educational system. Yet, although those who insist that gender does bear on education are correct, it is a grave mistake to adopt the extreme gender-bound approach to education that many do. Entailing separate educational tracks for girls and boys that lead in opposite directions, this stance effectively rejects both the common humanity of the two sexes and the centuries-old struggle for gender equality.

Fortunately, there is another answer to the gender question in education. It is possible to be sensitive to the workings of gender whenever and wherever gender makes a difference to education without endorsing the two-track system that was historically so oppressive to girls and women. In this volume, Ann Diller, Barbara Houston, Kathryn Pauly Morgan, and Maryann Ayim have adopted this alternative. Whether their subject be sexism or sex education, women's physical education or the ethics of care, political correctness or the androgynous classroom, or for that matter gender theory itself, they have unfailingly developed gender-sensitive analyses. In the process, they have cast education's aims, its curricula, its institutional structures, its pedagogies, and its practices in a brilliant new light.

Jane Roland Martin

Notes

1. See, for example, American Association of University Women, *How Schools Shortchange Girls* (1992); Peggy Orenstein, *School Girls* (New York: Doubleday, 1994); Roberta M. Hall and Bernice R. Sandler, *The Classroom Climate: A Chilly One for Women?* (Washington, DC: Project on the Status of Women, 1982); Margaret Clark, *The Great Divide* (Canberra: Curriculum Development Centre, 1989); Dale Spender and Elizabeth Sarah, eds., *Learning to Lose* (London: Women's Press, 1980).

Acknowledgments

The chapters in this book reflect more than two decades of philosophical investigations by all four of us. During these years so many people have contributed to our work that we cannot possibly name everyone here. Each of us has, therefore, forced ourselves to hone down our acknowledgments to a shortened list of persons vital to our work and to the production of this book.

In addition to our individual acknowledgments, we would like to express our collective gratitude to literally thousands of students and hundreds of colleagues at the University of New Hampshire, the University of Toronto, and the University of Western Ontario, as well as to the members of the Canadian Society for the Study of Education, the Canadian Society for Women in Philosophy, the Canadian Women's Studies Association, the National Women's Studies Association, and the Philosophy of Education Society for providing the occasions, audiences, encouragement, challenges, and critiques that fostered the growth of this volume.

We want to thank all of the staff at Westview Press for their fine work on this book. Spencer Carr, Cindy Rinehart, Jennifer Blandford, and Shena Redmond each played crucial roles at different stages. Linda Carlson's meticulous and thorough copyediting deserves special mention—any remaining errors are mine not hers.

This book is dedicated to our mothers. My own mother, Grace Hamilton Snelbaker, who graduated from Ohio State in 1926 with a degree in Home Economics, never could teach me how to sew; but she did teach me how to live, how to do philosophy, and how to practice an ethics of care. Completely honest and unwavering in her pursuit of truth, my mother would not let a perceived falsehood, hasty generalization, or unwarranted conclusion slip past her. She tempered her strong streak of Scottish skepticism with a cheerful sense of humor, compassionate action, and a sympathetic disposition. As a mother myself, I want to acknowledge my debt to my two sons, John Andrew and David Daniel Diller, who have not only brought much joy to my life but have also made me a better teacher, opened up my concept of gender, and expanded my sense of educational possibilities. Ever since the late 1960s my philosophic work has been sustained by the meetings of Phaedra. I am grateful to Phaedra's steadfast members, past and present, Nancy Clover Glock, Beatrice Nelson, Jane Roland Martin, Jennifer Radden, Janet Farrell Smith, Barbara Houston, and Susan Franzosa for the constructive candor of their critiques and the perceptive persistence of their encouragement. Other colleagues and friends toward whom I feel a strong debt of gratitude include

Michael Andrew, Ellen Corcoran, Margaret Crowley, Karl Diller, Carol Hochstedler, Susan Laird, Carl Menge, Nel Noddings, Stuart Palmer, Israel Scheffler, and William Wallace. A large heartfelt thanks goes to my co-authors Maryann Ayim, Kathryn Pauly Morgan, and especially Barbara Houston, for their contributions to this volume, for philosophical colleague-ship, and for wonderful friendships. The labors of Michaele Canfield, valued friend and invaluable secretary, have been vital to the production of this book at every stage. I cannot thank her enough.

Ann Diller

In many ways my deepest debt of gratitude is to my mother Ellen Houston who, with enormous courage, determination, and passionate hope, strug-gled to create for me educational opportunities that she herself never had. I am grateful to my father, Edward Houston, for his nurturance. Early morn-ing porridge and more recently seven-grain bread bespeak his love more than he knows. I thank him for teaching me to reason, to care about doing things well, to play baseball, and for cultivating my sense of morality and my sense of humor. His own sense of humor has made him a teacher I've wanted to listen to. John Diller I thank for his philosophically engaging conversations and for being so willing to share himself when it matters most. David Diller's quiet integrity and kindness are an inspiration, his hu-mor and sense of adventure a joy to share. The "Hags and Crones" of London, Ontario, in particular Gillian Michell and Kathleen Okruhlik, have provided me the best feminist counsel and support one could wish. I want also to enthusiastically thank many other friends and colleagues who have provided me with support, astute criticism, and stimulating conversa-tions. I cannot name them all, but special thanks are owed to Dwight Boyd, Kai Nielsen, Maureen Ford, Nel Noddings, Mike Andrew, Kay Munson, Barbara Brockelman, Denise Connors, Margaret Crowley, and the mem-bers of Phaedra: Jane Martin, Ann Diller, Jennifer Radden, Beebe Nelson, Susan Franzosa, and Janet Farrell Smith. I think no words can convey my profound appreciation for the wonderful philosophical friendships I have had with my coauthors: Maryann Ayim, Kathryn Morgan, and especially Ann Diller whose careful and caring labors are chiefly responsible for the publication of this book.

Barbara Houston

Many thanks go, first and foremost, to my mother, Estelle Kummer Pauly, for providing me not only with nurturance, understanding, and lunch but also with the striking image of a Catholic mother of five, up late at night, exploring tomes of speculative Thomistic metaphysics, her household finally at rest. My thanks, too, go to my father, Leon Pauly, M.D., who integrated his empirical bent as a much-loved physician with his support of his philosopher/daughter. I wish, too, to thank my son Daniel Christopher Pauly, whose antics, insights, and demands for integrity have found their way into my published work more than once. My appreciation should also go to my four brothers and to a series of ill-fated philosopher partners who have helped me sharpen my philosophical wits. I also wish to acknowledge the importance of Jane Roland Martin in being the first to say to me, "Your work is good enough to publish," and for continuing to affirm that throughout my personal and professional life. My students and colleagues in the Women's Studies Programme at the University of Toronto and my feminist colleagues at the Ontario Institute for Studies in Education have been a continuing source of support and courage in my "dark nights of the professional soul" when it looked like unemployment, part-time teaching, and sessional appointments might never end. Many friends and colleagues have provided me with invaluable challenges and reflections. I am especially grateful to Martha Ayim, Dwight Boyd, Paula Caplan, Roi Daniels, Maureen Ford, June Larkin, Nel Noddings, David Nyberg, Allen Pearson, Barbara Secker and Ronald de Sousa. Finally, last but certainly not least, this collection speaks to my experience of the delight, the power, and the fruitfulness of the rich philosophical friendships I have been privileged to enjoy with my coauthors: Maryann Ayim, Ann Diller, and Barbara Houston.

Kathryn Pauly Morgan

In a book dedicated to our mothers, it feels especially appropriate to me to formally acknowledge my daughter, Martha Ayim, who is for me a constant source of feminist inspiration and as much a friend as a daughter. I wish to acknowledge also the many years of competent and cheerful labor on these and other manuscripts by my co-workers/secretaries: Stephanie Macleod and Linda Colvin, in the Educational Policies Division, Faculty of Education, The University of Western Ontario. My indebtedness to colleagues who have encouraged my writing, who have engaged in passionate discussions of research topics I was exploring, and who have provided me with invaluable feedback on more and less primitive versions of my work is too extensive to be recorded here. Were I ever to catalogue this debt, however, my coauthors of this book, Barbara Houston, Ann Diller, and Kathryn Pauly Morgan, along with Joan Barfoot, Kathleen Okruhlik, Andrew Blair, Leslie Thielen-Wilson, Martha Ayim, and Jim Mullin would be at the top of the list.

Maryann Ayim

We gratefully acknowledge the following organizations for granting us permission to reprint portions of work that was first published in these publications: *Educational Theory*, Philosophy of Education Society; *Philosophy of Education: Canadian Perspectives*, Maxwell-Macmillan; *Women, Philosophy, and Sport: A Collection of New Essays*, The Scarecrow Press, Inc.; *Curriculum Inquiry*, Blackwell Publishers; and *Educational Philosophy and Theory*.

The Gender Question in Education

Introduction

ANN DILLER

We have designed this volume to be a clear, accessible introduction to gender questions in education. In one sense, this is a how-to book for anyone to use as a set of starting points and guidelines for sustained analysis of gender and education. In another sense, we envision the book as an open invitation to continue the conversation and to further advance investigations into the theory, pedagogy, and politics of gender in education.

Although the volume as a whole constitutes a series of inquiries into the gender question in education, the three parts mark a progressive differentiation in emphasis. Part 1 focuses on theory. Part 2 moves back and forth between theory and practical questions of pedagogy. And Part 3 applies theory to specific problems of practice and politics. Readers may, however, choose to jump about, or "read backwards" so to speak; those with urgent interests in pedagogy or politics may want to leap directly into Parts 2 and 3. For those who wish to read selectively, the next section of this introduction gives a preview for each part, with short chapter by chapter summaries. We do recommend, in any case, that you read this entire introduction first; it provides the contextual framework, and connecting links, for better understanding the individual chapters.

The central theme of the entire volume, both as text and subtext, is that of a *gender-sensitive* perspective on education. The concept of a gender-sensitive ideal for education was first suggested by Jane Roland Martin in a presidential address to the Philosophy of Education Society (Martin [1981b] 1994, pp. 70–87). Martin's gender-sensitive critique of the standard ideal of the educated person, which still dominated Anglo-American philosophy of education at that time, electrified, and in some instances horrified, her audience. When Martin made the case that this traditional ideal reflects a male cognitive perspective and does harm to both men and women, she catapulted the Society's members to a new level of public philosophical dialogue about gender and education.

1

Shortly after Martin's introduction of her gender-sensitive perspective, the four authors of this book came together, as feminist philosophers of education from Canada and the United States, to initiate plans for our first joint symposium: "Should Public Education Be Gender Free?" Thus began our ongoing collaborative inquiries and philosophical dialogues, which continue to the present day and led to this collection of essays.

All four authors use a gender-sensitive methodology in this book. The same persistent question recurs throughout our inquiries: What do we discover when we pay careful, systematic, sensitive attention to the difference that gender makes in educational thought and practice? And the answer, in broad terms, is that a gender-sensitive approach leads us to discover both new critiques and new possibilities. In some chapters we are more preoccupied with critique, in others with possibility; in a number of chapters we include both.

On the critique side, a gender-sensitive perspective uncovers the extensive effects and harmful consequences of society's gender discrimination, which inevitably intrudes upon education and can even undermine our best pedagogical practices. On the possibilities side, taking a gender-sensitive perspective on education can open up new angles of vision, expand our range of alternatives, alter our priorities, change our preoccupations, and help us to think more creatively about long-standing educational problems.

In Part 1 we begin with some theoretical basics: What do we mean by *sexism*? How can we explain well-intentioned disagreements over what counts as sexism? Which analyses lead us to say that someone can be well meaning and yet still be acting in a sexist manner? How can we recognize sexist education? Maryann Ayim and Barbara Houston discuss these questions in Chapter 1, where they guide us through the process of identifying and assessing various forms of sexism and sexist education. Ayim and Houston show how disagreements can arise when we shift our focus from questions about sexist intentions to ask instead about the existence of sexist content or to inquire into the occurrence of sexist consequences.

Ayim and Houston also address common concerns about the way we use the term sexism and draw helpful distinctions for its use. For example, they remind us to distinguish between the act of assessing something as morally objectionable (e.g., sexist) and the further, separate move of imputing moral blame. In the final section of Chapter 1, Ayim and Houston demonstrate the application of their analyses to five educational cases.

Once we glimpse the pervasive complexities of sexism and its links with our educational experiences, we start to question what we should do about all of this. In the first subpart, each of the three interconnected chapters sets forth an alternative vision of how gender should be treated in public education. The first alternative offers a traditional form of education in which girls and boys are taught their own clearly differentiated, socially determined gender roles (Chapter 2). The second alternative outlines an education that aims to free both sexes from externally imposed gender roles and from genderized expectations or restrictions by abolishing all gender differentiation from our schools and classroom practices (Chapter 3). Finally, the third alternative argues for the adoption of a gender-sensitive form of education that undertakes to eliminate gender bias by developing a critical awareness of the meaning and evaluation we attach to gender (Chapter 4).

The three alternatives discussed in the subpart do not, of course, exhaust the educational possibilities. Thus, in Chapter 5, Kathryn Morgan looks at another, sometimes popular, alternative. Well before the appearance of postmodernist deconstructions of gender, the ideal of androgyny provided one way to move beyond gender polarities. But when Morgan investigates the possibility of using androgyny as an educational ideal to remedy sexism in the classroom, she discovers three major difficulties: (1) conceptual confusions, (2) pragmatic problems, and (3) undesirable social consequences. Given these difficulties, Morgan concludes that the ideal of androgyny is neither an appropriate nor a feasible guide for classroom practices. This essay also illustrates a general point about the dangers of instituting any gender ideals, however wonderful they may appear to be.

We end Part 1 by returning to the larger overarching question: Theorizing gender: How much of it do we need? In Chapter 6 Barbara Houston examines one set of educational proposals that reflects the postmodernist interest in deconstructing gender. In her analysis, Houston uncovers key assumptions and addresses potential confusions. For example, she notes that efforts to abolish the whole concept of gender seem, at times, to be confused with efforts to reconstitute gender categories. She reminds us that abolishing gender as a category could be dangerous, as, for example, when it leaves us with no way to ground feminist politics. Her own analyses lead her to conclude that just which gender categories and how much attention to gender might best serve women remain unanswered questions. Houston also discusses both the possibilities and problems of abolishing personal gender identity. In her discussion she makes the important educational point that even if we cannot or do not want to abolish gender we can, nevertheless, alter the meaning of the categories; we can learn to change what it means to be a *girl* or a *boy*, a *woman* or a *man*; and we can learn to challenge the definitions that build subordination and domination into our gender categories.

In Part 2 our gender-sensitive search for new models leads us to consider an ethics of care (Gilligan 1982; Noddings 1984, 1992) as one new possibility for revisioning educational practice. In Chapter 7 I summarize the central tenets of an ethics of care, survey the criticisms leveled against this ethic, and classify the criticisms into two major groups: (1) those that claim that an ethics of care is applicable only to a limited domain of close personal relationships and (2) those that claim it is a dangerous ethic for women or for any other already subordinate group. After examining each of these claims, I argue for further discussion and exploration of educational applications; something that we return to in our second subpart as well as in Chapter 12. But before pursuing these possibilities, we shift to a critique in Chapter 8.

In Chapter 8, Morgan uncovers the complex ways in which our pedagogical practices continue to perpetuate gendered forms of educational empowerment and disempowerment. She exposes and describes what she calls three myths: (1) The Universality Myth, (2) The Coeducation Myth, and (3) The Equal Opportunity Myth.

At the end of the twentieth century we have become aware, often painfully so, of a multiplicity of axes of power and privilege that affect all of us in educational settings. As Morgan sets out to describe the "Emperor's New Clothes" she first pauses to diagram fourteen intersecting axes of privilege and domination affecting North American education. This diagram reminds us that sexism is only one axis of power among at least thirteen others, such as racism, class bias, heterosexism, ageism, ableism, and so forth. Thus, whatever our preoccupation with any single axis, such as gender, race, or class, we still need to strive for awareness and honesty with respect to our own differential positioning along all these multiple axes of power. In some cases we may discover that these myths, which camouflage gender bias, also serve to veil the faces of domination in force elsewhere. In such cases we might follow the same series of steps that Morgan uses in her critique as a means to challenge the myths and begin to free ourselves from their pervasive, often well-hidden power.

In our second subpart, we explore applications of an ethics of care approach within the context of feminist pedagogy. In Chapter 9, Morgan draws upon her own experiences as a feminist teacher and offers her philosophical observations on the difficulties attendant upon constructing an adequate, indeed a superior, model for feminist education. This chapter elucidates two common paradoxes we encounter as feminist teachers who attempt to bring nurturant models, such as the ethics of care, into our classroom practices: (1) the paradox of critical nurturance and (2) the role model paradox.

We encounter the first paradox when we find that feminist teachers are expected to be critical and nurturing at the same time; but students and teachers alike often experience nurturance and criticism as conflicting activities. This conflict becomes the topic of Chapter 10. Even though the general tension between nurturance and criticism is not a new educational problem, when we take a gender-sensitive perspective we discover further complications because of the powerful force exerted by genderized expectations. I begin by considering what we can learn from three standard attempts to resolve the paradox of critical nurturance. I then propose a new fourth alternative that is both gender sensitive and also in line with the ethics of care.

In Chapter 11, Houston addresses Morgan's second paradox, the role model paradox, which is found in the apparent contradiction between a student's identification with her feminist teacher as an ideal role model and the student's development of her own self-created autonomous identity. Using a number of biographical examples, Houston guides our study of the ways in which women have been helped and inspired by other women as role models, and she inquires into the conditions under which attachment to role models might constitute serious jeopardy for one's autonomy.

In Part 3, we address a number of practical political issues. As we note in Chapter 8, gender bias is only one among many axes of domination that serve to perpetuate inequities in school and society. Thus, in Chapter 12, we turn to the larger question of education for pluralism in general, not only for dealing with gender differences but also for learning to live well with multiple forms of diversity. Using the ethics of care as a framework, I propose a new approach to pluralism in education. I advocate four forms of pluralism: (1) co-existence, (2) co-operation, (3) co-exploration, and (4) co-enjoyment. When we see what is entailed in each of these, we find that all four are mutually compatible endeavors, appropriate and well suited to educational institutions. I conclude that true pluralism does have a chance in education if schools make a public commitment to teach and practice all four forms of pluralism.

In Chapter 13, Morgan investigates the controversial territory of sex education. She articulates a general framework of four questions designed to serve as analytic tools in unearthing the conceptual and normative presuppositions of pedagogical materials used for sex education. We then discover what happens when we apply these four questions to specific examples of liberal sex education materials. The imagery, the attitudes, and the recommended sexual behaviors turn out to contradict and undermine the liberal moral goals, such as individual self-determination and equality, that they purport to further.

Chapter 14 demonstrates one detailed application of a gender-sensitive perspective. This chapter can be read simply as an extended answer to the question: What would a gender-sensitive perspective mean for physical education? It can also be studied as a working model for confronting sex inequality and for handling an undesirable hidden curriculum in almost any subject area. We assume the viewpoint of an educator who is already committed to sex equality but is still faced with practical questions and policy decisions about the best way to proceed. We note that gender issues in physical education cannot be adequately addressed without asking what girls and women learn about themselves as physical beings from the powerful *hidden curriculum*. We offer a number of alternative approaches educators can turn to when faced with an undesirable hidden curriculum; and we show how some of these strategies can be used in a gender-sensitive approach to physical education.

In our final chapter, Maryann Ayim enters the debate over political correctness on two fronts. First, she exposes and critiques three erroneous assumptions made by those who rely on an unqualified First Amendment defense against campus speech codes. Ayim observes, for example, that such attempted defenses seem to take no cognizance of the fact that some forms of expression, in and of themselves, erode freedom of expression. Second, Ayim examines and calls into question the curricular justifications used for maintaining the centrality of a traditional male Eurocentric curriculum. She argues that these justifications fail to address the social and political implications of the whole process of defining knowledge. On both fronts we discover again how deeply moral as well as political our educational controversies turn out to be.

PART ONE

Theory

1

A Conceptual Analysis of Sexism
and Sexist Education

MARYANN AYIM AND BARBARA HOUSTON

A Conceptual Analysis of Sexism

Like a great deal of current academic research, the work described in this chapter has its roots in the feminist movement. We believe its contribution to this literature lies in its attempt to provide a clear and comprehensive conceptual analysis of the notion of sexism. The charge of sexism, carrying with it serious social and moral connotations,[1] is being leveled with even greater frequency and conviction at individuals, institutions, policies, and even language patterns. The result is a variety of books on such topics as sexism in religion, sexism in science, sexism in language, sexism in schools, and sexism in the workforce. Many writers seem to assume that the reader shares with them a commonsense notion of sexism, which equates it with sex discrimination, sex prejudice, or sex-role stereotyping. In her *Non-Sexist Childraising*, Carrie Carmichael (1977) equates sexism with being "prejudiced by a person's gender" (p. 1); hence, in her analysis, nonsexist child rearing becomes "free/fair-minded childraising" (p. 1). Mary Anne Warren (1980) defines sexism as morally "wrongful discrimination on the basis of sex" (p. 424). In the educational literature in particular, we see the phrase "sex-role stereotyping" used to define the concept of sexism. Sara Delamont (1980), for example,

---

In Chapter 1, we maintain the standard philosophical convention that places single quotation marks around words when their meaning as terms is under discussion. We do so in order to make it clear when we are speaking of the meaning of the terms 'sexism' and 'sexist' in contrast to when we are referring to the actual phenomena that we consider to be sexist. Except for Chapter 1, all the other chapters reflect the Westview Press policy of avoiding quotation marks for terminology.

claims that "sexism is a term meaning stereotyping people by sex" (p. 3). Eileen Byrne (1978, p. 148) uses the term in a similar way. Although such definitions succeed in capturing the ordinary language notion of sexism, they are not very helpful as tools for clarifying the meaning of sexism and distinguishing genuine from merely apparent instances.

Some considerably less simplistic conceptions of sexism have been advanced in the literature, and we will delineate some of these later. In explicating a term like sexism, it will be helpful to use as a model I. A. Snook's (1972a, pp. 16–45) categorization scheme for the concept of indoctrination. He presents four sorts of analysis of indoctrination typified by the central place given to content, method, consequences, or intentions. He argues that the intentional analysis is the only one that makes sense of the moral criticism implicit in the charge of indoctrination. More important for our purposes, however, is his claim that what counts as indoctrination is relative to which sort of analysis one assumes. The same observation should enable us to begin to unravel the ambiguity, confusion, and contradiction that characterize the use of the term sexism in feminist literature. What counts as sexism will depend upon the sort of analysis with which we begin.

Although Snook's (1972a) scheme is not a perfect model for our purposes, three of the characteristics that he investigates (content, consequences, and intentions) do seem to elucidate the different central features of alternative conceptions of sexism. Using these three analyses, we shall sketch out the form that sexism would take on each account, beginning with definitions from the literature itself.

Content

Examples of content definitions of sexism in the literature are more numerous than either of the other two categories. Two such definitions will be introduced and discussed here. One of the most detailed analyses of sexism appears on page 2 of Nancy Frazier and Myra Sadker's (1973) *Sexism in School and Society*, where sexism is defined as "(1) a belief that the human sexes have a distinctive makeup that determines their respective lives, usually involving the idea that one sex is superior and has the right to rule the other, (2) a policy of enforcing such asserted right, (3) a system of government and society based upon it." The second and third parts of this definition simply represent applications of the term sexism to the realms of policy and government.[2] There is a problem in the first, most crucial part: It says that sexism is "a belief that the human sexes have a distinctive makeup that determines their respective lives, *usually* involving the idea that one sex is superior and has the right to rule the other" (Frazier and Sadker 1973, p. 2, our emphasis). The term *usually* weakens the definition unduly, rendering it too inclusive. The fact that women, not men, bear children and that this is a determining factor in the lives of women would become, by itself, an instance of sexism on this analysis. Surely we would not want to allow this. Bearing this in mind, we would revise the definition of sexism as follows:

1. Sexism must involve a belief that certain differences exist between female and male human beings (Frye, 1975, pp. 68–69).[3]
2. These specified differences must be seen as relevant to justifying social and political arrangements whereby one sex has power and dominance over the other.

Some observations must be made about this definition. Can the beliefs specified in the first part be either true or false? Even this question offers too simple a dichotomy. For such beliefs are most likely to be neither clearly true nor clearly false but uncertain. Given the systematic entrenchment of sex roles in our socialization processes, it is almost impossible for us to decide whether many of the postulated sex differences are genuine—for example, mathematical and verbal ability and such personality characteristics as empathy and altruism. Nevertheless, it is important to ask whether the beliefs on which sexism is predicated could ever be true beliefs. The answer here would have to be "yes," as many (but not all) instances of sexism are in fact rooted in such true beliefs as the ability of women to bear children. It is the relevance that such beliefs are thought to have to other matters that is often at issue, as in an employer's refusal to consider a female candidate for a certain position simply on the ground of her childbearing capacity.

Another serious concern is whether a justifiable application of a true belief would be considered sexist on this analysis. Suppose, for example, that the higher testosterone levels of males rendered them unstable in power conflicts of international proportions. If this were true, it would seem highly relevant to justifying an arrangement whereby women held all positions of military and political prominence, particularly in crisis situations. Our working definition seems to assume that no application of a belief concerning sex differences could be legitimately used to justify power hierarchies based on sex. We feel that ruling out this possibility should not be condoned on scientific grounds. We want to leave open the question whether institutionalized gender-based dominance could ever be justified and to deny that dominance of this order would be sexist. Otherwise, as the definition stands now, the term 'sexism' cannot be seen as necessarily pejorative. Using such a definition, many cases of sexism would be morally unjustified; others would not. One problem with this usage is that it appears to violate the ordinary language use of 'sexism.' More serious, though, is the possibility that it might begin to weaken people's perceptions of the seriousness of all those clear cases of unjustified gender-based discrimination. Consequently, we would append to our two-part definition of sexism this third feature—that if the sex difference belief in question is true, it must in fact not be relevant to the social arrangements predicated upon it.

Two other observations apply to the second feature of our definition (that the specified sex differences must be seen as relevant to justifying social and political arrangements whereby one sex enjoys power and dominance over the other). First, the perceived relevance may not be merely tangential but must be much stronger, amounting in fact to a sufficient condition for the social and political hierarchy of the sexes. In other words, the perceived differences are not merely relevant to the sexual hierarchy but are actually adequate to justify such an arrangement. Second, the stipulated differences must be seen as relevant to nontrivial concerns. Linking sex differences to wage disparities, educational policies, and forms of government would count as sexist on this condition, whereas the linkage of sex differences to underarm deodorant marketing ordinarily would not.[4] Both these conditions are captured clearly by another content definition of sexism provided by Sheila Ruth (1980): "Sexism is a way of seeing the world in which differences between males and females, actual or alleged, are perceived as *profoundly* relevant to *important* political, economic, and social arrangements and behaviour" (p. 53, our emphasis). Taking all of these conditions into account, the following definition of sexism emerges:

1. Sexism must involve a belief that certain differences exist between female and male human beings.
2. These specified differences must be seen as relevant to justifying social and political arrangements whereby one sex has power and dominance over the other.
3. These perceived differences are seen as profoundly relevant or sufficient to justify the social arrangements in question.
4. These social arrangements are nontrivial.
5. Sexism must be based on either a false belief about sex differences or an unjustifiable application of a true belief about sex differences to the social and political context.

We shall conclude our discussion of the content analysis by mentioning one of its possible shortcomings. On this analysis, charges of sexism are leveled entirely without reference to whether or not those defending them had genuinely and sincerely, to the best of their ability, considered all the evidence available to them in formulating their beliefs in the truth or falsity of any of the component claims. Nineteenth century discriminatory practices against women could be judged just as culpable on this account as contemporary twentieth century practices; this seems unreasonable in light of the much more extensive body of research and knowledge available in the twentieth century.

Consequences

A very clear consequences analysis of sexism appears in *A Guide to Federal Laws and Regulations Prohibiting Sex Discrimination* (United States Commission on Civil Rights 1976).[5] Although the commission does not define the term 'sexism' specifically, the definition provided for the term *discrimination* is very helpful. We shall quote the definition in its entirety.

> *Discrimination*—Discrimination is the effect of an action, policy, or practice which selects a class of persons to receive unequal treatment. Discrimination may involve a single act or may be a continuing policy or practice. Discrimination may be intentional or unintentional; purpose or intent is irrelevant when the effects of a particular action, policy, or practice is to deny equal opportunity. Similarly, discrimination may be overt (that is, using sex or race to discriminate openly) or covert (that is, when a mechanism indirectly related to sex or race is used to discriminate) (p. 164).

Modifying this slightly, we arrive at the following definition of sexism:

1. Sexism is the effect of an action, policy, or practice that selects females (or males) as a class to receive unequal treatment.
2. Sexism may be intentional or unintentional—the test lies not in the intention but in whether the result has been unequal treatment.
3. Sexism may be either overt (that is, open or direct) or covert (that is, subtle or indirect).

The core of this definition lies in the first part, for, in identifying sexism with certain effects, we have captured the heart of the consequences analysis. Nevertheless, the second and third parts do provide useful clarification of what it *means* to identify sexism with effects or consequences. It means that establishing conscious intent to discriminate is not even relevant to identifying sexist behavior. It is worth noting that this does seem to violate our common understanding of sexism, which would see establishing intent as an entirely reasonable procedure. Conversely, the nonmoralizing stance of the consequences analysis may be viewed by some as a strength. In any case, intentions tend to be relatively inaccessible, at least in comparison with effects. If people deny having a sexist intention, for example, what evidence could be used to challenge their denial? How would we measure intensity of sexism intention (for presumably the moral weight of the sexism charge would vary with the degree of the intention)? These are hard questions that do not seem to arise on an analysis that assesses only effects.

Thus, it is not surprising that a political body whose task is to identify and redress instances of sexism would operate with a consequences analysis, for it appears that one of the primary virtues of such an analysis is the ease of identifying offending instances. The waters are not muddied by talk about intentions. Even subtle forms of sexism may be straightforwardly settled by simply looking at effects. Where one supports covert discrimination, the Commission on Civil Rights (1976) recommends simply carrying out "an examination of the *effects* of employment policies and patterns" (p. 7, our emphasis). An example of covert discrimination cited by the commission is establishing a certain minimum height as a job prerequisite, the effect of which would put female applicants at a disadvantage (U.S. Commission on Civil Rights 1976, p. 7).

It is not as easy as it may appear on first glance, however, to recognize consequences of certain actions or policies. Is it a consequence of sex-role stereotyping in school texts that the self-perception and self-esteem of female students are lowered? We do not know the answer for certain partly because we do not have a clear picture of the relationship between textbook characters and role models.

The term *consequences* itself must be scrutinized. Do consequences include actual consequences or predicted consequences? If the first, then it is not clear whether the consequences to be measured include only immediate ones or extend to more remote cases. To limit a tally to only immediate consequences would miss the point of much social criticism with regard to sexism. The most profound consequences of sexist childrearing, for example, only begin to emerge years later. Should more remote consequences be included, we have to decide how remote, and there is no clear basis on which to make this decision. However, if the consequences include predicted as well as actual ones, then what appeared to be the central advantage of this model—its clarity in assessing cases of sexism—is somewhat eroded. Will it be any easier to identify predicted consequences than to identify intentions, for example? (We might point out, however, that the public nature of predicted consequences does seem to make them a more reliable guide to action than intentions, whose nature is essentially private.)

Consequences are not things that can be determined independently of the context in which they occur. Is it sexist to refer to nurses as "she" and engineers as "he," given that this gender assignment does reflect actual employment trends, at least in North America? In an ideal nonsexist society, it might not be (although it would also be unlikely to obtain such employment patterns in a completely nonsexist society). Given the context of a highly sexist society, in which women are clearly and systematically disadvantaged in all areas and at all levels of employment, however, the reality-guided choice of pronouns may serve to further stereotype attitudes and expectations and, hence, further oppress women. Thus, this apparently innocent example, given its particular context, may well turn out to be sexist on a consequences analysis. What this means is that identifying consequences as positive or negative will be a highly complex undertaking, not blessed with any of the simplicity that the consequences model seemed to promise.

On the consequences analysis, sexism will have been wiped out when equal treatment of the sexes is achieved. One of the guidelines of the U.S. Office of Federal Contract Compliance (1976) illustrates this:

Women have not been typically found in significant numbers in management. In many companies management trainee programs are one of the ladders to management positions. Traditionally, few, if any, women have been admitted into these programs. An important element of affirmative action shall be a commitment to include women candidates in such programs.

Distinctions based on sex may not be made in other training programs. Both sexes should have equal access to all training programs and affirmative action programs should require a demonstration by the employer that such access has been provided (p. 177).

Although these guidelines are helpful in determining whether women as a class have been discriminated against, they are not nearly so helpful in determining whether an injustice has been done to any particular woman. Even in the case of class, however, the notion of equality is by no means a straightforward one; for example, it is not clear what evidence would be required to support a claim that both sexes had equal access to all training programs. Would the employers simply be required to inform both men and women clearly about the availability of the program? Would they have to ensure, by whatever means, that 50 percent of those enrolled in the training program were women? Suppose a disproportionate number of women expressed no interest in the training program. Should their employer require them to enroll in an attempt to offset the negative thrust of earlier socialization processes? What do we do when considerations of equality appear to conflict with those of freedom and self-determination? None of these questions admits of a clear, straightforward answer.

Intentions

The clearest example of an intentions analysis of sexism that we were able to find is provided by Devra Lee Davis (1972):

> The term "sexist" is equally applicable to male and female matters. "Sexist" refers to any attempt to understand, explain or predict a social phenomenon as naturally determined by the sex of the participants. The key word here is "naturally," for it implies necessity and inevitability. An immediate implication of the above delimitation of "sexist" is that glorifications of natural female or male characteristics are equally culpable (p. 25, n. 9A).

Modifying this somewhat, we arrive at the following definition:

1. Sexism is any attempt to understand, explain, or predict a social phenomenon as naturally (that is, necessarily and inevitably) determined by the sex of the participants.
2. Sexism may be directed against either females or males, both forms of which are equally bad.

The first part of this definition is the most important, and its wording leads one to expect that sexism could be directed against either females or males. The choice of words is also important in another respect. Sexism is described as "any attempt to understand, explain, or predict a social phenomenon as naturally determined by the sex of the participants." The key word here is 'attempt,' which presupposes an element of conscious intent on the part of the agent. We do not attempt to do things unconsciously or in spite of ourselves. The notion of attempting only makes sense in a context of conscious intent.

Somewhat similar comments apply to the terms 'understand,' 'explain,' and 'predict.' We can no more unconsciously and unintentionally understand, explain, or predict things than we can unconsciously and unintentionally attempt them. In precisely this sense, the notions of understanding, explaining, and predicting differ from that of *believing*; we can believe things unconsciously and unintentionally, and we can pick up beliefs unwittingly. It is this feature that distinguishes an intentions analysis of sexism from a content one. In the case of the term 'understanding,' an even stronger claim can be made—that understanding requires a context of critical evaluation as well. This strong feature is not required to justify the claim of conscious intent, however, and in any case does not necessarily characterize explaining and predicting; we can offer explanations and predictions that are by no means tied to a process of critical evaluation. Davis (1972) says, "An immediate implication of the above delimitation of 'sexist' is that *glorifications* of natural female or male characteristics are equally culpable" (p. 25, n. 9A; our emphasis). The word 'glorification' is important in that it suggests that sexism is not limited to explaining. Our amended definition is:

1. Sexism is any attempt to understand, explain, or predict a social phnomenon as naturally (that is, necessarily and inevitably) determined by the sex of the participants.
2. Sexism may also be identified with any attempt to see the value of persons or their activities as determined by their sex.
3. All of these activities involve conscious intention.
4. The understanding, explaining, predicting, or evaluating of the phenomenon in terms of natural sexual determination is inappropriate or unjustifiable.

Not surprisingly, the intentions analysis usually has to do with persons—we concern ourselves most with intentions in circumstances in which we want to evaluate persons and their actions from a moral perspective. Much behavior that may superficially appear to be morally unobjectionable turns out to be less innocent under careful scrutiny. On the intentions analysis, it is not required that one have the intention to be sexist. It is sufficient that one intentionally uses gender as the basis for evaluating persons or their behavior where such reference to gender is inappropriate. On this analysis, even the intention to compliment can be sexist if the complimentary evaluation is inappropriately based on the sex of the individual. Whistling at a woman in the street or referring to her as a "cute chick" will turn out to be sexist on this analysis provided that two easy conditions are met—first, that the agent is focusing on the woman's physical appearance in a way that would not normally be considered appropriate for the agent to focus on a man and second, that if the agent did want to call attention to a good-looking man, whistling at him or calling him a "cute chick" would be an unacceptable means of doing so. Using an intentions analysis, such behavior is sexist even if the agent actually intended to be complimentary. One can see the intentions analysis presupposed in some feminist writing. Pat Mainardi (1978, p. 36), in her feminist analysis of housework, presupposes an intentions analysis by suggesting that men support an inequitable division of household labor because they correctly understand this division to be one example of male privilege that they are reluctant to relinquish.

It is clear that the intentions analysis of sexism does provide leverage for moral criticism, and it does so in a stronger way than either the content or the consequences analysis. This is what we would have expected, given the necessary connection in our court system, for example, between intention and a strongly morally pejorative charge, like murder.

But it is exactly this notion of intention that is the most slippery feature of the definition. Following Snook's (1972a, p. 50; 1972b, pp. 155–157) analysis of indoctrination, the term *intention* may be seen to have two legitimate senses such that to intend a certain outcome would be either (1) to want or desire that outcome or (2) to foresee it as likely or inevitable that such an outcome would result from one's actions, where these actions are subject to one's control. The usefulness of the first sense is limited, for our purposes, by the difficulty involved in identifying wants and desires. History is filled with "justifications" like the following: Universities refused to admit women in order to protect women both from the strenuous working conditions, which would overtax their frail frames, and also from the harsh male environment, which would corrupt their innocent minds. How would one challenge this position, and what sorts of evidence would one use to illustrate that what the universities really desired was not to protect females but to protect male privilege by keeping females out of the running in the exclusive male preserve of academia?

It is the second sense of intention that seems to offer us some help here. It seems entirely plausible to suggest that one could foresee the oppression of women resulting from university policies that refused them admission and, hence, that such policies were sexist on an intentions analysis. Although this ameliorates the problem, it does not solve it, however, for there will still be significant dispute about what one could have reasonably been expected to foresee as consequences of one's action; neither does the account provide us with any clear mechanism for reconciling such disputes. Furthermore, this second interpretation of intentions allows the definition to take account of consequences—it defines intentions as foreseeing that one's actions will likely or inevitably result in certain consequences.

Critical Analysis and Comparison of Definitions

Thus far, we have been concerned not so much with particular definitions proposed in the literature as with types of definitions. Our comments have not provided conclusive objections to considered definitions but have simply raised some obstacles to the different kinds of approaches of defining sexism. We shall now proceed to briefly evaluate these three analyses of sexism on a somewhat broader scale than we have introduced to this point.

Of the three types of analysis available to us in the literature—the content, the consequences, and the intentions analyses—can we urge any one over the others? We think not. In general, the test of any definition is how well it serves the purpose for which the definition is required. Obviously, any adequate analysis of sexism must allow us to use the terms 'sexism' and 'sexist' with good sense over the whole range of contexts in which we do use them.

We shall argue that all three analyses are indispensable if we are to give a satisfactory account of the notion of sexism. However, we have suggested ways in which these analyses must be tidied up to better do the jobs for which they were designed. In most cases, our alterations have been such as to render the terms 'sexism' and 'sexist' unequivocally terms of negative evaluation. These alterations commit us to the view that sexism is morally wrong and that this is part of the meaning of the term. In short, we are saying that one could not say of something that "it is sexist but none the worse for that." But sexism is a complex moral phenomenon, and its complexity is reflected in the use of the term. The best way to argue for our claim that all three analyses of the term 'sexist' are indispensable and to further clarify the complex feature of its use as a moral term is to assess the analyses we offer against three standard criteria commonly employed to assess the adequacy of the analysis of any moral term. The three criteria that must generally be satisfied are these:

1. The term, as it is defined, must have a basis in use; that is, it must accurately reflect what ordinary people think sexism is.
2. The analysis must capture all the ethically significant cases.
3. The analysis must not settle genuine moral disputes by definition; that is, it must not settle a moral question by terminological fiat.

We shall address each of these criteria in turn.

Since the terms 'sexist' and 'sexism' have not been in existence long enough to bear any serious "scars of conceptual evolution" (Falk 1970, p. 390),[6] it is not particularly difficult to see that all three models are needed to satisfy the first criterion. They all can be claimed to have a basis in use.

The slogan "sexism is a social disease" reminds us that sexism is something that pervades a very broad range of human activity. It is tied up with our thinking, our everyday activities, our social institutions, laws, and policies as well as the most intimate of our relations with one another. It is indeed a multifaceted phenomenon. Since the central, primary use of the term 'sexist' is to describe and condemn a wide range of things such as institutions, policies, laws, theories, even language patterns and persons, we think it is pointless to suggest that any one model of analysis is better than another on this criterion. One can be better than another only for certain purposes. For the purpose of evaluating policies, the consequences analysis is likely to be more appropriate than the intentions analysis; for identifying sexist theories, the content analysis will obviously be more appropriate than the consequences analysis. Notice that no one model appears to rule out kinds of sexism that would be captured by the others. Any model could be used to assess different kinds of things. For example, although the content analysis is eminently suited to assessing theories, one could define persons as sexist if they held such theories; we could also judge policies as sexist if they were based on such beliefs. Similarly, although the consequences analysis is best suited to evaluating policies and practices, one could view persons as sexist if they engaged in behavior that had the stated effects. However, although it is possible to so use each of these analyses to evaluate different kinds of things, it would often strain them to do so. In the case of the moral evaluation of persons, for example, it is usually appropriate to examine their intentions, not just their beliefs or the effects of their behavior, for persons are held morally responsible precisely because they engage in behavior intentionally. No single one of the analyses we have considered will be satisfactory for describing all the phenomena we collect under the term 'sexism.'

It may appear that on occasion a single analysis can be used fruitfully, yet in many of our undertakings in which this seems to be the case, we very quickly realize that a single analysis is in itself inadequate. For example, if we wanted to understand the historical origin and processes of sexism, it would seem that we would do well to use the content analysis since it focuses on beliefs and the relations among beliefs that characterize thought that we label 'sexist.' Yet, the presence of sexist beliefs and theories about the role of women in a culture would not themselves be a guarantee that women were in fact oppressed at a particular time in that culture. In order to properly assess this, one would have to determine whether the beliefs were, in fact, shared by a minority or by the majority of people, whether they were influential, whether they captured the social reality of their time, or whether they represented a paradigm shift. One would also have to know whether such thought *prescribed* the behavior of women and whether it *described* it as well, whether it was used to justify policies, and whether policies of the day did, in fact, curb opportunities for women in ways that they did not for men. It would also be important to know how the beliefs functioned in policy formation. Were they used to justify what was conceived of as protective legislation that advanced the interests of women, or did they legitimate more maliciously motivated policies? In these few questions, we see that in writing the history of women one needs to be alert to all the different dimensions of sexism that are featured in the analyses we have examined.[7]

Consider another example that substantiates this point. It might be thought that, for purposes of eliminating sexism, we would do well to employ the consequences analysis and to formulate our antisexist legislation in accordance with it. But here again, one quickly realizes that legislation is only as effective as the support for its sanctions, and this is dependent upon the moral attitudes of those who are governed by the laws. Thus, it is often remarked in discussion of antisexist legislation that nothing effective can be done about the problem because "you cannot legislate attitudes." The point of this frequently made remark is to draw attention to the wide range of behavior that cannot be effectively legislated by law, either because it fails to have the support of the populace and so would be unenforceable or because use of the law would be thought to constitute an enormous invasion of privacy. In short, a large part of behavior that is sexist must be addressed, if it is to be addressed effectively, both as a matter of morality and as a matter of legal governance. Hence, we have a need for an analysis of sexism that is appropriate within the context of moral persuasion. We need an analysis of sexism that takes account of intentions. Yet, intimately tied to our intentions are our conceptions, our beliefs about how things are and how they ought to be. Thus, proper moral criticism, especially that involving moral blame, may require us to explore the individual's beliefs about the nature of the sexes and the perceived relevance of these differences. Our account of sexism can avoid clashes with ordinary usage only if it insists on noting the indispensable nature of all three types of analysis.

Given that the term 'sexism' was introduced to identify what is morally objectionable, the second criterion poses perhaps the most important test for any analysis of sexism: Does it capture all the ethically significant cases? Although it is easy enough to acknowledge the importance of any analysis satisfying this test, there is controversy over whether any one of the analyses does satisfy it. Part of the reason for this controversy is the ambiguity surrounding the phrase "ethically significant cases."

If by ethically significant cases we mean those instances of sexism that have moral importance, then we realize we are bound to have controversy in this matter because what is considered of moral importance varies with different ethical theories. Are the consequences of an action or practice more morally significant than the beliefs or intentions that underlie the action or practice?

Can the moral worth of an action be measured by its consequences? Can persons be morally evaluated solely in terms of their beliefs or their behavior? Is it of greater moral importance to assess persons or laws? It should be obvious, as we argued earlier, that the ethical significance of some of these issues cannot be purchased at the price of ignoring others. All these matters are of ethical significance, and only the use of several models will allow us to address all the cases of sexism that have moral importance.

There is, however, another possible meaning to the phrase ethically significant cases. The demand that the analysis of sexism encompass all such cases could mean, in a more substantive sense, that the best analysis will be the one that captures all the morally objectionable cases and includes none that are not. That is a more stringent criterion. Given that a term like 'sexism' is clearly employed in ideological disputes and is understood to have disapproval built into it, we should expect disagreement about its application. Predictably, there is disagreement about which of the analyses captures all, and only, the morally objectionable cases of sexism. In order to clarify this controversy, let us reexamine our critical commentary on the various types of definition. In our discussion of the content definition, we pointed out that charges of sexism could be leveled without reference to whether or not those defending sexist policies or beliefs had considered, to the best of their ability, all the evidence available to them. In our discussion of the consequences analysis, we noted that this definition of sexism did not answer the hard question of whether in a conflict between the ideals of liberty and sex equality one should choose sex equality. The problem we noted with the intentions analysis was that disputes would inevitably arise over which consequences it is reasonable to claim people intended. In all these cases, the deficiency of the definition is one that can only be rectified by further moral debate. Should we expect any satisfactory definition of sexism to resolve these questions? It is because we do not think it is appropriate to demand this of any analysis of sexism that we claim that our comments do not provide conclusive objections to these definitions. Such faults should not be remedied by an alteration of the definition of sexism, for they are genuine moral disputes that cannot and should not be settled by terminological fiat.[8]

We think that the analyses, taken jointly, do capture all the ethically significant cases. It is a matter for further moral debate as to which analysis is appropriate in which circumstances. In order to justify our position on this point, it is necessary to address directly some concerns and confusions people have had about the term 'sexist.'

Clearly 'sexism' is a pejorative term and, as such, carries with it moral disapproval. This makes some people want to be cautious in their use of it, which is as it should be since it is a serious moral criticism. But, on these same grounds, other people want to eschew its use altogether. This is a mistake that appears to arise from a simple confusion—that of confounding all moral appraisal with the attribution of moral blame. To say of something that it is sexist is to say that it is morally objectionable, but not necessarily to say that it is blameworthy. Sexism is, at heart, the mistake of an irrelevant use of gender in matters that are of moral concern. The morality enters by virtue of the domain within which the mistake is made. Like racism, sexism is deeply embedded in our culture and has been for a very long time; for many, it is still quite invisible. The question "Who is responsible for sexism?" can sometimes be answered equally well with "No one" and "Everyone." In any case, the question of who is responsible for particular instances of sexism is a separate question from that of what particular instances are identified as sexist, as is the question of whether anyone who is responsible should be blamed.

Disregard for the distinction between moral appraisal of something and imputing blame for it explains why people who clearly do disapprove of sexism are hesitant to use the term to describe it. It explains why people fail to take seriously charges of sexism leveled in what they take to be trivial matters. It explains why they think sexism must involve a negative evaluation of women, for only this could be blameworthy. It also explains why people think that a declaration of good intention is an appropriate disclaimer for sexist behavior.

It is true that we use moral terms both to condemn something and to impute moral blame, but not every use of a moral term does both. Moral terms do describe our moral evaluations, but not all our moral evaluations are evaluations of moral culpability. The question of assigning moral blame is itself a matter of moral concern, and we think it is a virtue of our analyses that they do not state the conditions under which it is appropriate to blame someone for sexism. On any use of the term, on any of the accounts we have considered, it is an open question whether or not anyone is to be blamed for instances of sexism.

Although it is appropriate for people to be sensitive to the responsibilities inherent in leveling a charge of sexism, it would be a serious error to decide never to use the term. Sex inequality is an intolerable evil and, like all other forms of injustice, it should be named, challenged, disapproved of, and eradicated. Moral language is an essential tool for this work.

Of course, the ultimate test of any accounting of the notion of sexism will be the use to which we can put it. In our case, we are particularly interested in having an account of sexism that helps us to understand and assess feminist criticisms of education.[9] As we noted earlier, feminists, like other social reformers, cite the educational system in the diagnosis and cure of social ills. Because the school is the one institution that declares itself formally responsible for the socialization of the young, because our society compels children to be in schools for approximately ten years, because of the power of the school experience in "its early, continuous and pervasive entry into our lives" (Ruth 1980, p. 384), and because of our reasonable conviction that the socialization that occurs in school is bound to reflect the values of the larger society, the educational system has been singled out by feminists for "vigilance and activity" (Ruth 1980, p. 384). It is wrong, these feminist writers claim, to socialize children to fit into a society that is unjust, whether this injustice takes the form of racism, classism, or sexism.

Kate Millett (1973) puts the feminist case succinctly when she charges that our society treats women as an oppressed group. "Oppressed groups are denied education, economic independence, the power of office, representation, an image of dignity and self-respect, equality of status, and recognition as human beings. Throughout history women have been consistently denied all this, and their denial today, while attenuated and partial is nevertheless consistent" (p. 365). If women indeed represent a group that is discriminated against in society, then it is as wrong to teach children sexist values as it is to teach them racist values.

Whether or not one thinks that Millett is correct in her claim that women are an oppressed group will depend very much upon one's critical scrutiny of the cases she mentions. The one we are most interested in is educational opportunity. There is an obvious sense in which women and men do appear to be treated equally in educational matters. After all, schooling is compulsory for both girls and boys alike in the United States and Canada, and women are no longer excluded from higher education or from the professional schools, as they once were. However, although it appears as though women and men do have equal access to education, it is not clear, feminists claim, that they have equal educational opportunities. If education is so structured that girls and women are disadvantaged by virtue of their sex, then they will be restricted in their growth toward autonomy and self-determination, their vocational aspirations and opportunities, and their abilities to enter fully into the creation of our culture. Thus, our analysis of sexism is important in helping us identify unequal educational opportunities for women and men, opportunities that have significant consequences.

Application to Education

Now we take up the question "Is education sexist?" From the first part of this chapter, one can see that it is not a simple task to determine an answer, for the single question must really be divided into many separate questions such as: Do the educational policies of the local, state, or provincial and federal governments result in disadvantages to either sex? Are the curriculum materials that express beliefs about the nature and social positions of women and men false and unjustified? Do teachers express attitudes intended to direct the development of girls and boys in ways "proper" to their sex?

Various facets of schooling at all levels have been criticized as sexist, including the curriculum, attitudes of the teachers and educational officials, achievement tests as well as academic and vocational counseling, the organization of extracurricular activities, and the administrative hierarchy of educational institutions. We cannot deal with all of these criticisms, but we can consider some of the common examples of educational practices that have been called sexist.

The following five incidents are representative of those we might expect feminists to object to. Employing our tidied-up analyses, we shall determine if they might usefully be labeled cases of sexism.

1. A teacher uses material that stereotypes females without commenting on the stereotyping.
2. A male coach of a grade 9–10 hockey team refuses to let girls try out for the team, even though there is no team for the girls in the school.
3. An elementary schoolteacher punishes a male student for misbehavior in the class by making him sit with the girls and then line up with them when it is time to dismiss for recess.
4. A school policy that discourages girls from taking industrial arts courses is defended by the industrial arts teachers and principal on the grounds that:

   • If the girls were in the class, there would be pressure to make crafts instead of real woodwork.
   • The tools are too heavy for girls to carry.
   • Since the unions will not admit them, there is no reason to train girls for jobs they cannot pursue.

5. A school dismisses classes early so that all students can attend the boys' football and basketball games but never does this for the girls' basketball and volleyball games. The school cheerleaders, all females, cheer only at the senior boys' games and not at those for senior girls.

The first case is one of the most familiar. There are many examples of material in all subjects, from kindergarten through university and professional graduate school curricula,[10] that are thought to stereotype women in various ways. It is objected that women are underrepresented and misrepresented when they do appear. The messages that are communicated about women are not flattering. In primary reading books, we find pictures of women having to be rescued by boys from simple situations that are hardly problematic for most adults; later, we find that history textbooks ignore women and their experiences or mention them only tangentially in their relations to men as mothers, wives, and occasionally as lovers (Trofimenkoff and Prentice 1977, p. 7).[11] Indeed, it has been claimed by many feminists that most of the scholarly disciplines are infected with a sexism that sociologist Jesse Barnard defines as

the unconscious, taken-for-granted, assumed, unquestioned, unexamined, unchallenged acceptance of the belief that the world as it looks to men is the only world, that the way of dealing with it which men have created is the only way, that the values which men have evolved are the only ones, the way sex looks to men is the only way it can look to anyone, that what men think about what women are like is the only way to think about what women are like (Gornick and Moran 1971, p. 25).

The objections to this form of sexism are many and varied.[12] And the defense of the stereotypes we find is often based on the claim that these are trivial matters and it is silly to get upset about them; especially when the authors are well intentioned.

We can still object that the material is sexist, however, on the grounds that, despite the author's beliefs and intentions, it may in fact disadvantage girls and women in a number of ways: (1) It puts them in a "double bind" when learning the material, (2) it places girls and women in a position of having to hear insults good naturedly, (3) it runs the danger of reinforcing a widely held stereotype of girls and women that is insulting and damaging to them. In these ways, the material discriminates against females.

Feminists point out that the matter is not trivial because the stereotypes are widely believed to be true, and there is a danger that in this context they will simply reinforce as true what, in fact, are mistaken beliefs. On the grounds of both the consequences and the content analysis, they claim that the charge of sexism is warranted. Conversely, defenders rely on an intentions analysis to dispel the charge of sexism. Knowing the three alternative ways of characterizing sexism helps us to focus on the real points of disagreement. But even on the basis of an intentions analysis, can we not say appropriately of people that they have been humiliated and insulted even though they may not have been aware of it and, a fortiori, not protested it? It is this question that underlies in part the controversy about sexist materials.

The second case, in which girls are denied the opportunity to try out for the hockey team, is perhaps the clearest case of sexism among those we are considering. On the consequences analysis, we have an obvious instance of a policy that has the effect of selecting a class (females) to receive unequal treatment. In order to show that this is a case of sexism, it is required on this analysis, as well as on the others, to demonstrate that the grounds for the unequal treatment be shown to be irrelevant. Now, that the individual is a girl cannot in itself be grounds since there is nothing about being a girl that entails that one cannot play hockey. Some girls have clearly demonstrated that they can play hockey well; besides, it is to be noted that the girls are excluded even from trying out for the team, so ability is not what is thought relevant. Some common reasons that have been advanced for such a policy are:

1. Boys do not like to defeat girls—it takes the thrill out of it for them.
2. Girls will be hurt too easily in this contact sport.
3. Boys do not want to play with girls.

Of these, number 2 might be a relevant consideration if universally applied. It just might be that all girls can be more easily hurt than boys; in which case, a rule excluding girls might be justified. But manifestly, girls do not injure more easily, and no attempt is made to invoke the principle. Some boys will be more easily hurt than others, and we leave it to their discretion whether they try out or not. Unless girls are less likely than boys to have discretion about what might cause them injury, we cannot use this as a relevant grounds for the policy. The other two considerations cannot be relevant inasmuch as they are not founded on a significant and relevant difference between males and females. Teams are not chosen, in general, by sampling players' views about who they would not like to defeat or who they want or do not want to play with. Thus, it appears that on the consequences, content, and intentions analyses, this policy would be sexist.

Let us now turn to the third case. The teacher, in punishing the male student, is clearly communicating and reinforcing faulty beliefs about the role of gender in relations between the sexes. Further, the gender of individuals is thought to be an appropriate feature to use as an everyday organizing principle and a management strategy for seating arrangements, lineups at recess, competitive games, and so forth. In this case, sex segregation is being used to motivate and control children. Other examples might include teachers saying "Boys, close your eyes. Girls, creep out, quietly get your coats. Don't let the boys hear you." Or "Boys, don't sing. Listen to the girls, make certain they sing nicely. Now it is the boys' turn. Get your best singing voices ready. See if you can beat the girls."

In these ways, children are constantly reminded that they are either female or male, even when this is irrelevant to the activity in which they are engaged. The message is also communicated that there is something wrong with boys and girls being work companions and allied with one another. It reinforces the idea that males and females are completely different, indeed even opposite. Any confusion on this issue is a source of hilarity or humiliation. In our example, the teacher can use gender as a feature of an individual to embarrass or humiliate the child only because children to some extent already share these beliefs. Further, for this to count as punishment it must involve something that the boy will not like—in this case, to be thought of as a girl. On the worst interpretation, the teacher is playing on a negative evaluation of girls or femininity, and at best, is communicating false and irrelevant beliefs about the importance attached to gender.

In our fourth case, it may appear obvious at first that the discouragement of girls from taking industrial arts courses is a clear case of sexism on the consequences analysis. However, it may be argued that advising girls not to take these courses is not the same as refusing to let them take them. They are not, by virtue of their sex, prohibited from taking such courses, which on the consequences analysis would be sexism, pure and simple. However, it is obvious that there are educational benefits and, perhaps, vocational benefits to be gained here, and girls are being discouraged from getting their fair share of the benefits on specious grounds. Let us look at the considerations offered to justify the belief and policy that girls should be discouraged from claiming what is rightfully theirs.

First, it is suggested that they would interfere with others in the course of doing what they want to do. This is not obvious. Would boys have to do crafts because the girls might want to do this? If so, and if in general it is expected that student interest dictates what is done in classes, then crafts should be done without complaint, otherwise one is committed to the blatantly sexist assumption that a student's interests should not count because they are those of a girl. Notice, too, that one might object that this "reason" rests on an assumption that is at best dubious—that girls will have different interests than boys. We may also have a differential evaluation of similar activity when it is done by a girl and when it is done by a boy reflected in the terms '*crafts*' as opposed to '*real woodwork*.'

The second reason offered for discouraging girls is that the tools will be too heavy for them. It is as likely as not that this is a false claim. But even if it were not, then anyone of whom this were true should be discouraged, not just girls. Or better yet, if we were concerned with giving everyone equal opportunity to learn industrial arts, we would provide strength training for those who are too weak, or we would provide lighter tools for those who needed them.

Finally, that the unions will not admit women cannot count as a relevant consideration either. Until shown otherwise, we can assume that the unions have no reasonable grounds for excluding a class of persons by virtue of their sex. But if the unions do not have a good reason for excluding them, then this action on their part is sheer prejudice, and it ought to be clear that other people's prejudices are not proper grounds for an educational policy. In short, this example is best revealed as an example of sexism by exposing the false, unfounded, and irrelevant beliefs cited in justification of a practice that clearly intends to exclude the members of one sex from a kind of education they choose to pursue.

The last example to be considered is that of a school's differential treatment of male and female athletic activities. It would likely be claimed that this differential treatment was sexist on the grounds that it is based on the beliefs that athletics are more important for boys than for girls, that it is more appropriate that students identify with the boys' teams than with the girls', that boys' athletics is more worthy of support than girls', and that it is appropriate for girls to cheer on boys but not vice versa. There are of course objections that readily spring to mind here. It may be protested that these practices simply reflect student interest and choice and cannot fairly be taken to express the beliefs cited. This objection readily shows us the weakness of the content analysis of sexism.

It may be that the justification for the practices is simply that students prefer to watch boys' sports and do not want to attend girls' games. But the question is whether the school ought to take these facts about student preference as relevant grounds for encouraging male and not female athletics. It is difficult to know what is responsible for what here. Given a context in which more space, time, money, and better coaching is given to male athletics, it is not surprising that these activities appear to be more highly prized by the students. But these facts might well be altered by different school policies. With more encouragement, better facilities, and coaching, girls' athletics may come to have a greater appeal, especially if one has the option of attending classes or the girls' games.

The important issue here is whether one is proposing to evaluate athletic activities for the pleasure they provide spectators or for the opportunities they provide talented young people to increase their competence and pleasure and perhaps even to improve their character. The other question is whether one differentially evaluates the pleasure afforded spectators or the opportunities provided the participants because of the sex of those involved.

We are now accustomed to the idea that few, if any, opportunities can be justifiably denied persons on the basis of their sex, but it is a revelation to some of us to discover that many of our most common preferences may be sex biased—that we prize things differently if we know the sex of their author or their recipient. The intentions analysis of sexism reminds us that it is as important to be fair-minded about our evaluations as our actions or our beliefs. A thoughtful application of that analysis in this particular case might reveal important prejudices that escape the nets of the other two.

Conclusion

In this chapter, we have not attempted to document the extent to which schooling in North America is sexist. This task has been undertaken by others. However, even a cursory investigation of the now voluminous body of empirical writing on the topic points to the need for having a clearer understanding of the concept both for designing empirical studies and interpreting their results. In this chapter, we have clarified the term sexism and exhibited important features of its use. Having honed this piece of moral language, we should find that instances of sexism are more easily identified and the ethical issues surrounding such practices are more easily examined.

Notes

1. Nevertheless, the charge of sexism is often not taken as seriously by offenders as that of racism. Complaints that would be worrisome were the victim a member of a minority race are all too frequently seen as humorous when the victim is a woman.

2. The distinction between institutional and private sexism cuts across all three of our analyses.

3. Marilyn Frye categorizes this belief component in three different ways as a function of its epistemological status. See Frye (1975), pp. 68–69.

4. An example of just such a situation is the recent controversy surrounding the advertisement and sale of potentially harmful feminine hygiene sprays.

5. A U.S. document is referred to here because Canadian antidiscrimination legislation does not provide such a clear definition of discrimination. The Canadian Human Rights Act, enacted in 1977, states that "every individual should have an equal opportunity to make for himself or herself the life that he or she is able and wishes to have, consistent with his or her obligations as a member of society, without being hindered or prevented from doing so by discriminatory practices based on prohibited grounds of discrimination as specified by the Act;

"Proscribed grounds of discrimination are race, national or ethnic origin, colour, religion, age, sex, marital status, conviction for which a pardon has been granted, and, in matters related to employment, physical handicap."

The concept of discrimination is not, however, defined within the Canadian Human Rights Act. (See sections 2 and 3.)

Nor is the term 'discrimination' defined by statute in the Ontario Human Rights Code. The legislation simply stipulates the grounds on which discriminatory practices will amount to a breach of the code. Judicially, the term 'discrimination' is defined very broadly as "treating differently."

6. Falk uses this phrase in his discussion of the concept of morality.

7. For a discussion of the importance of these and other questions in writing women's history, see Susan Mann Trofimenkoff and Alison Prentice, eds., *The Neglected Majority: Essays in Canadian Women's History* (Toronto: McClelland and Stewart, 1977), pp. 7–13. For a more elaborate introductory theoretical discussion of the nature of women's history, see especially the essays of Gerda Lerner, "New Approaches to the Study of Women in American History" and "Placing Women in History: A 1975 Perspective" in B. A. Carroll, ed., *Liberating Women's History: Theoretical and Critical Essays* (Chicago: University of Chicago Press, 1976), pp. 349–369.

8. The recommendation that the term 'sexism' not be defined so as to exclude the possibility that something could be morally justifiable may appear to conflict with our insistence that sexist is a pejorative term. It does not. Most moral terms function in such a way that they express disapproval yet leave open whether or not something may be wrong overall. Consider the term 'lying.' When we say something is a case of lying, we intend to say it is something wrong, but we do not mean that it cannot ever be right to lie. When we say something is a case of lying or breaking a promise, we mean that the fact that an action is of this description always counts against it. There can of course be cases in which an act of lying or breaking a promise might be morally justified; for example, if it were done to save an innocent life. Similarly, we might have a policy of granting mothers automatic custody of children in cases of marriage breakup. This policy would be sexist on our account, yet it is possible that this policy, although unfair, might in fact be in the interest of the children affected by it. The courts might simply rule that in cases of marriage breakup the interest of the children is to override the interest of either parent. Whether or not such a policy would be morally justified would depend on one's moral theory and various other moral consid-

erations; however, it is not difficult to imagine that someone might consider the policy sexist but justifiable. Still, the use of the term assumes that the onus lies with those who want to undertake sexist practices to justify them, and in this sense it is pejorative. For a more thorough discussion of the way in which different moral terms function, see Julius Koveski, *Moral Notions* (London: Routledge and Kegan Paul, 1967).

9. We are cognizant of the distinction drawn between education and schooling. Schools may undertake many things that are not, on some accounts, considered educative. Hereafter, whenever we use the terms 'education,' or 'educational policies or practices,' we mean to refer to those that are offered as part of one's education whether they would be judged as educative or not on some ideal analysis of education such as that of R. S. Peters, 1972.

10. For a pertinent review of teacher education texts, many of which are used in North American faculties of education, see Sadker and Sadker (1980), pp. 36–45.

11. These authors note that some of the most read texts on Canadian history treat women in this way. W. L. Morton, *The Critical Years* (Toronto, ON: McClelland and Stewart, 1964), mentions women eleven times. The authors cite Ramsey Cook and Craig Brown, *Canada: A Nation Transformed* (Toronto, ON: McClelland and Stewart, 1976), as slightly better but still containing only eleven items involving women. They also point out that Canadians still have to rely upon a U.S. woman historian for a scholarly, although now dated, account of the women's suffrage movement in Canada: Catherine Cleverdon's *The Woman Suffrage Movement in Canada* (Toronto, ON: University of Toronto Press, 1974). Apparently even this obviously significant event in Canadian women's history has received no close analysis in standard Canadian history texts.

12. Women's studies is born out of this recognized deficiency and is an attempt to correct it. In a word, it is about a revolution in knowledge, a change in perspective. Its single most distinguishing feature is that women are being studied, for the first time, from their own perspective. Women become investigators of their own experience rather than simply objects of study.

SHOULD PUBLIC EDUCATION
BE GENDER FREE?

Chapters 2, 3, and 4 set forth three different positions in answer to the same question: Should public education be gender free? Chapter 2 looks at the case for a traditional answer of No, education should not be gender free. Chapter 3 lays out a strong version of the answer Yes, education should be gender free. And Chapter 4 makes the argument that education should be gender sensitive rather than gender free.

2

Genderized Education: Tradition Reconsidered

MARYANN AYIM

The important social question, Should public education be gender free? is a complex one to which no obvious and easy answer corresponds. Nor does the prior query, What does freedom from gender entail? admit of a clear answer. *Gender free* cannot be identified in any straightforward sense with *nonsexist*, for a social scheme that takes cognizance of and makes allowance for the childbearing capacity of women, for example, may well be nonsexist but will not normally be gender free.

In the next three chapters, three contrasting possibilities will be explored—a gender-laden scheme that is sexist, a gender-free scheme that is nonsexist, and a gender-laden scheme that is nonsexist. Our first chapter in this subpart will be devoted to an explication and critical analysis of the traditional view that holds females and males to be different in respects that justify male dominance and female subservience in the social order. This traditional stance answers a decided No to our question Should public education be gender free? Our second chapter, answering the question in the affirmative, will present a feminist perspective based on a gender-free scheme. Our third chapter, by contrast, will provide a negative reply to the question, developing a contrasting feminist perspective based on a gender-laden scheme.

Each of the three chapters will explain the function of public education and the implications for actual classroom practice from within the context of the position being developed.

THE RESPONSE OF THE
TRADITIONALIST

The Function of Public Education
Within the Traditional Framework

On the good constitution of mothers depends in the first instance that of their children; on the care of women depends the first education of men; on women also depend our manners, our passions, our tastes, our pleasures, and even our happiness. Thus the whole education of women should be relative to men. To please them, to be useful to them, to win their love and esteem, to bring them up when young, to tend them when grown, to advise and console them, and to make life sweet and pleasant to them; these are the duties of women at all times, and what they ought to learn from infancy. Unless we are guided by this principle, we shall miss our aim, and all the instructions which we bestow on them will contribute neither to their happiness nor to our own (Rousseau 1964, pp. 220–221).

Worthy of note in this passage from Rousseau are his views that (1) the social roles of males and females are dramatically different, (2) female as well as male happiness depends on this role differentiation, (3) female virtue is defined largely in terms of catering to males, (4) early socialization practices are essential to the perpetuation of this social order, and (5) the impact that women, in virtue of their being mothers, will have on the proper molding of the young is of critical importance.

Rousseau is a paradigm of the traditional thinking about the role of women in society; he sees male and female nature as essentially different in respects that are relevant to the assignment of rights and responsibilities, duties, and privileges in the social order. In particular, male dominance is seen to be a logical outgrowth of ineradicable sex differences. Within the traditional framework, socialization into gender-based roles is assigned a high priority in the public education system. The perpetuation of society in a basically unaltered form is perceived as a social good, and schools are charged with clear responsibility in the maintenance of this good.

Examples of traditional thinkers span the historical gamut from early Greek philosophers like Aristotle to such contemporary figures as Steven Goldberg (1977) and J. R. Lucas (1977). Before proceeding to an explication and analysis of the traditional arguments for a gender-based education, it will be useful to provide, however sketchily, some indication of the sort of society and educational system the traditionalists wish to enshrine. To this end, I shall explore certain provisions of the Family Protection Act,[1] an omnibus bill proposed by such right-wing groups as the Moral Majority and the National Pro-Family Coalition. If successful in its quest for government endorsement, the Family Protection Act would:

> establish a legal presumption in favor of a broad interpretation of parental rights to supervise a child's religious or moral formation; exempt disciplinary or corporal punishment actions taken by a parent or person authorized by the parent from the definition of "child abuse and neglect."
>
> Prohibit any program receiving federal funds from providing services or counseling on contraceptives or abortion to an unmarried minor without first notifying the minor's parents. . . .
>
> Bar attorneys funded through the Legal Services Corporation from taking part in any litigation involving abortion, busing, divorce or homosexual rights.
>
> Prohibit federal funding of any group or individual advocating homosexuality as a lifestyle. . . .
>
> Prohibit . . . use of federal funds for educational materials that "do not reflect a balance between the status role of men and women, do not reflect different ways in which women and men live and do not contribute to the American way of life as it has been historically understood" (Pelham 1981).

It is important to be clear that supporters of the Family Protection Act are not simply pro-family but defenders of a very narrow notion of the family as traditionally defined. Contrary to what representative pro-family groups insinuate, it is possible to be pro-family and yet not favor the traditional nuclear family at all.

For those who mean by *family* the traditional patriarchal, heterosexual unit, however, the school is perceived as one of the cornerstones on which the very possibility of a desirable social structure rests; to this end pro-family groups advocate heavily gender-based education, to the point of withdrawing funds from schools that fail to perpetuate the differences in sex roles endorsed by society.

Traditional Arguments Against Gender-Free Education

Three of the standard arguments used to invalidate the concept of gender-free education will be summarized and critically assessed: first, the argument that gender roles are biologically determined and hence inevitable; second, the argument that gender roles are necessary to biological reproduction and hence to the survival of the species; and third, the argument that gender roles are necessary for the replication of cultural values.

Argument 1: Gender Roles Are Inevitable

The inevitable character of gender roles is sometimes tied to religious theories that see the creation of female and male as fulfilling two different but mutually coherent sets of purposes in God's scheme for the world. We shall not consider this view, however, but shall restrict our account to the argument that sees biology as the root of gender-role assignment. According to this view, innate sex differences, which are encoded in our instincts, our hormones, our genitalia, or our brains, dictate a social ordering in which roles are allotted to people on the basis of what are perceived as complemental principles. When these principles are actually spelled out, however, as in Goldberg's theory, they are clearly linked to patriarchal assumptions that justify both male dominance and a severe restriction of the options available to females.

A logical shortcoming of this argument is readily apparent. If the innate sex differences postulated are inevitable in some strong sense of the word, then prescription is pointless—sex-role socialization would be totally unnecessary, for males and females would monitor their behavior in accordance with sex-role norms with the same predictability that the life cycle of the monarch unfolds from caterpillar through chrysalis to butterfly. Thus, the very need for a mandate to schools to socialize children into sex-specific codes of behavior reveals that this notion of innate sex differences is unworkable.

If we attribute a weaker interpretation to innate sex differences, the prescriptive role of the school in its socialization practices is no longer logically ludicrous. However, the question as to whether the school ought to endorse such behavior now arises. Even if we grant that sex differences are biologically determined in some sense, this provides no guarantee of moral worth. Many biologically determined features (such as homicidal mania resulting from brain damage) are deemed undesirable and are interfered with via brain surgery or imprisonment. In other words, the moral worth of any action is not entailed by establishing a biological basis for the behavior. Hence the argument of the inevitability of gender roles fails to undermine proposals for gender-free education.

Argument 2: Gender Roles Are Necessary to Biological Reproduction

Although some formulations of this argument are patently absurd,[2] at a more sophisticated level, this may be the most powerful of the arguments against gender freedom. We might argue, like Richard A. Wasserstrom (1979), that gender is as irrelevant as eye color in every context except reproduction. But we have no clear and obvious notion of exactly what features are embodied in the reproduction context. Deep gender rifts have been a part of our society for so long that we really do not know how reproduction would fare if they were expunged. Perhaps we would find that men, like Broud in *The Clan of the Cave Bear* (Auel 1980), would be unable to perform their part of the reproductive function in a situation that denied them the power to humiliate their mate by so doing. If this were true, one might ask whether such a race is worth preserving, but that is a somewhat separate question. Perhaps the reproductive process would become distasteful in an otherwise gender-free society, but endured, like trips to the dentist, for the greater long-term good. Or perhaps in a gender-free society, reproductive sex would become truly a thing of joy, guaranteed by the pleasure that it promised. We really do not know where on this spectrum human sexual response would fall, for none of us has any significant experience of a gender-free society.

This argument that gender roles are necessary to biological reproduction is basically an appeal to ignorance. The claim is that since we do not know whether or how certain aspects of our gender roles are linked to a mating system that ensures the reproduction of the species, we ought not to tamper with these gender roles. In response to this argument, the research conducted by John Money and Patricia Tucker (1975, p. 193), for example, suggests that core gender identity should be pared down to the minimal belief items linked to reproduction—that is, that males ejaculate and that females menstruate, gestate, and lactate. No further item should be necessary to our perception of ourselves as female or as male. In other words, a wide variety of gender roles are compatible with a successful mating system. Furthermore, we have a social responsibility to explore alternatives, given that our traditional mating and reproductive arrangements are linked to such morally unacceptable practices as rape, sexual harassment, and wife battering.

A corollary of the reproductive argument is that child rearing would not be accommodated in a gender-free society. This view is generally based on the assumption that only females are biologically (or emotionally, it is sometimes argued) equipped to rear children. Such a position confuses childbearing, with which nature has favored only females, with child rearing; biology has nothing to do with the relegation of this latter process, with the single exception of breast-feeding. The claim that females are emotionally better equipped to rear children is more powerful, but only in the context of our present society; given that men are socialized into violent, aggressive forms of behavior, entrusting little children to their care might well be an unwise move. But this has no implications whatever for the division of labor in a gender-free society. Hence the argument that gender roles are necessary to biological reproduction fails to undermine proposals for gender-free education.

Argument 3: Gender Roles Are Necessary for the Replication of Cultural Values

This argument claims, essentially, that the replication of social traditions will be controverted by any move toward gender freedom. The official pro-family groups endorse this argument, and many of the clauses in the proposed Family Protection Act point to specific customs or aspects of institutions that those who back the bill wish to preserve.

The argument that *if* gender roles are abandoned or tampered with, *then* society as we know it will be significantly, perhaps even radically, altered is a valid one. Thus the claim of the Ontario Teachers' Federation (1982) that "girls must be encouraged to see the relevance of science and mathematics to their career plans. They must learn that scientific and technical occupations are interesting, rewarding, and do not conflict with their role as women" (p. 8) is misleading if not false. Such careers almost certainly would conflict with their traditional roles as women. A more fruitful line of approach is not to deny such conflict but to argue that one or the other (or even both) of the conflicting elements ought to be altered.

Any convincing critique of this second argument will focus not on the hypothetical claim, which in itself is perfectly acceptable, but on another assumption or claim that must be made to give the argument any force. For we must know not only that altering gender roles will change social norms but also that the current social norms are worth preserving before we reject the option to alter or eradicate gender roles. It is precisely this assumption or claim that renders the argument problematic. It is not obviously true that historical institutions and norms should be preserved. Many traditions, such as slavery, have been clearly bad, and the weight of morality has been on the side of eradicating them.

In other words, for any particular custom or tradition, simply citing historical grounding for it is not sufficient justification; an independent argument for its desirability must be produced. It is in neglecting to provide such an argument that the official pro-family groups err. The advocates of the Family Protection Act, for example, fail to provide justification for the particular historical version of the family that they endorse, apparently believing that this view of the family is a priori acceptable.

The discussion of this third argument will be concluded by examining the three most powerful justifications for replicating traditional sex-role arrangements: that these arrangements are efficient, that they maximize the interest of females, and that they commit us to minimal levels of public interference in private matters.

Traditional Sex Role Arrangements Are Efficient. The general efficiency claim is basically the view that our current sex-role arrangements are best for all concerned—that they are efficient because they offer us a clear set of rules for shaping our lives and our behavior without which we would be reduced to confusion and ambiguity. With the present arrangement, we all know where we stand and what we can expect. Three points need to be made here. First, the fact that a set of mandates is efficient by no means offers sufficient justification for adoption. The existence of a set of instructions for efficiently destroying the earth's ozone layer does not justify carrying out those instructions. Second, the efficiency of one mandate does not rule out the efficiency of a different, even opposing mandate; it is quite possible to offer people clear and straightforward roles that are not gender based—such roles might be age based, occupation based, or interest based. Third, there is some doubt that sex roles are clear, unambiguous, and efficient for women. Many women experience a "double-bind" that emanates from the conflicting messages prescribed by the female sex role and regard their lives as intolerably restricted by the traditional sex roles.

Traditional Sex Role Arrangements Maximize the Interests of Females. This view generally begins from the premise that the lot of woman is so confined by biology anyway that traditional sex roles optimize her interests as much as possible within these confines. Steven Goldberg (1977), for example, states that:

> if society did not teach young girls that beating boys at competitions was unfeminine (behavior inappropriate for a woman), if it did not socialize them away from the political and economic areas in which aggression leads to attainment, these girls would grow into adulthood with self-images based not on succeeding in areas for which biology has left them better prepared than men, but on competitions that most women could not win. If women did not develop feminine qualities as girls (assuming that such qualities do not spring automatically from female biology) they then would be forced to deal with the world in the aggressive terms of men. They would lose every source of power their feminine abilities now give them and they would gain nothing (pp. 203–204).

A problem with this justification of traditional sex roles is its assumption that women are indeed weakened in the manner specified by the constraints of biology. It is not obvious that the childbearing capacities of women, or their hormone makeup, render them constitutionally unable to take on the running of the world and relegate them forever to the realms of child rearing and housekeeping.

However, suppose it were true that a large proportion of women are naturally unfit for the competitive endeavors traditionally associated with the male sex role. It is not clear that the unhappiness they would suffer in failing at male endeavors would be greater than the unhappiness suffered by women denied access to these realms or the unhappiness resulting from curtailed freedom of choice in general (Treblicot 1977, pp. 121–129).

An additional problem with the Goldberg argument is its assumption that the world should be defined in male terms. It may be true that in a world that defines success in terms of aggressive competitive behavior, females are ill equipped to succeed. It is far from clear, however, that this notion of success is a worthy one. It could be argued that correlating success to the nurturant affiliative behavior traditionally valued in females is much more conducive to a cohesive and smoothly functioning society.

Traditional Sex Role Arrangements Lead to Minimal Public Interference in Private Matters. J. R. Lucas (1977), for example, argues that sexual equality is not an appropriate social ideal because the range of controls that would be necessary to institute and monitor such equality would necessitate a totalitarian form of government (pp. 255–280). Thus we would be ill advised to attempt any egalitarian-motivated change in the traditional sex role standards. Lucas is correct in pointing out that a higher level of social control would ensue as a result of taking seriously a mandate for sexual equality. He is also right that such controls would eat into those aspects of our lives typically regarded as private. Although it is clear that male rights and privileges would be decimated by the institution of such controls, it seems equally apparent that females would generally stand to gain from measures that guaranteed them equal access to traditional male realms. Furthermore, if the public realm were to be redefined in terms of some of the traditional female rather than male values, we could argue that the habitation of this world would be a more pleasant venture for all concerned—male as well as female. As we have seen, the three standard arguments for retention of gender roles are seriously problematic and the typical justifications for *traditional* gender roles do not work either.

Implications of the Traditional Thesis for Classroom Practice

The traditional beginning of the traditional classroom day may well be some such phrase as, "Good morning, boys and girls," emphasizing the teacher's perception of males and females as vastly different creatures. Consequently, much of the teacher's methodology, from lining the children up into male-female rows, streaming them into sex-stereotyped subject areas, pitting male and female teams against one another whenever they do occupy the same classroom, maintaining different standards of excellence for males and females, particularly in physical education, math, and science, and even standard greetings and language patterns will highlight these perceived differences.

Boys' sports will receive more emphasis, better coaching, superior equipment, more encouragement in the form of cheerleaders, and so forth, than girls' sports, because physical strength will be perceived as more important in the male sex. More will be demanded of boys in the areas of mathematics and science, whereas females will be prepared for the gentler tasks of motherhood and all its associated roles—such as child nurturer, cook, nurse, and seamstress. The school board, the librarian, and the classroom teacher will all cooperate to ensure that textbooks, curriculum materials, and the library holdings endorse these views about sex-role behavior. Far from being imaginary, such a school, even today, is sadly commonplace.

Notes

1. This bill (S1373, HR 3955) was referred to five different Senate and House committees.

2. An example of the argument at its worst occurs in Michael Levin's attempt to persuade us of the evils inherent in parallel terms of address for males and females, in particular, the evils of a term such as *Ms.*, which, in failing to reveal the marital status of an adult female, threatens the survival of the species. Michael Levin, "Vs. Ms.," in *Sex Equality*, ed. Jane English (Englewood Cliffs, NJ: Prentice-Hall, 1977), 216–219.

3

Freeing the Children:
The Abolition of Gender

KATHRYN PAULY MORGAN

TWO INSTRUCTIVE ANECDOTES

Anecdote 1

I am fortunate to be able to teach a course entitled "Philosophy of Human Sexuality." One of the course materials I use is a story by Lois Gould called "X: A Fabulous Child's Story" (1974, pp. 281–290). Gould describes the adventures, challenges, and perils experienced by a child named X, whose gender goes undetermined for the entire story. She observes the behavior of X's committed parents who frequently consult their several-thousand-page *Instruction Manual* on how to raise a gender-free child. She notes the delighted reactions of X's gendered peers, reactions that are in striking contrast to those of their increasingly disturbed parents. Apart from the intrinsic interest of the story, I have noticed that whenever I read the story, I find *myself* desperately wanting to know X's gender. I search, time after time, for microscopic clues in the text that would reveal this information. I share the frustration and the curiosity of the other parents who want to know about X. At the same time, I realize well that I have no justification that would entitle me to that gender knowledge. And yet I still want to know. I do not regard my reaction as idiosyncratic or pathological. Rather, I see it as instructive, for it points to the centrality of our gender categories and gender assignments in mediating how we identify and understand others and ourselves.

Anecdote 2

I have recently acquired, as part of my politically correct set of feminist possessions, a bumper sticker that reads "Sexism Is a Social Disease." This bumper sticker complements a matching T-shirt and button bearing the same message. I want to stress both aspects of this claim: (1) that sexism is a profoundly crippling *disease*, and (2) that like some other diseases conspicuously communicated in a social context, sexism, too, is fundamentally social in nature and "caught" through social intercourse.

In this chapter, I argue that because sexism is social in nature, those institutions of a culture that serve as the primary transmitters of that sociality should work to eradicate the disease by striving for gender freedom.[1] It is not sufficient simply to develop some sort of inoculation to a disease that continues to threaten.

In order to effect a complete social cure, we must perceive sexism's tenacious, multifaceted nature and come to understand how different aspects interact and mutually reinforce each other. Only in this way can we come to comprehend how completely human life and sensibility can be infected and destroyed by this disorder.

In his essay "Racism and Sexism," Richard Wasserstrom (1979, pp. 5–20) distinguishes three separate domains for social analysis: the domain of social reality, the domain of social ideals, and the domain of optimal means for implementing those social ideals given a particular social reality.

Social Reality

The social reality of our situation is that people are not only distinguished on the basis of but discriminated against and harmed by the use of gender categories. Our situation is one of patriarchy in which males are accorded supremacy in theory, policy, and practice (even if not at the level of explicit political ideology). In her book *Sexual Politics*, Kate Millett (1970, pp. 23–58) argues that in a patriarchal society three important societal dimensions need to be integrated if male dominance is to come to be experienced and accepted as natural by virtually all the participants in that society, women as well as men. She maintains that such a society needs to construct some account of *personality* (mythic, commonsense, or theoretical) that holds that human beings are psychologically gendered at birth and that one's gendered personality is given, natural, and fixed. Any such view holds that such gender-normal personalities are properly ascribed, involuntarily, *at birth* on the basis of biological sex. Second, such a society must establish a functional set of social *roles*, called *sex roles*, which are normative regulatory principles assigned, again, at birth on the basis of biological sex. And third, a patriarchal society must accord differential *status* to the particular occupants of these sex-role clusters. This introduces a political element of differential social power. In practice, this will mean granting advantages and privilege to those biological males who automatically belong to the social category of men *and* who publicly and privately conform to the norms of the masculine sex-role system.[2] Our situation is further corrupted by the fact that our society is not only male supremacist; it is also racist, class biased, and oppressively heterosexist. Any adequate diagnosis, then, must keep all these lethal disease dimensions in mind.

Diagnosis is a complicated process. In what used to be phallocentrically described as a "seminal" article, Ayim and Houston (Chapter 1, this volume) analyze at least three logically independent forms of the disease. The first form they discuss is the content of an ideology or belief set. They claim that central to any constellation of sexist beliefs is this axiom: that certain natural differences exist between female and male human beings, which are seen as morally relevant in justifying social and political arrangements wherein men, by virtue of belonging to the category of men, are entitled to dominate and exercise legitimate authority over women. Second, sexism may manifest itself as the consequences of policies, practices, and institutional norms. Just as we inadvertently can set up optimal conditions for catching various diseases, so, too, can sexist consequences result from policies and practices that did not have sexist outcomes as part of their intentional program. In the more difficult case, we can be consciously trying to avoid a particular infection but become infected nevertheless. So, too, with sexism. We, as individuals, may try hard to avoid gender bias and oppression; nevertheless, sexist consequences may result from our practices. (How this might work in an educational setting is explored briefly later.)

Third, Ayim and Houston note that sexism may occur in the form of intentions. This intentionalist form may be present in explicit and deliberate words and actions that are designed to communicate sexist convictions and promote sexist aims. But sexism can also infect our intentional behavior, understood in a much broader sense to include our a priori conceptual frameworks and the use we make of them to understand and interpret the world and to predict and evaluate the significance of events in the world. In this more general case of a naive sexist, sexist derangement is at work, although the individual in question does not entertain the deliberate intent and purpose of being sexist or operate with an explicit, theoretically grounded sexist conceptual framework.[3]

Transposing the Ayim/Houston analysis into a specific social setting enables us to attend to systematic and complex forms of the disease. Let us look at a hypothetical classroom. Using the content criterion we can look at curriculum materials. Considerable critical progress has been made in this area concerning sexist stereotypes, but more needs to be done. For example, we need to assess counseling materials, personality tests (Bem 1976, Constantinople 1976), achievement tests (Nicholson 1983), and the operative principles of curriculum design to determine whether or not the educational process has been infected. Using the diagnostic instrument of the consequentialist analysis, we can scrutinize classroom dynamics and school policies. In many classrooms, interaction patterns between female and male instructors and female and male students differ demonstrably and significantly according to gender. There is now ample documentation showing that when other variables such as class and race are held constant in coeducational classrooms, male students are encouraged to ask questions. Males are called on more often than female students (despite a gender-equal distribution among raised hands), and the amount of time and quality of response given to questions asked by male students are greater than those accorded to female students.[4] The consequence of this practice is that not only are male students taken more seriously, they are seen by females and males alike to be entitled to be taken more seriously as participants in the kind of dialogue that is central to the educational process. This is an example of how sexist practices might operate in an educational setting, even though the instructor in question might be consciously trying to avoid sexism. Good intentions do not cure a sexist pedagogical dynamic and its harmful consequences.

Finally, using the diagnostic instrument of an intentionalist analysis, we might, for example, draw attention to the way teachers use labels such as *objective* and *rational* as forms of praise and devalue their alleged antithesis: the *subjective*, the *personal*, and that which *involves feelings*. In a sexist intentional context, boys and men will be expected to be, will be seen as striving for, and will be evaluated as producers of rational, objective knowledge. Such behavior will come to be seen as the mark of achieved masculinity as well as definitional of genuine knowledge. Analogously, concern with the subjective, the personal, and the emotional will be expected of and seen to be characteristic of normal women. What marks this as a sexist framework of interpretation is the simultaneous denigration of the latter focus and praise of women whose behavior is most accurately described as "thinking like a man."

A similarly complex sort of analysis must be carried out with respect to the other diseased dimensions of our society: our racism, our class bias, and our heterosexism. We live in a society in which oppression operates as a virtual epidemic for many people. It is clear that, unfortunately, these forms of oppression infect our classrooms as well.

Social Ideals and Values

What values and social ideals would justify striving for gender freedom as one focus of public social policy? Surely the top contenders—a kind of list of moral Oscar nominees—must include the following: social justice, equality, liberty, security, happiness and the avoidance of harm, equality of opportunity, autonomy, and privacy. Many moral conflicts derive not from the question of whether these are genuinely worthy moral goals, but from differences in ordering one's moral priorities. I claim that a social policy of gender freedom gives equality and justice pride of place alongside liberty and self-determination. It accords secondary importance to such values as privacy and security in realizing a healthy society that is genuinely gender free.

Optimal Means

Gender freedom, gender justice, and gender equality are inconsistent with any form of sexism. Sexism is conceptually and pragmatically dependent upon a complex structure of personal intentions, theories of personality, sets of roles, and differential gender-based assignments of power. I argue that the eradication of sexism demands the abolition of gender altogether. Because our lived experience of gender in patriarchy involves such multifarious domains and is such a systemic infection in our lives, gender must not only be deinstitutionalized,[5] it must be abandoned altogether. Moving to an individual and social world of gender freedom will involve profoundly altering our sense of personal identity, our fundamental conceptual schemes, our seemingly most intimate private actions,[6] and most of our social and political practices. We must degenderize our sense of self-identity so that gender no longer functions as a crucial social variable in understanding ourselves. Sex roles must disappear altogether as gender stops functioning as any sort of social and political category (whether power-laden or not) in determining how we conduct our lives. Gender will no longer function as an operative category of classification, prediction, interpretation, or evaluation. As a consequence, our psychological attitudes and social and moral postures around considerations of gender will be genuine puzzlement and profound indifference. Like freckles, gender will be regarded as something intrinsically irrelevant, though potentially dangerous insofar as it could again interfere with principled impartiality.

   Clearly this process must be carried out on a comprehensive scale, because the disease is highly contagious. One setting in which it is transmitted on a large scale is public education since schools are engaged in long term normative socialization directed toward producing acceptable adult members of the society.[7] I believe it is morally permissible for schools to take a relatively conservative stance with respect to the process of normative socialization when the society to be conserved is a morally justified one, one that is worthy of being perpetuated in subsequent generations. But when we can point to social realities in the dominant culture that are significantly morally defective, public education has a commitment to move toward morally acceptable political and social ideals. U.S. and Canadian society already has an explicit, articulated set of political and social ideals that stress individuality, freedom, and justice at the heart of its classical liberal ideology. What I am arguing is that gender freedom is necessary for the full implementation of those ideals.

Two Separate Cases

Not all societies are equally sexist. In some patriarchal societies where the norms of masculinity are wedded to violence the disease proves terminal or permanently maiming for many. In other cases, it is less threatening. I want to examine both ends of the spectrum, in other words, those societies that are horribly mutilated by sexism and those that seem relatively unaffected. The second case refers to (fictitious but logically interesting) gender-egalitarian societies, which could not be classified as practicing gender bias but which, nevertheless, retain an institutionalization of the category of gender. I wish to argue the more radical case for gender abolition and not restrict myself to manifestly sexist societies.

The first case is easy. The morally objectionable features are clear and readily observable. We are familiar with the history and practice of the systematic denial of human rights and full personal respect to women in such societies. We can document the widespread exploitation of women as unpaid workers in the home and low-paid, sexually harassed workers in the paid labor force. We know that many girls and women are the victims of sexual violence in the form of sexual abuse and incest as children and as targets for rape, mutilation, battering, and murder. All these phenomena are crucially bound up with not seeing women as fully developed human persons, a view entrenched in much of Western philosophy.[8] These ideas and practices have a devastating effect on a woman's own sense of self-respect and self-esteem. Moreover, as John Stuart Mill (1970) pointed out, the virulent form of the disease takes a moral, social, and psychological toll on men as well (although this cannot be equated with the harm experienced by those in a position of formal powerlessness). According to Mill,

> all the selfish propensities, the self-worship, the unjust self-preference which exist among mankind have as their source and root in, and derive their principal nourishment from the present constitution of the relation between men and women. . . . people are little aware, when a boy is differently brought up [from a girl] how early the notion of his inherent superiority to a girl arises in his mind; how it grows with his growth and strengthens with his strength, how it is inoculated by one schoolboy upon another; how early the youth thinks himself superior to his mother, owing her perhaps forbearance, but no real respect; and how sublime and sultan-like a sense of superiority he feels, above all over the woman whom he honours by admitting her to a partnership of his life. *Is it imagined that all this does not pervert the whole manner of existence of the man, both as an individual and as a social being?* (pp. 218–219, emphasis added)

This "perversion of the whole manner of existence" is caused by a situation of inequitable male supremacy, according to Mill. Moral, social, and personal alienation and corruption are inevitable outcomes of this sexist contagion. In this case, only the complete abolition of gender can eradicate the harm caused by the disease of sexism.

The second case is more challenging. I envision a society that I would describe as nonsexist and egalitarian but that continues to use the category of gender as a principle of social organization. I believe that there are, nevertheless, three morally objectionable features of this society. First, to the extent that gender categories would continue to be ascribed at birth on the basis of biological sex, they would interfere with the *voluntary* taking on of gender as a set of social roles.[9] Traditional definitions of the role set of marriage can be criticized on liberal grounds as unfair, because the people entering into the traditional contracts do not really have a choice as to who is going to play the role of husband and who is going to play wife (Ketchum 1979, pp. 184–189). Similarly, if the members of this egalitarian society do not have any choice about the gender they are expected to belong to, then this involuntary aspect of gender ascription is at least a prima facie reason for questioning the fairness of the process of gender ascription.

Second, insofar as a society uses gender as a principle of social organization, it must be, as a minimal logical requirement, a gender-dichotomized society. In the most exaggerated form, that society would speak (as we ourselves speak) in terms of "the opposite sex" and would likely support research (as we do) that would be published in the *Journal of Essential Sex Differences*, considering only that research publishable that uncovers statistically significant differences between or among the various genders. Regardless of the degree of opposition, any such genderized society would necessarily sever a sense of social community by splitting the members of that society in mutually exclusive gendered groups. Again, insofar as using the category of gender produces that loss of integrated community, I would see it as contributing to a sense of social disintegration while potentially obscuring important human continuities. Eliminating the category of gender would avoid both these dangers.

Third, it is likely that particular individuals will not feel comfortable with the prescribed norms definitional of their particular gender. To the extent that they are described in terms of and punished for *gender deviance* in their personalities, their behavior, their preferences, their mode of cognition, and their aspirations, their right to self-determination will be interfered with. And it is difficult to imagine a situation in which gender would function in a normless fashion.

Thus, I would conclude that the abolition of gender in the name of individual autonomy and social welfare is morally desirable in this second case as well.

Healthy Moral Benefits

I conclude by noting four healthy benefits of the campaign to eradicate gender. First, dismantling gender as a norm-laden category would alleviate an enormously destructive source of immoral gender coercion in the direction of gender conformity. This would have a liberating effect on our imaginations in exciting ways almost impossible to predict, although we are beginning to catch glimpses of this effect as gender categories become more blurred in our society. In a gender-free society we could explore life in the areas of work, sexuality, physical movement, speech, dress, learning patterns, personal relationships, virtues and vices, and forms of creativity in ways that would not be artificially created or constrained by gender. Second, the eradication of gender could provide us with a pragmatic model for striving for person-respecting equality in other areas of oppression such as race, an area in which analogously pseudonaturalistic arguments have been constructed to support a situation of white supremacy. Third, it is important to note that the virus of heterosexism feeds off sexism. Heterosexist oppression fueled by feelings of homophobia against those individuals attracted to members of their own gender is conceptually dependent upon being able to make gender distinctions. Abolishing those distinctions would make the practice of heterosexist persecution and discrimination impossible to pursue. Fourth, and finally, the abolition of gender and gender distinctions would serve to promote in a deep and rich way an integrated sense of human community consistent with the flourishing of genuine individuality.

Notes

1. Note that I am arguing for a stronger position than simply equating gender freedom and gender blindness. The term *gender blindness* can mean ignoring, not attending to, or refusing to take notice of *existing* gender. I am not interested in this sense of the term. Gender freedom can also be understood as *gender sensitivity*, as this term has been developed by Jane Roland Martin and others in the literature. As I understand this notion, it is directed toward the elimination of gender bias, a goal that may require attending to gender as a matter of social practice. It is in this sense that gender freedom is understood by Barbara Houston, the author of Chapter 4. I reject this use of the term in favor of a third, strong reading, which entails the total obliteration of gender as an operative social category. I argue for the abolition of gender in the public domain where it may be appealed to to support differential access to rights, obligations, powers, privileges, burdens, and roles. I also argue that as a social category with normative implications it should be eliminated in the informal private domain as well. See Jane Roland Martin's work, in particular, "The Ideal of the Educated Person" (Martin [1981b] 1994); "Excluding Women from the Educational Realm," *Harvard Educational Review*, 52, No. 2 (1982), 133–148; "Bringing Women into Educational Thought," *Educational Theory*, 34, No. 4 (1984), 341–353.

2. It should be noted that this twofold condition is crucial. Not all men gain access to power in a patriarchal society. In particular, those men who are labeled "effeminate" are socially punished and lose such access.

3. Part of the elegance of the Ayim-Houston analysis derives from the power it gives one to identify and distinguish the unreflective, naive sexist, the well-intentioned but inadvertent sexist, and an explicit, theoretically grounded sexist. Analogous but sketchy categories are worked out by Marilyn Frye in an otherwise well-argued

paper. See Marilyn Frye, "Male Chauvinism: A Conceptual Analysis," in *Philosophy and Sex*, ed. Robert Baker and Frederick Elliston (Buffalo, NY: Prometheus Books, 1975), 65–79.

4. This phenomenon is now documented and discussed in a voluminous literature. See, for example, the Association of American Colleges, *The Classroom Climate: A Chilly One for Women*, a report issued by the Project on the Status and Education of Women, 1982; Dale Spender, *Man Made Language* (Boston: Routledge and Kegan Paul, 1980), especially "Constructing Women's Silence"; and Barrie Thorne and Nancy Henley, eds., *Language and Sex: Difference and Domination* (Rowley, MA: Newbury House, 1975).

5. I am using this term in the technical sense introduced by Alison Jaggar (1979) in "On Sexual Equality," in *Philosophy and Women*, 77–87. Jaggar argues against the institutionalization of sexual differences where an *institution* is understood as a "relatively stable way of organizing a significant social activity," which defines "socially recognized roles and thus enables prediction of what those participating in the practice are likely to do. It also . . . provides a standard of correctness by reference to which the propriety of certain kinds of behaviour may be judged" (78).

6. One of the fundamental insights of feminism, both historically (e.g., in the work of John Stuart Mill and Charlotte Perkins Gilman) and in its contemporary articulation, has been the illuminating of the dark side of sexual politics as it has permeated the domain of the apparently most intimate and private.

7. For a normative philosophical analysis of this process, see Kathryn Morgan, "Socialization, Social Models, and the Open Education Movement: Some Philosophical Speculations," in *The Philosophy of Open Education*, ed. David Nyberg (Boston: Routledge and Kegan Paul, 1974), 278–314. See also Kathryn Morgan, "Socialization and the Impossibility of Human Autonomy" (Paper presented at the American Philosophical Association, Western Division, 1977).

8. For an examination of the concept of "seeing X as a fully developed person," see Frye, "Male Chauvinism." For useful historical anthologies documenting this claim, see Rosemary Agonito, ed., *History of Ideas on Woman: A Source Book* (New York: G. P. Putnam's Sons, 1977); Martha Lee Osborne, ed., *Woman in Western Thought* (New York: Random House, 1979).

9. From M. Wollstonecraft onward, many liberal feminists have voiced this concern. See, for example, Alison Jaggar, "On Sexual Equality"; Joyce Treblicot, "Sex Roles: The Argument from Nature," in *Sex Equality*, ed. Jane English (Englewood Cliffs, NJ: Prentice-Hall, 1977), 121–129.

4

Gender Freedom and the Subtleties of Sexist Education

BARBARA HOUSTON

Discussion of the question, Should public education be gender free? should begin with a sorting out of the different possible meanings of the term *gender free*.[1] In the context of our discussion I consider three distinct meanings. In the first sense, the strong sense, a gender-free education would be one that made active attempts to disregard gender by obliterating gender differentiations that arose within the educational sphere. Ruling out items on IQ tests that gave sex-differentiated results in scores is an example of a gender-free educational practice in this strong sense. Such efforts are sometimes described as attempts to deinstitutionalize sex differences in order to create a form of gender blindness.[2] Another example of this approach is the elimination of activities, such as wrestling, in which there are thought to be significant gender differences in achievements due to natural and ineradicable biological differences between the sexes.[3]

In the second case, the weak sense, gender free means that gender is ignored, not attended to. On this meaning a gender-free education is one that refuses to take notice of gender. No longer using gender as an admissions criteria to educational institutions or to specific educational programs is an example of this weak sense of gender free.

In the third sense I take gender free to mean freedom from gender bias. On this understanding, a gender-free education would be one that eliminated gender bias.

In this last, weakest sense, we could all be said to favor gender-free education. Even the traditionalist who holds to false accounts of sex differences and inadequate justification for gender roles within education might well argue that gender differentiations within education are not meant to constitute a gender *bias*. So the interesting interpretation of our question, Should public education be gender free? is *not*, Should public education be free of gender bias? This question is not an issue, since all positions, at least in their rhetoric, already agree that public education should be free of gender bias. The question is rather what is the best way to achieve this freedom from gender bias. Should we undertake to ignore gender or to obliterate gender differentiations, or should we in some way pay deliberate attention to gender?

I assume, in this chapter, the viewpoint of an educator who is already committed to sex equality and to equal educational opportunity but who recognizes that a number of practical questions and policy matters are still undetermined with respect to the question of whether we should or should not institute a kind of gender blindness. I shall argue that in the present circumstances, the adoption of either a weak or a strong version of gender-free strategy is problematic in two different ways. It is problematic, first, because the use of either version of the strategy is likely to cause us to miss, or even to reinforce, the more subtle form of gender bias. Through an examination of three prevalent forms of gender bias and actual examples of the gender-free strategy, I shall show that a general adoption of this strategy would likely ensure that females continue to have unequal educational opportunity. The strategy is problematic in a second way, because both versions of it presuppose an ideal of sex equality that prematurely forecloses on important questions central to the issue. In conclusion, I shall defend a more promising strategy for achieving freedom from gender bias, a strategy first suggested in the work of Jane Roland Martin (1981), which she labeled *gender sensitive*.[4]

Gender Bias: Unequal Access, Unequal Opportunity for Participation, and Genderized Valuation

That girls and women have had unequal access to educational institutions is news to no one. Undoubtedly significant progress toward sex equality was made when it was decided that we should ignore gender, that is, no longer pay attention to it in deciding who should get an education, who should be admitted to schools, allowed to study certain subjects, and have access to particular educational activities. Having come to the realization that much sex-segregated education has been both different and unequal, we made the choice to ignore gender, which has enabled us to move to coeducation in a stricter sense. For example, no longer do we have home economics and typing for girls only or physical sciences and industrial arts for boys only.

Physical education is an especially interesting case in point. Sex-segregated classes have fostered different and unequal education for boys and girls in this domain.[5] One reasonable attempt to eliminate the gender bias that has developed in physical education has been to adopt both the weak and strong versions of what I have called the gender-free strategy. This approach has urged that we ignore the gender of those in the physical education class and ignore the gender of those on the teams, allowing all to have equal access to the educational resources. Under such a policy, one would expect girls' and women's opportunities to increase. But often quite the opposite is true. Solomon's observations of game interactions in a fifth-grade coed class showed that

> girls tended to be left out of game interactions by the boys. This was true even when the girls had a higher skill level than boys did. Additionally, both girls and boys regarded boys as better players even when the girls were more highly skilled. Boys preferred to pass the ball to an unskilled boy rather than to a skilled girl. Girls tended to give away scoring opportunities to boys. Unskilled girls were almost completely left out of game action. However, both skilled and un-skilled girls received fewer passes than boys did (Griffin 1980, p. 10).

Of course, it is a good thing to remove access barriers to education, and in this case ignoring gender has allowed us to do that. However, equal partici-pation in the educational process is also a crucial dimension of equal educa-tional opportunity. In this case, the strategy that removes access barriers has also had the effect of bringing about a *greater loss* of educational opportunities for girls (Diller and Houston, Chapter 14, this volume).

Research findings suggest that this basketball game, where males keep passing the ball to each other, is a metaphor for all types of mixed-sex class-rooms and activities. From the research we have on student-teacher interac-tions and on student-student interactions, essentially the same picture emerges, although there are some differences dependent upon the race and class of the students.

Studies on teacher-student interactions indicate that within coeducational classrooms, teachers, regardless of sex, interact more with boys, give boys more attention (both positive and negative), and that this pattern intensifies at the secondary and college levels. Girls get less teacher attention and wait longer for it. When they do get attention, it is more likely that the teacher will respond to them neutrally or negatively (although this depends some-what on the girls' race and class). The reinforcement girls do get is likely to be for passivity and neatness, not for getting the right answer (Frazier and Sadker 1973; Mahoney 1983; Spender 1982; Spender and Sarah 1980; Stacey, Bercaud, and Daniels 1974; Stanworth 1983).

Equally distressing is the indication we have from research findings that student interactions with one another also appear to dampen female partici-pation in mixed-sex classes. At the postsecondary level often the brightest women in the class remain silent; women students are in general likely to be less verbally assertive, they are likely to be called on less often than men stu-dents, and those who do participate may find that their comments are disproportionately interrupted by teachers and male classmates and that teachers are less likely to develop their points than those made by men students.[6]

Part of the explanation for these classroom inequities may be that the everyday linguistic patterns of how women and men talk together in mixed-sex groupings is carried over into the classroom. In mixed-sex groupings men talk more than women; men talk for longer periods of time and take more turns at speaking; men exert more control over the conversation; men interrupt women more than women interrupt men; and men's interruptions of women more often introduce trivial or inappropriately personal comments that bring women's discussion to an end or change its focus. It is also indicated that what men say carries more weight. A suggestion made by a man is more likely to be listened to, credited to him, developed in further discussion, and adopted by the group than a suggestion made by a woman (Spender 1980a and 1980b; Spender and Sarah 1980).

There are also linguistic styles of speech that can affect women's participation opportunities in the classroom. For example, there are certain features that occur more in women's speech than in men's, such as hesitations, false starts, a questioning intonation when making a statement, an extensive use of qualifiers that serve to weaken what is said, an extensive use of modals and forms of speech that are excessively polite and deferential. In addition, in mixed-sex interactive patterns the speech of women is more supportive than that of men, inasmuch as it exhibits an effort to elicit and encourage the contributions of the other speakers to the conversation. Male patterns, in contrast, include highly assertive speech, an impersonal and abstract style, and "devil's advocate" exchanges (Ayim 1982; Key 1975; Thorne and Henley 1975).

The problem, as one researcher suggests, is that in the school setting these "male" ways of talking are often "equated with intelligence and authority" (Association of American Colleges, 1982). If someone speaks hesitantly or with numerous qualifiers, she is perceived by her teachers and classmates as unfocused and unsure of what she wants to say. It is also clear that an overly polite style more easily allows interruptions or inattention from both teachers and students (Spender 1980b, p. 150). The same points made in a "masculine," assertive way are taken more seriously. But more significant perhaps is the fact that although it is thought to be perfectly proper for boys to "conduct argument, air their views and query information," it is not thought proper for girls to do the same thing (Spender 1980b, p. 150). This genderized valuation of classroom talk poses special problems for girls who seek to take on those ways of talking associated with "intelligence and authority."

What are the consequences for girls if the classrooms are male-dominant in this way? Clearly, we think it important that learners be able to talk about their own experiences as a starting point for learning; we regard the classroom as an opportunity for discovering new insights and understandings that need not depend upon received knowledge. Here, we say, "Students can find out things for themselves, they can ask questions, make new connections, describe and explain the world in different ways" (Spender 1982, p. 61). Indeed, we even claim they can criticize the received texts. But what if one-half of the students are not free to make such explorations, to take up the topics of their choosing, to articulate and validate their own experience? What if this opportunity is blocked for them?

Teacher behavior can directly or inadvertently reinforce those patterns that make it difficult for half the class population not only to talk, particularly to the teacher, but also to have their own experience be perceived as interesting and appropriate topics to discuss. If teachers fail to notice the gender of the student who is talking, if they pay no attention to who is interrupting whom, whose points are acknowledged and taken up, who is determining the topic of discussion, then they will by default perpetuate patterns that discourage women's participation in the educational process.

The teacher may well try to ignore gender, but the point is that the students are not ignoring it in their sense of how the interactions should go and who is entitled to speak in the educational arena. Gender may be excluded as an *official* criterion, but it continues to function as an *unofficial* factor.

In a study (Tavris 1983) designed to measure the effects of efforts to correct sexism in education, a tenth-grade girl said, "If I were a boy I would be more outspoken and confident, but I really don't know why" (p. 94). It has been suggested that "the why is that boys usually know that they are valued whereas girls are not always sure" (p. 94). Although they may not articulate it, students of both sexes have a clear perception of the devaluation of girls in the culture (p. 94). Obviously, in these circumstances if we simply ignore gender differentiations in the mode in which students can participate in the educational process, we will reinforce the message that girls do not count, or at least they do not count as much.

This suggestion of some of the influences of gender in educational interactions has been necessarily brief. The picture is not nearly as simple as time forces us to sketch it. Nevertheless, although gender bias will vary in texture and complexity depending upon many other factors, notably race and class, our picture points to the fundamental issue with which we should be concerned: the manner in which the school can confirm girls in subordinate positions. This, I would stress, should be a matter of concern regardless of girls' school achievements.

Evaluation of the Gender–Free Approach

When gender differentiations exist in the opportunity to participate in the educational process, what are we to do to eliminate bias? Within the gender-free strategy there are two approaches, one more radical than the other. We have seen that the first approach, that of deciding to ignore gender by no longer letting it count where it had before, is certainly effective in removing gender as an access barrier. However, we cannot count on this passive ignoring of gender as an effective means of eliminating other types of gender bias. In fact, it appears that it may simply have the effect of masking other types of bias, for example, in opportunities for participation.

There are two general difficulties with the approach suggested by the weak sense of gender free. First, it is doubtful that teachers *can* ignore gender in this sense, because they often do not recognize when gender is exerting an influence. It is startling just how unaware teachers are of the phenomenon we have described. Their perceptions of how they interact with students are often grossly inaccurate. Having claimed that they treat girls and boys equally in the classroom, they are shocked to discover through objective observation measures that they spend over two-thirds of their time with boys who compose less than half the class; or that they reward boys for getting the right answers and girls for neatness; or that they criticize boys for poor work and criticize girls for being assertive; or that they explain a boy's achievements in terms of his abilities and a girl's in terms of the degree of difficulty of the test or in terms of luck (Spender 1982, p. 82). Students, however, are often clear in their perceptions of the gender differences in student-teacher interactions (Sarah 1980; Stanworth 1983).

But the second and equally important difficulty is that even if the teacher were successful in ignoring gender, it is obvious that students do take cognizance of it. The gender-connected conventions and expectations that students themselves bring to their classroom interactions will continue unaltered, if not actually strengthened, if teachers do not intervene to change the patterns.

Perhaps mindful of these difficulties, the other version of the gender-free strategy would have us press for interventions to eliminate any gender differences in achievements in the hopes of creating in us a kind of gender blindness. As with the first approach, this more active pursuit of gender blindness can be useful. But it is also problematic. There is the very real danger that in restructuring activities we are likely to be unduly influenced by a male valuation scheme. For example, it would have us intervene to eliminate or restructure sports at which either of the sexes had a natural advantage because of physical differences, such as football, in which males are favored, or certain forms of gymnastics work, such as the balance beam, in which girls are favored. The idea behind restructuring sports activities has been to allow girls and boys equal rates of success. However, there are a number of dubious assumptions at work here, for instance, the assumption that girls' performance levels are accurately perceived and that these levels do determine their opportunities.

But the case is not that simple. The problem is not how well girls do in relation to boys; the problem is that *even when girls do as well as or better than boys at the same activity*, their performance is undervalued by themselves and by others, and their opportunities remain relatively limited (Stanworth 1983). A more radical critique would note that, even if we could straighten out the misperceptions about performance and opportunities, we should still question the further value assumption that only winning matters, rather than the enjoyment of playing or the development of a sporting attitude (Diller and Houston, Chapter 14, this volume).

In the case of gender-differentiated speech patterns, a male valuation scheme might well recommend a single classroom speech pattern, an assertive one, and offer girls and women special training in this form of "educated speech." But giving girls lessons in how to be assertive in the classroom can be problematic when it merely puts girls in a double bind in which they must adopt what are perceived as "masculine" speech patterns if they are to succeed. As we have noted earlier, the patterns of speech in boys and men that are regarded as forceful are often regarded as negative and hostile when used by girls and women (Spender 1982, pp. 60, 64).[7] More to the point, women's conventional patterns of speech have been demonstrated to be helpful insofar as they foster participation by others and encourage a cooperative development of ideas rather than adversarial relations (Fishman 1977, pp. 99–101). If we attempt to eliminate gender differentiations, we will have to bear in mind that often our evaluation of the differences has itself been gender biased.

There are two other significant problems that need to be addressed in our discussion of the interventionists' gender-free approach: How accurate are teachers' perceptions of fairness? And more significantly, what influence can we expect students' efforts to have on teachers' efforts to bring about change?

Even those teachers who undertake to correct genderized patterns of participation have been, in the words of one of them, "spectacularly unsuccessful." Dale Spender (1982, p. 55) notes with dismay how she and others seriously underestimated the amount of attention they gave to boys as compared to girls, *even when they were trying to be fair about it.* When teachers feel they are being fair, or even showing favoritism to girls, the empirical evidence shows otherwise. For example, giving 35 percent of one's attention to girls can feel as though one is being unfair to boys. Giving just over one-third of one's attention to girls can feel as though one is making a significant effort, even compensating girls.

It is important to notice that students share this perception. For example, when a teacher tries to eliminate gender bias in participation by giving 34 percent of her attention to girls who compose one-half of the class, the boys protested: "She always asks girls all the questions"; "She doesn't like boys and just listens to girls all the time" (Spender 1982, p. 57). In a sexist society boys perceive that two-thirds of the teacher's time is a fair allotment for them, and if it is altered so that they receive less, they feel they are being discriminated against. And of course they resist, and they protest, and teachers often give in in order to foster the cooperation that gives the appearance that they are in control of the classroom. Anyone who has tried to correct the bias will recognize the phenomenon.

In other words, even a strong interventionist strategy may at best achieve a gender-free inequality that gives two-thirds time for attending to males. As Spender notes, even when teachers do want to treat the sexes equally, the difficulty is that "our society and education is so structured that 'equality' and 'fairness' means that males get more attention" (Spender 1982, p. 55). Our own existing perceptual frameworks are themselves too gender biased to provide reliable guides as to whether or not our approaches are actually gender free. Of course these difficulties will plague all methods we use to get rid of gender discrimination. However, their presence represents a powerful argument against the suggestion that the best route to sex equality in education is simply to ignore gender and, as I shall argue, careful attention to these difficulties can point to a better approach to the problem of the elimination of gender bias.

Thus, as with the weaker version of the gender-free strategy, I find two major difficulties with the stronger version: (1) It fails to aid us in the identification and elimination of genderized valuations and (2) because of this, in employing the strategy we run a serious risk of encouraging an assimilation of women's identity, interests, and values to men's.

It should be clear that I do not object to all suggestions coming from the gender-free approach. As I have indicated, I think it is useful, indeed imperative, at times to ignore gender in the weak sense, and at other times I think it is useful to try to obliterate gender differentiations to ensure the absence of improper gender influence. However, it is also clear that both recommendations may, on occasion, fail to eliminate bias. More importantly, on some occasions we may need to use gender as a criterion in designing a practice useful to eliminating gender bias.

For example, we might restructure the basketball game so as to introduce new rules requiring alternative passes to females and males. In other sports such as volleyball one might introduce a temporary rule change: Boys must set up spikes for girls. We may even want to introduce single-sex schooling. Some studies indicate that in certain contexts it may be necessary to have single-sex classrooms for particular subjects such as math or science for a period of time to ensure that in coeducational classrooms girls will have an equal opportunity to participate and attain equal educational results (Finn, Reis, and Dulberg 1980; Laviqueur 1980). The point is that these equalizing practices require those involved to be sensitive to gender in a way that appears to be ruled out by the gender-free strategy.

My most general objection then to the gender-free strategy, both the strong and the weak versions, is twofold: (1) It is likely to create a context that continues to favor the dominant group and (2) it undermines certain efforts that may be needed to realize an equalization of educational opportunities.

The central problem with the gender-free mandate is that it misleadingly suggests that in order to free ourselves of gender bias, we have to stop paying attention to gender. It is singularly odd to call this approach gender free or gender blind if it involves paying attention to gender. If we look closely, we find that any significant success of the gender-free strategy would require that one continue to pay scrupulous attention to gender to make sure that the strategy is effective in eliminating bias. Either the strategy recommends this attention to gender or it does not. If it does, its rhetoric is misleading; if it does not, its method is mistaken.

In response to my evaluation of the gender-free strategy, it may be said that I have created a straw strategy. In particular, a gender-free enthusiast might claim that the strategy can be more effectively used than is suggested by my choice of examples. This response to my criticism has some merit. It is not ever wholly convincing to argue that a strategy or method is a poor one because its use is liable to error. In the wrong hands, or in difficult circumstances, any method for eliminating gender bias will suffer an increased likelihood of failure.

A critic might also contend that any persuasive force my remarks or examples may have is due to my equivocation upon the notion of ignoring gender. Proponents of the gender-free approach would undoubtedly claim that the gender-free strategy, in recommending that we ignore gender, is not recommending that we stop attending to it. But no, my criticism cuts deeper than this. My point is that the gender-free strategy presupposes that we have a priori decided that gender should have no educational relevance attached to it. This, I contend, could never be decided once and for all a priori. The greatest danger of the gender-free approach is that it prematurely forecloses on two important questions: (1) Are there gender-related differences? and (2) How are we to evaluate them?

With the growth of women's studies in the past decade we are only now beginning to catch a glimmer of the powerful and subtle ways in which gender has been and continues to be a basic social organizing principle in all known societies. In taking gender itself as a matter of study, women's studies has produced a revolutionary means of viewing the form and subject matter of a variety of disciplines. It is too early to pronounce that we know all the forms of gender bias and that we know that they are best eliminated by invoking a gender-free ideal and a gender-free strategy. We need to pay yet *more* attention to gender, not ignore it. We need to inquire further into gender differences, not try to get rid of them.

For the first time in history, we are now actually in a position in which women are beginning to create a study of themselves by themselves. There is now the opportunity for us to articulate systematically, theorize about, and evaluate our own experience. We need this opportunity especially to investigate what is or might be uniquely female experience in order better to understand the human condition. We will not achieve the understanding we seek if we ignore or try to obliterate gender differences, or attend only to those experiences that the genders share in common, without first being sure that we have accurate information about differences and a proper evaluation of them.

Assumptions About Gender

Thus far I have attempted to show that the gender-free strategy is suspect because both versions of it, the strong and the weak, fail us in the identification and elimination of the type of gender bias I have called gender valuation. I wish now to explain why the strategy has this effect in some cases. The explanation lies in an examination of the assumptions about gender that underlie the strategy and the ideal of sex equality at which it aims.

The ideal of sex equality urged by those who advocate the gender-free strategy is one that gives gender the status that eye color now has in our society. In short, gender is taken to be totally irrelevant to social organization. I have no special quarrel with the claim that this is precisely how a good, just society ought to treat gender. My worry is that this ideal is not especially helpful in the detection and elimination of existing gender bias.

This difficulty arises, I suspect, because there is a tendency to see gender as a trait of individuals. If gender were simply a characteristic of individuals that was linked to sex, could be easily marked, correlated with achievements, and used as a criterion for qualification or exclusion, then it would make good sense to talk about ignoring gender or treating it as an irrelevant characteristic. However, although we do speak of individuals as gendered, if we see gender solely or primarily as a trait of individuals, we shall be seriously misled.

Gender is also a structure of power; it is a structuring *process*. As one group of researchers puts it, we are better to "treat gender not just as a matter of existence of two categories of people, male and female, but primarily as a pattern of *relations* among people" (Connell, Ashenden, Kessler, and Dowsett 1982, pp. 34–35). They note further: "Relationships between the sexes are not just a matter of distinctions leading to inequalities. They are also relations of power. When we talk about gender we are talking about ways in which social relations get organized in the interests of some groups, overriding the interests of others" (p. 173).

It is equally important to notice that these social relations are systematic, not random and historical, not static. They change constantly, and they are influenced by other social structuring processes such as race and class. But matters are extremely complex, because the influence of race and class is not in any way straightforward. "Class and gender do not occur jointly in a situation. They abrade, inflame, amplify, twist, negate, dampen and complicate each other. In short, they interact vigorously, often through the schools and often with significant consequences for schooling" (p. 182).

If we want to make any significant difference in the educational opportunities of girls, we shall have to take cognizance of the precise nature of the femininity the school is helping to construct, how it is aided or subverted by race
and class influences; and we shall have to map the consequences of alternative
interventionist policies. This will not be an easy task. The structuring
processes of race, class, and gender have different dynamics, and attempts to
remedy unequal educational opportunities from the point of view of one of
these interests can have different and even contrary effects for the others. We
have learned, for example, that in some cases policies undertaken with class
interests in mind have had differential effects for girls and boys (p. 181). In
other instances we have learned that the educational sex segregation of girls,
which once served to marginalize them and socialize them to a subordinate
role, now works, in some class contexts, to erode their subordination (p. 182).

Because gender is a set of relations that is constantly changing and is constantly affected by other structuring processes in social relations, the gender-
free strategy has to appear somewhat simplistic. It is misleading to think of
gender as something that can be ignored or treated as irrelevant. Gender relations can be ignored, but only at the risk of entrenchment; and although
they are changeable, it misses the mark to think of them as something that
can be eliminated. Eliminating gender bias may often be a matter of seeing
gender differently rather than becoming blind to it. It is not always a question of making some characteristic of individuals irrelevant; it is often a matter of recognizing that some activities, characteristics, or interests of individuals are more valuable than we thought. We need to learn to assess them
independently of their location in gender relations.

A Gender–Sensitive Perspective

But there is another, a better, approach to the elimination of gender bias, one
that is conceptually distinct from the gender-free approach, although it does
not necessarily foreclose on any particular suggestions recommended by that
strategy. Jane Martin (1981) has suggested that we employ a gender-sensitive
perspective, which recommends that we pay attention to gender when by doing so we can prevent sex bias or further sex equality. This perspective requires careful monitoring of our gender interactions and urges direct intervention when necessary to equalize opportunities. In considering alternative
strategies for eliminating bias, I think it is Martin's that is the most defensi-
ble.

The difference between a gender-*sensitive* strategy and a gender-*free* one is
that a gender-sensitive strategy allows one to recognize that at different times
and in different circumstances one might be required to adopt opposing policies in order to eliminate gender bias.[8] A gender-sensitive perspective is not a
blueprint for education that will answer all our questions about particular

practices. It is, rather, a perspective that constantly reminds us to question the ways in which students and teachers make sense of and respond to a sexist culture. It is a situational strategy, one that lets the patterns of discrimination themselves determine which particular action to take to eliminate bias. This is an important feature to bear in mind. It is the chief virtue of this perspective, for new unsuspected types of gender bias will continue to emerge.

We have already seen how a significant school policy on gender relations (coeducation) that was designed to remove access barriers has revealed that women do not have equal participation in the educational process. Once equal participation is achieved, it will become more evident that women do not have an equal say about what knowledge is to be distributed, or about what the styles of pedagogy should be, or about what the goals and ideals of education should be (Martin 1981b).

A gender-sensitive perspective is a higher-order perspective than that involved in the gender-free strategy. It encourages one to ask constantly: Is gender operative here? How is gender operative? What other effects do our strategies for eliminating gender bias have?

A gender-sensitive perspective can also be differentiated from a gender-free strategy by the kinds of questions it leaves open—questions that a gender-free strategy threatens to close, for example, questions about possible differences in learning that might be correlated with gender relations. It is not that a gender-sensitive perspective claims there *are* significant differences, only that there *could be*, given the way in which gender has functioned as a species creator within our culture.

The superiority of the gender-sensitive perspective is secured by the fact that it can yield a methodology that is self-correcting. For it is a view that can acknowledge that gender is a set of relations between the sexes, a process that is constantly organizing and reorganizing our social life. It can recognize the dynamic nature of the gender system, one that exerts pressures, produces reactions, and generates changes (Connell et al. 1982, p. 30). It is the only perspective of the three considered that maintains a constant vigilance and reckoning on the significance gender acquires in particular contexts. Only if we adopt a perspective of this sort will we be able to catch our own errors, alter policies and practices that no longer work, and introduce new policies for new circumstances. It is in this sense that a gender-sensitive perspective can be a self-correcting methodology for realizing the elusive ideal of sex equality.

Conclusion

In this chapter I have tried to address the transitional problem of moving from a gender-biased education in a sexist culture to an unbiased education that will continue for some time to be influenced by the wider culture. I have argued that the most effective way to deal with gender bias is to adopt a gender-sensitive perspective, which is fundamentally a perspective that encourages a critical and constant review of the meaning and evaluation attached to gender. In this it offers greater hope for the elimination of all types of gender bias than does a gender-free strategy.

Notes

1. One of the common distinctions employed in the literature on sex roles and sex equality is that drawn between sex and gender. When the distinction is drawn, *sex* refers to the biological differences between females and males and *gender* refers to the social differences between the sexes. However, the matter is far from simple; usage of the terms is often inconsistent, and some have argued that the distinction itself is unsuccessful because of the complex linkage between the biological and social aspects of sex (see Eichler 1980). I grant the difficulties and nevertheless employ the distinction in this chapter. I use the term gender free precisely because I believe that not only biological differences between the sexes are relevant to the discussion of sex equality in education. I do not wish to beg any questions about the nature or causal explanation of gender differences, but I am interested in the implications we think gender relations should have for educational theory and practice. Hence I invoke the notion of gender, but I use it solely as a descriptive term. For an elaborate clarification of the notions of gender, gender identity, and gender role and a discussion of their related implications for education, see Ayim and Houston (1985).

2. As far as I know, the term *gender blindness* was first introduced by Richard Wasserstrom (1979).

3. For a discussion of the merits and difficulties with this attempt to pursue gender blindness, see Wasserstrom (1979) and Boxill (1980).

4. For further discussions of Martin's critique of philosophy of education and her views about the best ways to include women in educational theory and practice, see the bibliographic references listed for Martin.

5. This point has been argued in many places. Noteworthy discussions occur in Fischel and Pottker, eds. (1977), Saario, Jacklin, and Tittle (1973), and Eitzen, ed. (1979).

6. For a summary and discussion of these findings, see the report issued by the Project on the Status and Education of Women of the Association of American Colleges, entitled *The Classroom Climate: A Chilly One for Women* (Washington, DC: Association of American Colleges, 1982).

7. For a more general discussion of the genderized valuation of educational traits, see Martin (1981b).

8. If the complexities of gender relations were acknowledged and taken seriously in education, one should expect those interested in sex equality to recognize that different social contexts can make the same educational policy at one time effective in realizing equality and at another ineffectual. A differential evaluation of the effectiveness of a particular educational policy such as a common curriculum need not make us think the ideal of sex equality has altered, nor should it lead us to doubt either the sincerity or intelligence of feminist reformers who offer differential evaluations of it at different times. For an example of just this sort of a serious misunderstanding of fem-

inist proposals for reform that is based on an ignorance of the complexities of gender, see Parrington (1984).

This chapter has benefited from my discussion with Susan Franzosa, Jennifer Radden, Janet Farrell Smith, Gillian Michell, and especially Jane Martin and Ann Diller.

5

The Androgynous Classroom:
Liberation or Tyranny?

KATHRYN PAULY MORGAN

Many human beings never experience autonomy and self-determination in any meaningful sense. There are intelligible explanations for this: mass starvation, plague, war. There are other equally devastating but less intelligible situations that prevent the development of full individual personhood. Two such situations are the color of one's skin and the configuration of one's genitals, in other words, racism and sexism.

In this chapter, I describe sexism, which pervades schools. I then critically examine one alternative that has been proposed as a remedy for the ills of sexism: androgyny.

Sexist Schools

I define *sexism* as a range of attitudes, beliefs, practices, policies, laws, and behaviors discriminating against women or men on the basis of their gender.[1] Often sexism is a deeply entrenched ideology that functions as an a priori conceptual framework that is institutionalized and justified as the cultural reflection of the natural order.[2] For example, we find Rousseau (1976) stating, in *Emile*, that

> woman is expressly formed to please the man. . . . This, I must confess, is not one of the refined maxims of love; it is, however, one of the laws of nature. . . . [Women's] education must be wholly directed to their relations to men. To give men pleasure, to be useful to them, to win their love and esteem, to train them in childhood, to care for them when they grow up, to give them counsel and consolation, to make life sweet and agreeable for them: these are the tasks of women in all times for which they should be trained in childhood (pp. 322–328).

64

Modern educators have taken Rousseau sufficiently seriously that sexist education can be found throughout the world: in developing Third World countries; in socialist countries such as the former USSR, Hungary, Poland, and Czechoslovakia; in industrialized countries of North America and Western Europe; and in allegedly "liberated" countries of Scandinavia.[3]

In order to perceive how sexism is institutionalized in North American education, let us examine a typical contemporary sexist classroom. At first glance, it might appear that if we concentrate on curriculum materials, the charge of sexism is misplaced. Gone are the readers with their blatant sex-role stereotyping. Gone are the fairy tales with their incessant parade of passive, semicomatose, or dead damsels, for example, Sleeping Beauty, Snow White, Cinderella, and others, and their heroes who are *never* allowed to fail. What is not gone are seemingly less suspect curriculum materials. Take, for example, the mathematics textbook, *Seeing Through Arithmetic Five* (West 1973; Frazier and Sadker 1973). In one set of ten problems, five problems deal with girls cooking and sewing. The remaining problems deal with fathers taking boys on camping trips while their mothers stay home and bake; fathers going out planting with their sons while their mother stays home and bakes. In general, girls and women are characteristically portrayed as involved in such activities as babysitting, sewing, cooking, shopping, and buying ribbons.[4] Boys and men, however, are portrayed in a variety of activities such as building, earning money, hiking, camping, planting, driving cars, and traveling. Girls are seldom, if ever, portrayed as engaged in stereotypical boy activities. Boys are *never* shown sewing, babysitting, cooking, baking, and staying home. Through the seemingly abstract medium of the arithmetic problem, the message is clear: For each sex, there is something like a fixed and preordained gender essence and set of corresponding available social roles. This essence is seen as rising out of the natural order and is represented by the natural family. (Think of "The Three Bears.")

Consider a second case. In the spelling texts adopted by the state of California during the 1960s and early 1970s, consonants were represented as boys whereas vowels were represented as girls.[5] Following are some characteristic lines found in the texts.

Boy Consonant Lines

It looks like we are stuck again;
We much prefer to work with men.
You don't look like very much;
You'd probably break at the slightest touch.
The girls are really getting out of hand.
I think I'll hit them with a rubber band.

Girl Vowel Lines

And when our sounds are short and weak
You must make it safe for us to speak.
Protection is what our short sounds need;
The boys should protect us—is that agreed?
Oh please, Mr. R. don't change me.
I don't learn too easily (Nilsen 1977, pp. 166–168).

Although the content of this program has been altered in response to re-search findings on sex-role stereotyping,[6] altering the content will not affect the deep-level sexist assumptions at work here. The stress in the program continues to be on the difference between consonants and vowels, how differently they behave, and how vowels are dependent on consonants for their identity and their worth. That is, sexism is built into the conceptual structure of the program not merely into specific stereotypes at the level of content.

Sexist assumptions are also at work in the hidden curriculum (Jackson 1968, Silberman 1971). In order to determine how a hidden curriculum operates, we need to look at the methods of interaction and organization that function in the classroom and the school. That is, we need to look at the patterns of interaction that develop and are reenforced among the students, at how specific teachers use power in praising and reprimanding pupils in their classrooms, at the rule structure in the classroom and school, and at the principles of staffing in the school. In each of these areas, sexism may be rampant although all those concerned maintain scrupulous guard over curriculum materials.

Suppose you are a child. What would you infer from the following?

1. the fact that your school has a dress code that requires boys to wear pants and forbids girls to wear pants:

    Who can run? Who can do somersaults? Who can climb trees? Who is active?

2. the fact that chores in the classroom that require heavy manual labor are assigned to boys even though the biggest and strongest students in the classroom are girls:

    Who is *expected* to be strong? Who is *expected* to be weak and passive?

3. the fact that almost all teachers in the preschool, the kindergarten, and elementary school are female, that almost all the teachers in the secondary school and university are male, and that virtually all principals are male:

    What do you infer here about power? About authority? About respect? About ability? About who defers to whom? And what do you infer when you discover that the same male-dominated pyramidal structure (which is almost always racist as well) replicates itself in the business world, the medical world, the world of politics, the world of religion, and is reenforced by portrayals of the "normal family" in your culture?

4. the fact that many school personnel, especially guidance counselors, use different criteria for describing good male and female students:

> For example, good female students are described as appreciative, conscientious, considerate, cooperative, sensitive, obliging, and dependable. Good male students are described as adventurous, assertive, curious, energetic, enterprising, frank, independent, and inventive.[7]

5. the fact that in many classrooms, boys receive eight to ten times as many prohibitory control messages as girls; that when teachers criticize boys, they are more likely to use harsh, angry tones than when speaking with girls who have committed the same or an equivalent offense; that girls but not boys are praised for their neatness, their conformity, their docility, and their cooperative behavior:

> Who is learning to be active and independent? Who is learning to be conforming? Whose courage in taking intellectual risks is more likely to be undercut, especially in adolescence? (Bardwick and Douvan 1971; Frazier and Sadker 1973).[8]

In these areas of the hidden curriculum, sexist practices and assumptions are at work. As suggested above and elsewhere sex-role polarization into stereotypes is dangerous, impractical, and inherently unjust for girls and boys, women and men (Chesler 1972; Maccoby 1988). For both groups, successful socialization into stereotypical sex roles and attitudes entails the loss of both autonomy and the possibility of self-determination. I wish now to turn to a critical assessment of one of the alternatives that has been proposed: the alternative of androgyny.

The Ideal of Androgyny

A characteristic definition of androgyny is the following:

> the androgynous ideal which combines the two (that is, the Masculine principle and the Feminine principle) seeks to offer the full spectrum of experiences and feelings covered by both principles to every human being regardless of sex. In an androgynous society when a child is born, no longer will its genitals determine what his or her parents expect in terms of personality, behavior and work. Furthermore, in an androgynous society . . . everyone would have a new sense of wholeness both socially and psychically (Bazin and Freeman 1974, p. 186).

The notion of androgyny suggests completion and unity. If we become androgynous persons, we become "more truly whole, more truly human" (Block 1976, p.78). Those who advocate androgyny see it as a moral imperative, a religious vision, a metaphysical and cosmic call to unity. For those who view sex-role polarization as leading to psychological fragmentation and distortion of individual identity, the alternative of androgyny appears as a powerful alternative promising wholeness and integrity.

There are theoretical differences among those advocating androgyny. Several theses are advanced in the literature.[9] These are:

1. Androgyny is primarily a psychological process or state.
2. Androgyny involves extrapsychic factors (e.g., biological, social, political, cosmic) as well.
3. Androgyny is innate but buried or thwarted by socialization.
4. Androgyny is acquired through socialization.
5. The definition of androgyny is *inclusive*, that is, it involves reference to all sex-coded characteristics.
6. The definition of androgyny is *selective*, that is, it is phrased in terms of "most valued" sex-coded characteristics.
7. The definition of androgyny is based on the assumption that sex-codings have *universal* validity.
8. The definition of androgyny is based on a view of sex-codings as *culture-specific*.
9. The androgynous person will strive for totality through *balance* (which suggests a *single* ideal).
10. The androgynous person will choose from an optimally large spectrum (which emphasizes choice, differences, *plurality*).

It is clear that many important philosophical assumptions underlie the claims of the androgynists. What is also clear is that there is very little agreement on those assumptions. I will not deal with these internal disagreements in this chapter.[10]

Before moving to a critical discussion of three difficulties I see with the androgynous ideal, I will first sketch an imaginary androgynous classroom. One of the explicit goals of the androgynous educational process will be the fostering of androgynous children and students (regardless of whether one takes an innatist or non-innatist line here). This requires an androgynous teacher and support staff. The teacher will need measures of assessment to mark the progress of the student. Not only will curriculum materials need to satisfy the requirements of being nonsexist, they will also have to provide explanations for earlier texts and traditions in the Savage Ages of sexual polarization. All the elements of the hidden curriculum mentioned above will need to be set up to encourage the androgynous person.

Thus far, it appears relatively easy to specify the formal requirements of the androgynous classroom. But, I would suggest, appearances here are deceiving.

Three Difficulties with the Androgynous Ideal

A Conceptual Difficulty

As mentioned above, one of the conflicts among androgynists concerns whether or not androgyny is defined by reference to culture-specific sexual stereotypes or whether the principles of masculinity and femininity have cross-cultural, suprahistorical validity. Some theorists argue for the former, suggesting, for example, that the meaning given these terms derives from early divisions of labor and sex roles associated with those divisions (Bazin and Freeman 1974, pp. 187 ff). The implication here is that if such divisions change, so, too, does the content of the terms *feminine* and *masculine*. This position derives considerable support from the findings of anthropologists and social historians. In some centuries, for example, the feminine was identified with the dark, the earthy, and the passionate; in others, such as the Victorian period, it referred to the asexual, the pure, and the highly moral. Similar variations can be traced with respect to the content of masculine. Given this variability, it would seem reasonable to define androgyny in culture-specific relative ways.

What does this mean for our androgynous classroom? In a culturally pluralistic society, the content of feminine and masculine can vary so widely that, in principle, the successful androgynous student in classroom X in school X might have little in common with a similarly described student in androgynous classroom Y. As we look more and more closely at specific androgynous classrooms in specific subcultures and examine the specific constituent definitions of masculinity and femininity, any semblance of universality vanishes. And with it goes much of the original appeal of the androgynous ideal. In short, if one attempts to incorporate social and cultural diversity and pluralism in the educational setting, one is led to form androgynous *multiples* rather than arriving at a more cosmopolitan, integrated definition of human beings.

If, however, we try to transcend the cultural pluralism, searching for a more universal definition of androgyny, we encounter other sorts of difficulties. Our task is to uncover commonalities among variation in sexual stereotypes in order to determine potentially universal characteristics. But present data suggest there is little, if any, universality among cross-cultural sexual stereotypes even though sexual polarization itself is common (Mead 1935; Rosaldo and Lamphere 1974). To construct a working definition of androgyny out of the remaining crumbs and fragments is not an inviting prospect. Nor does it represent full humanity, the original promise of androgyny.

The universal, inclusive definition of androgyny might be salvaged in one way, that is, by assuming that *all* human qualities were sexually coded as either masculine or feminine. If that were the case, then the precise difference in masculine and feminine codes would be irrelevant. This is an appealing assumption. Unfortunately, it is not a real option because we know that the assumption is not true. There are many human characteristics that are presently nonsex-coded in our culture, for example, being sincere. Similarly, in many classical texts in moral philosophy, morally worthy characteristics of being just or trustworthy are not sex-coded.[11]

The upshot of these remarks is this: Androgyny is unworkable in either its culture-specific or universal form. But if neither of these is workable, then it is not an attainable ideal. What this means for the androgynous classroom is that if this split is irresolvable, it will be impossible to staff the androgynous classroom. Neither the androgynous teacher nor the androgynous students can, in principle, be described in a concrete way that both satisfies the requirements of the theory and avoids paradoxical inconsistencies of multiple androgynous ideals at the level of practice. These difficulties, I have argued, follow directly from the incoherence built into the concept itself.

Suppose, *per impossibile*, we provide an androgynous teacher. Will this teacher be able to operate in the androgynous classroom? In particular, will the androgynous teacher be able to assess the progress of the children and students with respect to the ideal of becoming androgynous persons?

A Pragmatic Difficulty

In general, it is important to be able to assess one's students. With respect to progress in the area of androgyny, it will be relatively easy to assess it in a negative direction insofar as the display of sexist behavior and attitudes will indicate an absence of androgynous behavior and attitudes. It is, however, fallacious to infer that simply because nonsexist behavior is manifested, androgynous behavior is. Many liberals who are convinced by arguments against sexist discrimination nevertheless believe quite firmly in sex-role polarization.[12] And it is quite consistent for them to advocate reform of existing sex-role stereotypes while preserving fundamental sex-role dichotomization. Androgynists, conversely, argue that sex-role dichotomization per se must be eliminated.

Therefore, if the androgynous teacher is to assess androgyny in the children and students, some form of assessment that measures androgyny is necessary. It is not surprising that instruments for assessment have been proposed in the psychological literature. One of the most well known of these is the Bem Sex-Role Inventory (BSRI) (1976), which attempts both to operationalize and to measure androgyny. In the literature (Constantinople 1976), some psychologists have documented and criticized the practice of using tests that assume and reenforce sexual polarization. Most frequently this is done by assuming that masculinity and femininity are unidimensional, bipolar opposites that are negatively correlated. In the BSRI, masculinity and femininity are independent categories. Bem (1976) operationalizes androgyny in the following way: "If a person's masculinity and femininity scores are approximately equal, that person is said to have an androgynous sex role. An androgynous sex role thus represents the equal endorsement of both masculine and feminine personality characteristics, a balance, as it were, between masculinity and femininity" (p. 51). Although this sounds promising, there are problems involved. First, if we apply the BSRI, we will discover that, in our classroom, we will have high androgynous individuals, medium androgynous individuals, and low androgynous individuals (since only equality is required). But this sounds rather odd since we had been told that androgyny made us more fully human.

Second, if we take actual items from the scale, the BSRI requires us to say that someone who is athletic, aggressive, individualistic, childlike, flatterable, and gullible is an example of an androgynous individual. That is, at best, a counterintuitive consequence. Third, Bem's own columns leave out what are well-documented sex-stereotypic items in our culture (such as weak, narcissistic, tactful, fastidious, rational). As such, the BSRI is incomplete. Finally, when we face the issue of how particular characteristics are placed in particular columns, all the problems cited previously concerning culture-specificity versus universality reappear.

A further drawback of the BSRI and any similar device is that, like the concept of androgyny itself, it requires us to postulate clusters of characteristics associated with masculinity and femininity. Although the empirical and historical evidence suggest that these stereotypes are inherently variable, placing them in an instrument such as the BSRI freezes them in time. This carries with it the reactionary suggestion that these stereotypes are naturally given, permanent definitions of what *constitute*, necessarily, masculinity and femininity. Thus, at the very time that we are trying to decode personality traits, we find ourselves, as androgynous teachers, having to sex-code many (and possibly all) human characteristics in order to measure androgyny in the classroom. This is a pragmatic paradox, which, I would argue, is generated as soon as we try to operationalize the notion of androgyny. But operationalize that notion we must if it is to serve the demands of educational practice.

This pragmatic difficulty is closely related to a third weakness of the androgyny ideal and highlights the social undesirability of applying the androgyny measure.

An Undesirable Social Consequence

In general, I believe that the ideal and implementation of androgyny leads to sex-role tyranny. Although its formulation promises an expansion and rich-ness of human possibilities, the concept of androgyny leads, in fact, to a monolithic pattern of human development. It works like this.

Prior to the introduction of androgyny, human beings had at least two op-tions in any sexually dichotomized society. Although it has been (correctly) argued that dichotomized sex roles can be despotic in nature, nevertheless, fluctuation over time in the content of those sex roles was possible. Moreover, any member of the culture has, in principle, the option of switch-ing from one legitimized sex role to another or moving to a culture in which different sex roles are in operation. The coming of androgyny ends all that. Whether the androgyny measure is culture-specific or universally defined is irrelevant here insofar as the claim for the particular androgyny formula in operation will be the same. And it is that claim that, I argue, is tyrannical in its implications.

First, I am assuming that only one formula of androgyny is possible for a particular group such as the classroom in question, and that all individual members of the classroom will be measured according to the same yardstick. The alternative, that is, to use multiple definitions, would only result in chaos. Given a general distribution of human characteristics, what is likely to happen in this classroom is that a small percentage of individuals will score high on the androgyny scale. Now it is important to note that, in this context, such an individual will exemplify the norm for androgyny, not the exception. That is, if full humanity is what is expected of any androgynous person, a high score on the scale will simply establish that one is a normal androgynous person not a special case. As a consequence, all the other children and stu-dents will be described as inadequate, low, or subnormal androgynous per-sons. Moreover, any individual who appears to be developing as a girl *or* as a boy will be perceived as a deviant, subnormal androgynous person. Now, rather than having two, socially approved, valued personality patterns avail-able, which a large number of people could achieve, the members of the class will have only one, the high demand pattern of androgyny. In general, the use of practices that establish and augment feelings of personal inadequacy and failure should be avoided because they involve pain. Thus, the use of any standard that, when applied, would increase and intensify such pain is, at best, questionable. I believe that the androgynous role is such a standard. (It should be noted that this is not an argument for sexual polarization; many of the same remarks apply to that practice as well. Androgyny and sexual polar-ization do not exhaust the alternatives open to us.)

Moreover, it is not clear that from a long-term social point of view pro-ducing generations of androgynous students is desirable. We now know that persons who are likely to be highly creative and theoretically inventive are persistent and single-minded in specific tasks; socially, intellectually, and familially independent, adventuresome, ambitious, and self-reliant (Rossi, in Bardwick 1972). It is quite possible that socializing these students to be warm, empathic, sensitive, and compassionate will undercut precisely those qualities that mark them out as creative individuals.

In short, the social cost in terms of generating widespread feelings of inadequacy in the population is likely to be high. Moreover, the application of androgynous norms to particularly gifted individuals—in one direction or another—could erode their potential, lead them to regard themselves as social deviants (a consequence that could also undercut their individual potential), or both.

Although androgyny is an ideal of liberation, it is an ideal that lacks intellectual coherence, involves pragmatic paradoxes, and can lead to a situation of psychological and social tyranny. It is too dangerous an ideal to implement in the educational process. Liberation from the injustices endemic to sexist polarization is possible but not through androgyny.

Notes

1. This definition is adopted from C. Safilios-Rothschild's work (1974). It is the standard definition in the literature.

2. For an excellent analytical discussion of various forms of sexism, see Marilyn Frye (1975), pp. 65–82.

3. *Women and Social Policy*, C. Safilios-Rothschild (1974), pp. 25–39, covers the international literature on the subject.

4. This research is reported in Frazier and Sadker (1973), pp. 137–141. Similar examples can be found in Scandinavian texts. See Safilios-Rothschild (1974) for a review of this literature, pp. 26–27.

5. These are used in the Alpha Time and Alpha One reading programs. This curriculum material is analyzed by Alleen Pace Nilsen (1977), pp. 166–168.

6. The effect of these texts on sex-role stereotyping has been documented by Jenkins. See Nilsen (1977), p. 168.

7. This research is reported in Frazier and Sadker (1973), pp. 137–141. This same sexual dichotomizing of expectations is reflected in the therapeutic community at large. High school counselors may be considered a subset of this larger community. See, for example, the research of Broverman, Broverman, Clarkson, Rosencrantz, and Vogel (1970), pp. 1–7. Two startling implications of Broverman et al.'s research are (1) that according to the clinicians' stereotypes, it is impossible for a woman ever to be an integrated woman *and* a healthy adult; adulthood must be purchased at the cost of womanhood; (2) only masculine characteristics, which are *equivalent* to the characteristics desired in a healthy adult, are valued; masculine characteristics are the only properly adult human traits.

8. John Stuart Mill accounts for the lack of spectacular achievement by women in the arts and sciences through the same sort of argument. See John Stuart Mill (1970), pp. 202–215.

9. Here are some typical sources. In each case, I have listed their theoretical orientations by reference to the thesis number. Bem (1976), (1, 4, 6, 8, 9); Bazin and Freeman (1974), (2, 3, 5, 7); Daly (1973), (2, 3, 5, 7, 9); Eliade (1967), (2, 3, 5, 7, 9); Heilbrun (1974), (1, 6, 8, 9); Heilbrun (1973), (5, 7, 10); Kaplan (1976), (1, 6, 10); Rossi (1964), (2, 4, 6, 8); Singer (1976), (1, 3, 5, 7).

10. For a more extensive analysis of the internal difficulties, see my paper, "Androgyny: Vision or Mirage? A Philosophical Analysis," presented to the Women's Research Colloquium, York and University of Toronto (January 1978). Unpublished.

11. This is, however, not true for all philosophical theories. See Beardsley (1967), pp. 285–293.

12. For a subtle and sensible philosophical discussion of this position, see Hill (1975), pp. 171–186.

6

Theorizing Gender:
How Much of It Do We Need?

BARBARA HOUSTON

Do we need to abolish gender in order to realize sex equity? What would life be like beyond the male-female duality? What would it mean not to have gender identity?

These are the sorts of questions raised by a deconstructionist approach to gender equity issues in education. In an influential and compelling paper Bronwyn Davies (1989) shows the inadequacies of two common theoretical models used to study sex bias in education, sex-role socialization theory and reproduction theory. In their place she argues for a different theoretical model, one she thinks is better equipped to do the job. She offers a deconstructionist approach; that is, an approach that requires attention to and an analysis of the discursive and textual practices through which the constructs male and female are established and maintained as fundamental structures of society. To better study sex bias in education, she claims, we need a better account of the relations between social practices of sexism and gender equity and the symbolic systems in which people grasp, justify, and enact these practices.

Along with other feminist thinkers, Davies views the sex gender system as a sociocultural construct, *a system of representation* that assigns meaning (identity, value, prestige, location, kinship, status in the social hierarchy, etc.) to the individual within a society. The notion of representation is understood very broadly, not simply as cultural images and narratives but also as the arena of formal and abstract knowledge in fields defined by the social sciences and humanities as well as the arena of specific, concrete social practices (Leach 1989). The construction of gender duality goes on "in the laws, the family, and private and public schools. It also goes on in the social science models, in the academic and intellectual community, in radical theories, and even, indeed especially, in feminism itself" (p. 30). So in Davies's discussion of discursive practices she includes not only language, the linguistic forms, but also the intellectual symbolic order and concrete social practices, for she posits a "material existence" to discursive practices. They work to contribute to the sense humans make of the world, not just a cognitive sense but, as she says, "a sense . . . apprehended bodily."

In this way the embeddedness of the oppositional male-female duality within our consciousness constrains thought and action within and toward gendered "subjects" in our society. The consequences of that duality has led to women's subordination to men (Leach 1989, p. 30). The deconstructionist believes that the oppositional duality can be systematically linked to the organization of social inequality. If this is the case, then the requirements of equity will not be satisfied by equal access to the (male) system of education. Davies believes that establishing equitable practices in schools, indeed in all social institutions, requires the abandonment of the categories of male and female altogether.

In this chapter I reflect upon the changes recommended by the deconstructionist approach. I argue that although it seems reasonable to accept the deconstructionist substantive claims about gender and sex and how we both constitute them as social categories and become constituted by them through discursive practices and material social interactions, nevertheless, we should be wary of the proposed recommendations for change that are alleged to follow from the theory.

I argue first that the recommendations are ambiguous: It is not clear whether we are to abolish gender altogether or reconstitute it. I then argue that the descriptions of the options Davies and some other deconstructionists present obscure alternatives available to us; they also mask the political dangers associated with some of the alternatives. Finally, I query whether a deconstructionist theory of gender such as Davies presents *can* support the changes she desires.

Although I accept that the deconstructionist approach Davies advances is useful, indeed very important to us in examining sex equity issues, I dispute the proclaimed desirability and necessity of the specific proposals for change. I also challenge Davies's claim that the deconstructionist's theory of gender does indeed hold "the greatest potential for establishing equitable practice."[1]

Moving Beyond Gender: Abolition or Reconstruction?

Very broadly, the deconstructionist solution to the problem of sexism in education, at least as Davies sets it out, is clearly stated in her claim that we need to (1) identify and change discursive practices and (2) challenge male-female duality as it is incorporated into each person's identity. However, a perplexing ambiguity emerges when we look for more specificity about what changes are needed and precisely how we might bring them about. On the one hand, we find Davies claiming that "it is clear that the abandonment of the categories [male and female] is essential if the fabric of patriarchy is to be undone" (p. 14). On this strong interpretation of the changes needed we are urged to abolish gender both as a social category and as part of our personal identity. On the other hand, Davies elsewhere appears to be offering a weaker proposal, that we might reconstitute the categories male and female as reproductive categories only. She suggests that they be "no longer central to our identity, . . . no longer polar opposites, but categories relevant to little else than biological reproduction" (p. 8).

Our task of the determination and assessment of Davies's proposals for change is made difficult by several factors. First, nowhere does she mention the distinction many people draw between sex and gender.[2] Consequently, we are left wondering whether she is speaking of the sex categories (usually referred to by the terms *male* and *female*) or the gender categories (usually designated by the terms *girl, boy, woman, man,* or *masculine* and *feminine*).[3] I assume, therefore, that Davies uses the sex and gender categories interchangeably, recognizing no viable distinction between them.

Difficulty arises also because of the ease with which a number of issues concerning the origin, relevance, and changeability of the gender categories are confounded. The confusions arise in part from the assumptions that underlie Davies's discussion of the deconstructionist position, assumptions that underlie her view but are not articulated or acknowledged. These assumptions are:

1. Deconstruction of gender involves or results in a dispersal of the category, a demonstration of the irrelevance of the category.
2. If gender categories are not based on natural, immutable essential characteristics, then gender identity need not be central to personal identity, and gender as a social category is largely irrelevant.
3. If gender is not a product of biology, then we have some choice about and some responsibility for the part it plays in our identity.
4. If gender is socially determined in precisely the way Davies's theory of gender describes, then it can be abolished or wholly changed.

These assumptions obscure at least the following alternatives:

1. Gender is not fixed, immutable, natural; it is changeable, but it still is, and ought to be, central to our identity.
2. Gender is socially constructed, plays a central role in our identity, but it is not changeable, that is, it is learned and fixed.

3. Sex and perhaps gender categories are partially biologically determined, largely culturally mediated, with some parts fixed and some
   parts not.

In my discussion I will reveal how these assumptions come into play and
argue that the alternatives Davies's deconstructionist position offers us are
neither the only alternatives nor the obviously most desirable changes we
need in order to realize sex equality.

Another major source of trouble is Davies's use of Kristeva's (1981, 1986)
description of the struggle for sex equality as a framework for her own discussion. Julia Kristeva has suggested that the feminist struggle is best seen
both historically and politically as a three-tiered struggle in which we fight
for (1) equal access to the male symbolic order; (2) equal right to have one's
way of being legitimated by the educational system; and finally (3) the right
to a symbolic order that does not rest on the male-female duality, where
women reject the dichotomy between masculine and feminine as metaphysical (Davies 1989, p. 1). Davies writes as though her proposal for change
would fit Kristeva's characterization of "moving beyond the male female duality." However, her description of the debate surrounding Carol Gilligan's
work to illustrate this particular aspect of the struggle for equality is misleading. I shall show that this mischaracterization of what is involved in moving
beyond the gender duality is worrisome because it camouflages dangers inherent in abandoning the gender categories: dangers I want to draw out.

The Dangers of Abolishing Gender Categories

The problems I have mentioned can be illustrated in Davies's efforts to chart
feminist discourses about women's morality. The implication is that progressive movement occurs when we shift from the second to the third tier of the
struggle, from defining and celebrating women's difference to deconstructing
it. Davies suggests that the criticism of Carol Gilligan's work moves beyond
the gender duality. However, if we look closely at this move in the literature
on Gilligan's work, we can see how it provides only the illusion of having
moved beyond the gender duality and only an illusion of progress toward sex
equality.

Gilligan (1982), quite rightly, I think, challenges the adequacy of Kohlberg's theory to account for all of women's moral thinking. On the basis of
her own empirical work she draws a stronger differentiation between (some)
women's and (some) men's moral reasoning, and she asserts the value of the
ethic of care she discovers among her women subjects. This is characterized

by Davies using Kristeva's framework as a struggle to define femaleness and to celebrate it. Fair enough. Difficulties emerge with the characterization of the next level of the struggle, the level at which there is an attempt to move beyond the male-female duality. Davies cites as an example of discourse at this new level some of the common criticisms of Gilligan's (1982) work, summarizing them as a complaint that "it [Gilligan's work] ignores the way in which women's subject positions are created through the narrative structures, the texts, and discursive practices such that she comes to see herself as only able to have what she needs through caring for others" (p. 13). The assumption is, as I have stated, that deconstructing Gilligan's subject in this way moves us beyond the gender categories. But it does not, at least if "moving beyond the male female duality" means abandoning gender as a focus of analysis, not using or having recourse to the categories "woman" and "man" in discursive practices or in identifying ourselves.

Feminist criticism of Gilligan's work is varied. It asserts, among other things: (1) that Gilligan does not have the empirical support for claiming that this is an ethic that all and only women have (i.e., it cannot underwrite some claim for a distinctive women's morality in any essentialist sense); (2) that the ethics of care does not have the value Gilligan claims for it; and finally, (3) that the morality that Gilligan ascribes to her subjects is not an authentic morality at all; it is a product of women's self-deception.[4] Obviously, from a feminist point of view, some of these criticisms are more helpful than others.

In the first instance what is being challenged is the femaleness of the ethic on the grounds that some women do not share it. In the second criticism the critics challenge the value of the ethic because as John Broughton (1983) says, it "perpetuates the status quo, affirms the established division of labour, and forecloses on the possibility of a radical transformation" (p. 626). In short, because it is not an ethic that will help women resist and challenge their oppression. But notice that in neither of these cases could we say that the critics had moved beyond the male-female duality. Indeed, both appeal to the category "woman" to make their point. And the second does so quite strongly and obviously: It criticizes the ethic for failing to meet the needs of women. If we did move beyond the gender categories in the sense Kristeva seems to be suggesting and Davies endorses, that is to say, abandon them, such an appeal to the needs and interests of women would no longer be open to us. This is one political danger of the proposal to move beyond the gender duality.

Another political danger arises with the third sort of criticism, the one that most obviously involves a deconstruction of female subjectivity. In this criticism Broughton complains that Gilligan fails to consider that her subjects have an interest in not knowing themselves, in particular in not knowing that they are mystified by cultural norms of femininity. The effects of this deconstruction of the subject are devastating: Women no longer have an authentic moral voice, even a mistaken one; they no longer have real moral agency. What we are left with are suspicions about women's ability to theorize about themselves.[5] Women's subjectivity has been determined; it has in fact been overdetermined. Thus we can see that, despite Davies's categorization of them, none of the feminist criticisms of Gilligan's work challenges the gender duality in the strong sense. Deconstruction itself need not entail that we abandon gender altogether. It may simply involve recognizing that gender is a social construct and leaving entirely open the questions of whether it is or is not possible to change it and whether it is desirable to do so. Gender categories may be socially constructed and changeable or they may be incorrigible. They may be socially constructed and not useful or very useful. Thus, whether the gender categories posit an essential nature is irrelevant to other questions we might ask and does not foreclose on the issue of whether we should continue to use the categories. By understanding some alternatives as "moving beyond gender" when they do not, we mask the dangers that can occur when we really do move beyond gender.

Linda Alcoff (1988) elaborates in a general way on the political dangers inherent in a poststructuralist theory of gender such as Kristeva's, which moves us beyond gender categories, and which leads us to what she calls a *nominalism* with respect to gender. "What can we demand in the name of women if 'women' do not exist and demands in their name simply reinforce the myth that they do? How can we speak out against sexism as detrimental to the interests of women if the category is a fiction? How can we demand legal abortions, adequate child care, or wages based on comparable worth without invoking the concept of 'woman'?" (p. 272) The point is, the proposal to abolish gender offers us no way to ground feminist politics. "Nominalism threatens to wipe out feminism itself" (Alcoff, p. 272). It at the best leaves us with a purely negative struggle, that of reaction and deconstruction of the fiction "woman." But as Alcoff reminds us, "a movement cannot be only and always against. It must have positive alternatives, a vision of a better future that can motivate people to sacrifice time and energy towards its realization" (pp. 270–272).[6]

The Possibilities and Dangers of Abolishing Gender Identity

It is difficult to think that there are not also comparable dangers in Davies's intriguing but disquieting suggestion that we try to abolish gender as part of personal identity. The "fear of dispersing gender" (Todd 1988) is something that we have probably all experienced personally and as parents and educators who have seriously entertained feminist revisions of early childhood rearing and education. Do we really want to pursue programs that might leave a child not knowing whether she is a girl or a boy (or neither)? Can we, do we want to, throw adults into some doubt about whether they are gendered? Or would these efforts unjustifiably jeopardize psychological integrity?

Both the possibility and dangers of abolishing gender as part of our personal identity are difficult to determine unless we know precisely what gender identity refers to. If it refers to those features that summarize the culturally approved characteristics for females and males, then it seems to me we have less to worry about on both counts. It is easy to think of these as changeable; after all, they vary enormously across cultures. Further, it is so easy to see them as often damaging to an individual and constraining. It would be better if girls thought themselves intelligent and competent as well as nice and boys thought themselves nurturant and attractive as well as big and strong. The real fear of gender dispersal does not rest here. However, when gender identity is understood to include the individual's sense of belonging to one sex or the other (or to neither), then we might well wonder whether change is possible or desirable.

The sense of myself as gendered is sometimes called "core gender identity" (Money and Erhardt 1972; Money and Tucker 1975; Stoller 1968) and refers to the "infant's developing sense of self as a boy or a girl in the second year of life" (Money and Erhardt, p. 282). Core gender identity appears to be acquired in the first few years after birth, and once established, it is said by some theorists to be absolutely unalterable. Money characterizes the fixity of core gender identity in the following way: "Once a sex distinction has been worked or pressured into the nuclear core of your gender schema, to dislodge it is to threaten you as an individual with destruction. The gate is as firmly locked there as it is on your chromosomes and gonads" (1975, p. 30). So, for some gender theorists, core gender identity, once it is established, is locked tight forever and any deliberate attempts to tamper with it after this point in time are both futile and morally reprehensible in terms of their potentially disastrous consequences for the subject.

There is no doubt about the enormous difficulty in reassigning a gender identity; that is, in getting someone who thought they were a girl to now think that they are a boy. But it is not clear what the precise implications of this psychological fact are for efforts to abolish gender as part of our identity. It may be that the claims that it is both impossible to do and wrong to try are mistaken (Ayim and Houston, 1985). My point is that Davies does not appear to consider them and fails to give us an inkling of *how* it might be done. But these matters need to be investigated if Davies's proposals are not to be dismissed as utopian.[7] A more promising deconstructionist position is advanced by Judith Butler (1994), who suggests that we learn to play with our gender identities. Such play can confirm suspicions that gender categories are not part of our essential nature but can, to some extent, be put on, taken off, and changed.

Is It Necessary to Abolish Gender to Realize Sex Equity?

By now we may want to ask the question, Do we really need to abolish gender to realize sex equity? Davies's answer, as far as I can tell, is an unequivocal yes. But as I see it, the answer is yes *only if* we accept some highly questionable assumptions.

Davies argues that the (current) requirements for being successfully female and male "potentially override the logic of quality" (p. 9) because female and male are constructed as bipolar opposites and gender is the primary defining feature of each person. What she needs to add but does not, presumably because it is so evident in her detailed examples, is that the male-female categories carry a dominance-subordinance structuring. But this can only entail that "abandonment of the categories is essential if the fabric of patriarchy is to be undone" (p. 14) *if* we *additionally* assume: (1) that gender differentiation itself causes male supremacy or (2) that gender structures are necessarily and unavoidably hierarchical in the way they are now, that is, that oppositional difference always involves a dominance. The truth of these assumptions is difficult to establish[8] but unless Davies defends them, we do not have sufficient reason to think we need to abolish gender in order to realize sex equality. Given there are some questions about both the possibility and the desirability of abolishing gender, we may want to consider the alternative—changing it.

Reconstituting Gender: A Test of Adequacy

Even if we could demonstrate the possibility and the warrantability of abolishing gender, perhaps we would do better to take more seriously Davies's weaker interpretation of "moving beyond the male female duality." On one reading Davies can be understood to be declaring the distinction between sex and gender anachronistic (Butler 1987) and to be wishing to construct gender categories around the following pivotal points: Women menstruate, gestate, and lactate; men impregnate. If the categories under this meager description seem too role-ridden, we might restrict them further: Women have ova; men have sperm. The clear understanding would be that gender has relevance only in the context of reproduction. It would remain an entirely open question whether gender has any relevance for erotic roles.

Such changes, radical enough in themselves, must be predicated upon the belief that even core gender identity is corrigible in some sense. I think it can be shown that core gender identity is mutable in the sense that we can change the *meaning* of what it is to be a girl or a boy, a woman or man, even if we cannot or do not want to abolish gender in the sense of changing an individual's sense of themselves as being one or the other (Ayim and Houston 1985). If we can alter the *meaning* of what it is to be female or male then, even if the categories continue to be bipolar, the dominance-subordinance structuring can be removed.[9] However, the task is far from easy. The question is: Can Davies's theory of gender support the sorts of changes we want and need from it?

Davies claims to choose her preferred theory of gender on the grounds that it, better than the leading alternatives, explains and allows for change in the gender system. But, from the point of view of individual human agency, it is not clear that her theory is more useful than the others, or as useful as it needs to be.[10]

When we are considering change in personal identity, we are necessarily talking about changes involving personal agency. Who we are is how we respond to what we are.[11] Therefore, given Davies's proposals for change, requiring us to either eliminate or radically alter our gendered identity as part of our personal identity, the onus lies with Davies and any other deconstructionist to clarify precisely how her preferred theory of gender can allow for these changes. A successful deconstructionist approach needs to avoid the conclusion that "our very experience of our gendered subjectivity is a construct mediated by and/or grounded in a social discourse beyond (way beyond) individual control" (Alcoff 1988, p. 268).

One danger with theories of gender that rely upon analyses of discursive practices and textual forms is a tendency to reify and rigidify the gender categories in such a way that we fail to make a satisfactory critical move from the feminine to the political potential of actual women (Cornell and Thurschwell 1987, p. 149). I think this has been shown to be true of Kristeva's own theory in which woman gets defined as (only) subordinate and (only) the other (Cornell and Thurschwell 1987; Alcoff 1988). Happily there are features of Davies's view that resist these tendencies and allow us to recognize the "imminent potential in the gender system" (Cornell and Thurschwell 1987, p. 159). Specifically there is an insistence that the gendered subject is active in the processes through which she becomes gendered, that our subjectivity can be reconstructed through reflective practice and that discursive practices are fluid interactions open to alterations by self-analyzing practice. Indeed, these are necessary features if we are to avoid "an overdetermination that erases agency" (Alcoff 1988, p. 277). However, they are not sufficient. We know, and Davies reminds us, that individuals cannot alone change discursive practices; but they can initiate shifts in discourse. The question is: Can they change their own identity?

Alcoff suggests, I think rightly, that any adequate theory of gender will have to have attached to it a politics of identity. It will need to recognize and explain how one's identity can be taken and defined as a political point of departure, a motivation for action. It will need to explain how gender is a constructed position, but still one from which women can act politically.

Once we recognize a politics of identity at work[12] we need to examine carefully what exactly is it that does disrupt the discursive practices, what does empower women. Is it from revaluing the feminine or is it negating divergence? Or something else? The answer to our question, How much gender do we need? will not come easily. At the moment it seems to me to be an open question just which gender categories might empower women. It may be no gender categories, it may be the sparsest of gender categories. Some even hold out hope that with the current gender categories deconstruction can open up the possibility of "communicative freedom" in which "the Other is not there as a limit but as a supportive relation, the 'ground' of my own being" (Cornell and Thurschwell 1987, p. 161).

It is obvious, as Davies insists, that an adequate theory of gender is going to have to allow for radical change if we are not to foreclose on the stages feminist transformations must take. But, if we mean to get at the deepest resistance to change and allow for the abolition or reconstitution of gender *identity*, then an adequate theory is also going to have to provide a good, detailed accounting of the possibility of individual agency in these matters.

Notes

1. All quotations from Davies (1989) are from "Education and Sexism: A Theoretical Analysis of the Sex/Gender Bias in Education," *Educational Philosophy and Theory*, 21(1), 1–19.

2. When the distinction is drawn, *sex* refers to the biological differences. To determine sex one takes into account the following physical conditions: chromosomes, external genitalia, internal genitalia, gonads (ovaries, testes), hormonal states, and secondary sex characteristics. *Gender* is a term whose psychological and cultural connotations outweigh the biological connotations. It usually refers to the social differences between the sexes. Usages of the terms are often inconsistent and some argue that the distinction itself is unsuccessful because of the complex linkage between the biological and social aspects of sex. See Margrit Eichler (1980) for an illuminating discussion of the dispute concerning the variability of the distinction.

3. It is only in the discussion of Kessler and McKenna's work that it becomes clear that Davies thinks both sets of categories are culturally constructed and rejects the claim that bipolar sex categories match our biological nature. Oddly, it is here that we find the hint that we might simply reconstitute the gender categories to match (broadly speaking) the biological reproductive sex categories.

4. The term *deconstruction* undoubtedly has many meanings. I have found Alcoff (1988, p. 267, note 24) the most helpful in clarifying it. She notes it to be "a term

principally associated with Derrida, for whom it refers specifically to the process of unraveling metaphors in order to reveal their underlying logic, which usually consists of a simple binary opposition such as that between man/woman, subject/object, culture/nature, etc." The term's more general meaning refers to "any exposure of a concept as ideologically or culturally constructed rather than natural or a simple reflection of reality." I use it in this latter sense.

The critiques I have in mind are those produced by Broughton (1983), Card (1985), Houston (1987), Ringelheim (1985), and Walker (1983). For a summary of the more powerful criticisms of Gilligan's work and the political implications of these, see Houston (1988a).

5. See especially Ringelheim (1985).

6. Davies recognizes that "work at the second tier is and will remain essential as long as the male female duality is a crucial thread in the social fabric" (p. 2). She acknowledges that "relegating male and female to the metaphysical could seem to negate that work" (p. 2) Yet she appears to accept Kristeva's view that "all three tiers . . . though appearing in sequence must have a parallel existence . . . in the same historical time, or even . . . interwoven one with the other" (p. 2). However, I am suggesting that not all forms of positive revaluation of the feminine need involve a form of essentialism (see Ruddick 1983 for a good example that does not), and some forms of deconstruction deny women as subjects. This should suggest to us that we need not nor should we accept what Kristeva says we must. The idea is to look beyond the struggle as Kristeva formulates it.

7. Judith Butler (1987) strongly reminds us that if a theory of gender is to have "emancipatory potential" it must provide us with "specific cultural innovations rather than myths of transcendence." We need to avoid a notion of radical invention that "lacks a reality principle" (1988, pp. 137, 140).

8. Nancy Chodorow (1978) argues for a version of (1) claiming a strong connection between masculine domination and the process of gender-personality differentiation, but her account arguably makes serious category mistakes. See Young (1983) and Nicholson (1986). Kristeva's theory appears to assume the truth of (2) that oppositional difference always involves dominance, but this "truth" is purchased with questionable assumptions and procedures: abstraction from the meanings of male and female as they are constructed in specific situations and practices; a characterization of the gender categories as rigid and unitary such that woman is defined as pure negativity. For an illuminating discussion of Kristeva on these points, see Cornell and Thurschwell (1987) and Weedon (1987).

9. For example, Kagan (1964) found that to be a boy meant being dominant in a boy-girl relationship. Presumably we could change this meaning and still keep the categories girl and boy. It is also obvious that although the categories girl and boy are bipolar, that is mutually exclusive, the activities that are associated with each need not be. Rough and tumble play and preference for dolls are discrete but not mutually exclusive. For a more detailed discussion on this point, see Ayim and Houston (1985).

10. Davies says of her preferred theory of gender, "the means of change are available within the analyses because forms of discourse can be changed . . . as can textual forms" (p. 8). True, but when we examine the nature of agency attributed to the subject, it seems to be limited to making sense of "one's place in the narrative structure in the culture" (p. 8) and to experiencing the "subject positionings made available

through interactions with others" (p. 8). Individual agency seems restricted to learning one's place and getting it right. Additionally, Davies explicitly notes that "the structures created by the forms of practice that constitute them do have sufficient force to undermine the attempts of isolated individuals to change them" (p. 8). With her theory, individuals may still be "lost in the overpowering controlling social structures" (p. 8). It seems that discursive practices are no easier to change than other social structures and practices.

11. For further discussion on this point see Houston (1988b).

12. One of the best examples and beginning formulations of a politics of identity can be found in Adrienne Rich (1986).

PART TWO

Pedagogy

7

The Ethics of Care and Education:

A New Paradigm, Its Critics, and

Its Educational Significance

ANN DILLER

In 1982, Harvard University Press published a modest-sized monograph (less than 200 pages) entitled *In a Different Voice*. In its pages Carol Gilligan described what she discovered when she listened closely to what women had to say about personal problems, such as abortion decisions. One striking discovery Gilligan chronicled was that of recurrent divergences in the ways that male and female subjects discussed moral issues and decisions. Whereas many men talked fluently about questions of rights and justice, the women were more often preoccupied with questions of responsibilities and care. We now realize that Gilligan's book was like an indicator light for the visible tip of a huge iceberg representing what is variably called the ethics of care, female ethics, or feminine ethics.

Carol Gilligan was not the first or only person to write about women's moral experience and the ways in which its major features or preoccupations differed from the dominant ethical talk of rights and justice. But Gilligan's eloquent exposition and her effective use of examples taken directly from interviews set off a strong chord of recognition for many women and for a still undetermined number of men. Women resonated with what Gilligan and her subjects had to say about women's own moral thinking, feelings, and concerns. Women resonated with the emphasis on care, nurturance, human connections, and responsibility. Many women said that here at last was a morality they could recognize as their own.

Although it seemed clear that this submerged ethics of care was a powerful reality for many women, possibly for most of us, we still had only rough soundings, or sketches, of what this reality was. A philosophical delineation, precise analyses, and definitions of key terms were still missing. Then in 1984 the University of California Press published *Caring: A Feminine Approach to Ethics and Moral Education*, by Nel Noddings. Here we have set forth for us, in bold outline and in analytic detail, a sustained philosophic account of an ethics of care. With the publication of *Caring*, the growing contention that care-based morality constituted a new ethical paradigm became a full-fledged, well-developed claim.

The Ethics of Care

Noddings makes it clear that she is setting forth a new paradigm that requires a radical reconstruction in standard ethical thought, beginning with how we define *ethics* itself: "It sounds all very nice, says my male colleague, but can you claim to be doing 'ethics'? After all, ethics is the study of justified action. . . . Ah, yes. But, after 'after all,' I am a woman, and I was not party to that definition. Shall we say then that I am talking about 'how to meet the other morally'? Is this part of ethics? Is ethics part of this?" (p. 95)[1] In addition to this redefinition of ethics itself, there are a number of other distinctive features essential to understanding an ethics of care. Using Noddings (1984) as our primary text, let us look at some key features in Noddings's account that are also roughly representative of what is intimated, if not explicitly stated, by other ethics of care advocates.[2]

Relational Ontology

The first claim that resounds throughout discussions of female ethics is that relation is ontologically basic. The nature of being for us humans is to be in relation. This is a given; it is how every one of us survived infancy. As one woman philosopher has observed, we are not mushrooms.[3] We humans do not spring up like mushrooms out of the ground; we are born in relation and we grow in relation.

For Noddings the starting point is that "relation will be taken as ontologically basic" (p. 3). And the point to which she returns again and again is, "I am not naturally alone. I am naturally in a relation from which I derive nourishment and guidance. . . . My very individuality is defined in a set of relations. This is my basic reality" (p. 51).

The ethics of care then moves directly from a relational ontology to a relational ethic. Our being-in-relation, this interdependence, is not only natural, it is also deemed morally desirable. We do not become ethically mature by achieving independence but rather by participating responsibly in caring relations. Just as relation is ontologically basic, the caring relation is viewed as ethically basic, as well as a moral achievement.

In her own extensive analysis of the caring relationship, Noddings uses a dyadic schema in which the caregiver is named the *one-caring* and the recipient is the *cared-for*. According to Noddings both parties must contribute to this relationship if caring is to be complete.

Attention as Engrossment

Another prominent feature that recurs throughout women's ethics is the high regard for certain forms of attention-giving. Noddings's own term for this concept is *engrossment*, and she claims it is a necessary condition for caring. "At bottom all caring involves engrossment. The engrossment need not be intense nor need it be pervasive in the life of the one-caring, but it must occur" (p. 17). Engrossment is, in brief, "feeling with" another person.

There is a crucial and important distinction here between engrossment or feeling with and the more analytic task of imagining what I would feel in someone else's situation. It is not a question of my feelings at all. My entire attention is taken up with what the other person is feeling.

> I do not "put myself in the other's shoes," so to speak, by analyzing his reality as objective data and then asking, "How would I feel in such a situation?" On the contrary, I set aside my temptation to analyze and to plan. I do not project; I receive the other into myself, and I see and feel with the other. I become a duality. . . . The seeing and feeling are mine, but only partly and temporarily mine, as on loan to me (p. 30).

Noddings then goes on to describe an experience in which she finds herself unexpectedly moved to engrossment. "It is as though his eyes and mine have combined to look at the scene he describes. I know that I would have behaved differently in the situation, but this is in itself a matter of indifference. I feel what he says he felt. I have been invaded by this other" (p. 31). This form of engrossment, or feeling with, when one temporarily suspends the preoccupations of self so that another person can fill the field of attention, is perhaps best recognized by our experiences of its absence. We find ourselves saying or silently thinking, "You're not really paying attention to me!" or "This person isn't really listening to what I'm saying."

In fact such experiences are sufficiently common that we could conclude engrossment is a fine art rarely achieved by ordinary people. But the ethical point is rather that it demands a serious effort and discipline. Part of what is entailed in this discipline of giving our concentrated attention to the present other is a concomitant respect for the singular character of each person and situation. Any summary of an ethics of care must, therefore, note the favored status of concrete particulars.

Primacy of the Particular

Ethics of care advocates have in common an explicit methodological commitment that favors judgments based on detailed, in-situation perceptions. Priority is given to one's sense of the total concrete particularity of an immediately present set of circumstances. And there is a sense of loss, distortion, or danger associated with moving to a more general level of rules, principles, or ethical universals. Also in some cases there is the belief that any particular situational whole forms a unique gestalt that cannot be generalized without ethical distortion.

One of Noddings's major objections to the search for justification is that it misdirects our ethical attention and energy.

> As one-caring, I am not seeking justification for my action; I am not standing alone before some tribunal. What I seek is completion in the other—the sense of being cared-for and, I hope, the renewed commitment of the cared-for to turn about and act as one-caring in the circles and chains within which he is defined. Thus, I am not justified but somehow fulfilled and completed in my own life and in the lives of those I have thus influenced (p. 95).

But it's not simply the misdirection of ethical energy that is at issue here. There is also a worry about the misuse of principles. "Too often, principles function to separate us from each other. We may become dangerously self-righteous when we perceive ourselves as holding a precious principle not held by the other. The other may then be devalued and treated 'differently'" (p. 5). And finally there is a fundamental skepticism about whether the notion of universalizability can have any valid, meaningful application; when "so much depends on the subjective experience of those involved in ethical encounters, conditions are rarely 'sufficiently similar' for me to declare that you must do what I must do" (p. 5).

Responsibility Includes "Motivational Displacement"

We now come to a feature whose precise characterization is difficult or elusive. I think there is no question that something akin to Nel Noddings's concept of *motivational displacement* is central to an ethics of care. But her characterization may not be equivalent or even acceptable to other versions. Nevertheless, Noddings gives us the specifications for perceiving and understanding the powerful motivational shift that occurs for many of us when we take responsibility for a caring relationship.

In Noddings's analysis, caring engrossment is only half of the story for what happens when one cares. The other half, the other necessary requirement for the one-caring, is what she terms motivational displacement:

> When I care, when I receive the other in the way we have been discussing, there is more than feeling; there is also a motivational shift. My motive energy flows

toward the other and perhaps, although not necessarily, toward his ends. I do not relinquish myself; I cannot excuse myself for what I do. But I allow my motive energy to be shared; I put it at the service of the other (p. 33).

In her analysis Noddings identifies two levels of response for the one-caring: first a natural, spontaneous shift and second an ethical commitment. She seems to treat the first as a natural correlate of engrossment; so that when I begin to feel another person's "reality as possibility . . . I feel also, that I must act accordingly; that is I am impelled to act as though in my own behalf, but in behalf of the other" (p. 16).

Noddings then goes on to say that "this feeling that I must act may or may not be sustained. I must make a commitment to act" (p. 16). It is this commitment and its renewal that are essential to an ongoing caring relationship. Furthermore, for Noddings, this sharing of my motive energy is a requirement for full caring. It may not always result in my taking action, but this would be only "if I believe that everything I might do would tend to work against the best interests of the cared-for" (p. 81). In any case, caring "requires me to respond to the initial impulse with an act of commitment: I commit myself either to overt action on behalf of the cared-for . . . or I commit myself to thinking about what I might do" (p. 81). Before we conclude that this is an overly strenuous ethic, we should remember that one thing I might do is find someone else to help the cared-for, or even simply direct them to the appropriate source of aid.

A Primary Ethic

The strongest proponents for an ethics of care make a number of primacy claims. They claim that caring comes first in importance, first in time, and first in the construction of human morality. Our survival as humans depends upon our being cared for and ultimately it is in caring relationships that we achieve our highest moral ideals. Human relationships constitute the necessary ground of our being, and friendship, social community, parenting, and mutual love provide some of our most rewarding and desirable goods.

In fact, caring relationships are so basic and so elementary to our experience that we too easily forget their role and importance. As Annette Baier has observed, other ethical systems that fail to recognize and acknowledge the indispensable role of these caring activities and relationships are, in a sense, ethics of "bad faith"—insofar as they deny their own ground and the necessary origins for any moral practices (Baier 1985, pp. 56–57).[4]

Furthermore, once we acknowledge the relational ground of morality, some standard ethical puzzles lose their force. For example, Noddings explicitly rejects the standard contractualist account of moral motivation as the "desire to be able to justify one's actions to others on grounds they could not reasonably reject" (Williams 1985, p. 75). In place of this rationalist view,

Noddings identifies two sources, one primitive and one ethical: (1) our natural sympathy, which arises out of experiences and memories of caring and being cared for; and (2) a concern for oneself as one-caring, that is, a commitment to the ethical ideal, or vision, of our "best self" (p. 80).

On Noddings's account the problem of how to explain *altruism* and *moral motivation* must be recast. One can still ask, Why be in human relationships? But the reformulation has lost the power of perplexity.

As I read Noddings, she certainly does not exclude the consideration of other ethical principles and concerns, including those of contractualists, utilitarians, existentialists, and so on. The key point, and the one that makes caring primary, is that the first and last question to be asked in a moral situation should be, How can caring relationships best be sustained or created in this particular case? All other considerations must ultimately be tested and weighed at the tribunal of what constitutes caring in the immediately present relationship.

In sum, the ethics of care as primary ethics calls for a radical paradigm shift in which moral agents redirect attention and energy away from concerns about right judgments and their ethical justification in order to focus instead on how we can best meet each other as ones-caring and how we can create and enhance caring relationships.

Now that we have a sense of the major tenets in an ethics of care, it is time to consider, first, some critical responses to this ethic and, second, some of the educational implications and questions that follow both from the ethic itself and also from the criticisms.

Two Criticisms

In order to provide a brief representative characterization of the critical responses to an ethics of care, I have divided critics into two major groups: (1) those who hold that an ethics of care is a domain ethic; and (2) those who hold that an ethics of care is a dangerous ethic. We shall first consider the domain ethic position.

A Domain Ethic

A sympathetic skeptic might grant most of what has been said so far about an ethics of care and then go on to note that even if caring is perhaps an essential foundation for human moral practice, comes first as a necessary prerequisite for moral development, and must continue to play a crucial role in our close relationships, there are nevertheless vast arenas of human experience that do not fit this model and are not amenable to such structures of interaction. What about the areas of national and international politics, economics, business, large impersonal institutions, the world of law, the military, and so on?

The central notion in a domain ethic is that we need different moral procedures and priorities for different contexts, or domains. A domain ethic could expect that the best moral approach to education would not be the best for economics or for the law or for international politics, but rather that each of these domains, or moral territories, would need its own ethical theory. Thus, a domain ethic approach to the ethics of care would, in a sense, be one that would "put it in its place." But this place may be great or small, central or peripheral, and it may be perceived as significant or trivial.

Nel Noddings unabashedly ties her exposition of the ethics of care to the mother-child relationship as one of the central paradigmatic cases for understanding what is entailed in the actions, experiences, and deliberations of caring and being cared for. Other relationships that are characterized by physical proximity and some degree of nurturance are also taken as of central importance—such as between teacher and student, between friends, colleagues, and spouses. Thus one might characterize this ethic as one that belongs to the domain of *special relations*.

Historically the domain associated with women's territory and responsibilities, such as the family and special relations, were often considered peripheral, insubstantial, or, perhaps worst of all, uninteresting for ethical theory. And even today certain responses to an ethics of care do not merely relegate it to a peripheral place but also dismiss moral preoccupations with caring as no more than personal problems for women's ego development.[5] But, given the context of present-day discussion and debate, such cavalier dismissals of care-based moralities seem to be not so much domain ethics as dominance ethics, whose advocates still believe that their own position determines the boundaries for the universe of moral discourse.

A more representative and generous version of a domain ethic is the one found in the work of Virginia Held (1984). Her book *Rights and Goods* provides a detailed, systematic account of what I am calling a domain approach.

In some of her work since the publication of *Rights and Goods*, Virginia Held (1986) applies her approach directly to an examination of the mother-child relationship, or more precisely to the relationship between child and "mothering person" (male or female). In a conference presentation, Held reiterated her stance as a domain ethics advocate: "I doubt that we should take any one relation as paradigmatic for all the others . . . I am inclined at this point to think that we will continue to need conceptions of different types of relations for different domains." But then she proceeded to argue that "to think of relations between mothers and children as paradigmatic may be an important stage to go through in reconstructing a view of human relationships . . . since the image of rational economic man in contractual relations is absolutely pervasive in this society, and expanding every time one looks around" (Held 1986).

Held's comments illustrate the most sympathetic version of a domains response to the paradigmatic claims of an ethics of care. Held acknowledges
the timely importance of a care-oriented position and she gives serious attention to its implications for the reconstruction of all moral domains.

But Held and Noddings would disagree on whether an ethics of care is a
stage to go through, or a stance to take. Noddings's position seems to require
a radical questioning of the whole structure of the domains themselves,
rather than an acceptance of the prevailing political, social, or economic
structures as necessary givens. What she would do instead is to use an ethics
of care as a critical tool for rethinking and restructuring these arrangements.
Noddings articulates this point when she discusses her own refusal to think
like a utilitarian. "I suggest that we make an error when we think of the moral
good in terms of acts that produce the greatest good for the greatest number,
even among human beings. Such thinking may be as close to the ethical as we
can come in the contemporary political arena, but this seems to count against
our political machinery rather than for utilitarian thinking in social life" (p.
154).

If the applicability of an ethics of care appears to be severely limited within
the prevailing political, legal, social, or economic conditions, this may be an
indictment of the prevailing structures that support these conditions.
Noddings's position implies that we should question these structures and
presumably try to widen the range of viable caring by altering such limiting
conditions.

I say "presumably" because Noddings has not yet told us how to proceed
to alter the prevailing structures that are antithetical to caring. Furthermore,
some critics, both sympathetic and unsympathetic, suggest that an ethics of
care may itself constitute one obstacle in the way of making the requisite
changes, that it may, in fact, be a dangerous ethic for those who practice it,
particularly if they are women (or other subordinate social groups).

A Dangerous Ethic

The central sources for what I am calling the dangerous ethics criticisms are
found in some feminist writings, in particular those writings that focus on the
question of an ethics for feminist political movements.[6] In contrast to those
who relegate caring to the sidelines of a special relation, these critics give full
recognition to the widespread appeal of care-based moralities; and they acknowledge the force of an ethical vision that sustains well-established forms
of practice.

The defining tenet of this position is the observation that, in one way or
another, the practice of such a morality may require either servility or
supererogation. Given this common belief that an ethics of care can be dangerous for its practitioners, there are at least two variations that we should

distinguish from each other. Some critics consider an ethics of care *contingently* dangerous whereas others find it *necessarily*, or essentially, dangerous.

As I read them, a number of contemporary feminists would argue for contingent dangers, although a few would maintain that at least some aspects of an ethics of care make it a necessarily dangerous ethics. The contingent version need not be without sympathy for an ethics of care as such. The ethics is found dangerous because in its presentation there is a lack of attention paid to the conditions that exploit caring and to the systematic deforming of women's caring.[7]

An example of the basic difficulty arises in the very presentation of an ethics of care as primarily a women's or feminine ethic, this phenomenon of the gendered division of moral labor that Noddings portrays and describes so vividly.

For many feminists, the power, accuracy, and richness of Noddings's descriptions are a valuable contribution for understanding the enormous work, the complex skills, and the value of what goes into the labors of caring and the ways in which women constantly reconstitute the social fabric of human life. But what feminists object to is a lack of critical consciousness or a kind of naïveté about the costs and consequences for the women who must do these caring labors.

One danger here is that unless we consider what is actually happening, in our present economic, social, and political contexts, to those who do these caring labors, we fail to talk seriously about the costs of women's caring labors. It is easy, then, to perpetuate inequality and subordination by default or by not challenging the facile inference that caring is naturally feminine work. For example, Noddings's (1984) well-meant use of the feminine pronoun *she* for the one-caring and the masculine pronoun *he* for the cared-for is all too accurate as a description of the status quo, but it becomes unfortunate, misleading, and dangerous, if it encourages us to infer that such a gendered division is desirable, natural, or acceptable.

If we, as gendered men and women, especially women and girls, are to ever have real choices about our own ethics and moral directions, then we need to have the sort of critical consciousness that comes from making explicit what we have learned and internalized as the meanings for *good girl, good boy, good woman, good man, good mother,* and so on. Once these are made explicit, they become directly available to us for our inspection.

But it is also imperative that we, as educators, distinguish between our assessment of the accuracy of given accounts of caring and our assessment of their ethical and educational desirability, the grounds upon which we would consciously adopt them for ourselves, insist on them for our children, or teach them to our students. These are some of the issues that an ethics of care raises for teachers and other educators.

Once educators recognize an ethics of care, the hard questions of educational implications must also be asked. As a teacher and parent herself, Nel

Noddings suggests a number of educational changes and presents us with some clear challenges. She also leaves us with unanswered questions and puzzling dilemmas.[8] Let us turn now to this meeting between education and the ethics of care.

The Ethics of Care in Education

In addition to her use of educational examples throughout *Caring*, Noddings devotes her final chapter completely to educational questions and applications. Here she makes her position unequivocally clear: Not only is the ethics of care the primary human ethic, it should also be the primary educational aim. "The primary aim of every educational institution and of every educational effort must be the maintenance and enhancement of caring. Parents, police, social workers, teachers, preachers, neighbors, coaches, older siblings, must all embrace this primary aim" (p. 172). Noddings hastens to add that "educational institutions may still differ in their secondary aims." The school should not "abdicate its essential responsibility to train the intellect." But the forms that intellectual training takes should not "put the ethical ideal at risk," for to do so would mean that we had "confused our priorities dangerously"— making primary what should be secondary.

This leaves open two interpretations of what is meant by *primary aim* within formal schooling: (1) a constraints interpretation, and (2) a central focus interpretation. In the first interpretation the ethical requirements of caring relations would function for the most part as a constraint or limitation on the range of behaviors, tasks, interactions, and so on, that are used in carrying out specific educational projects such as the teaching and learning of traditional academic subject matter. Under the second interpretation the "maintenance and enhancement of caring" would be the central or foremost focus, something to be kept consciously before us as always more important than anything else. Noddings leaves room for us to apply both interpretations at different points.

In her article "Fidelity in Teaching, Teacher Education, and Research for Teaching," Noddings (1986) further clarifies the ways in which an ethics of care can be an integral part of traditional academic teaching. She gives an example in which the teacher starts with an academic difficulty, but then notices, by practicing engrossment, that if she simply proceeds on course then what is happening will violate caring for several students. At this point the constraint becomes a central focus while the teacher considers what can be done for these students.

Following is Noddings's account of a math teacher reflecting on whether to give retests to several students who have failed a test. The teacher considers and rejects the idea of merely giving them some extra remediation, by saying, "No, that won't do. The bad grade on this test is itself a handicap. It makes them feel scared and hopeless. They need time to learn more and a chance to improve their position. I'll have to give retests" (1986, p. 500). When the teacher focuses directly on the maintenance of caring, the answer to her methodological question becomes clear.

Further on in the example Noddings's teacher takes up the question of whether a retest is fair to the other students who passed the first test. Her reply makes the paradigm shift particularly evident. "I'm not sure fairness is the right criterion here. This isn't a *contest*. Why should there be any winners and losers? Those who pass the first time don't lose anything—they don't have to prepare for a retest" (1986, p. 500). She thus illustrates how a contest view of education can be more effectively challenged from a base within an ethics of care that functions both as a constraint and a central focus.

One example of a central focus application is Noddings's recommendation that schools have "caring apprenticeships" for *all* students; these apprenticeships "should have equal status with the other tasks encountered in education" (p. 188). Here Noddings places the students' explicit acquisition of caring skills and propensities on an equal footing with other academic aims, as one primary aim but not as the only one. But she is also well aware of the fact that in moral education we have no clear separation between the explicit curriculum and the hidden (or latent) curriculum. Noddings puts the point succinctly when she says: "A teacher cannot 'talk' this ethic. She must live it" (p. 179).

Caring apprenticeships are, therefore, simply one form of practice that occurs within a caring community, where through "dialogue, modeling, the provision of practice, and the attribution of best motive, the one-caring as teacher nurtures the ethical ideal" (p. 179).

This is no piecemeal, added-frills approach that Noddings is advocating, but rather a thorough, pervasive transformation of the way teaching is practiced and subjects are taught. One might well ask, How could anyone ask for more than this? But we have not yet confronted the dangerous ethics critics.

Recall that the critics who worried about the dangers attendant upon the ethics of care noticed that the feminine nature of this ethics could be a mixed blessing when it locked women into positions of servility or sainthood as the sole bearers of caring responsibilities. And, second, when political change or reform is needed, an ethics of care seems to be, at best, unclear or hesitant, and at worst an obstacle for its adherents.

Do these dangers pose any problems for Noddings's approach to education? Let us start with the identification of caring as feminine. Noddings is certainly right in her insistence that "all of humanity can participate in the feminine as I am describing it" (p. 172). But is she overly sanguine about the ease with which education may alter the genderized nature of morality, which she herself so accurately describes?

When Noddings associates caring with the feminine, she highlights the way in which our moral propensities often reflect genderized values—perhaps especially with our public ways of behaving as gendered beings. To the extent that our moral propensities are highly genderized, we may have self-imposed gender constraints operating on us where ideally we should, instead, be following our own freely and thoughtfully chosen ethical convictions.

Thus, one thing that follows from acknowledging the tie between caring and the feminine is that as long as gender identity is of central importance, those who have acquired certain standard gender conventions may not be free to choose caring if they conceive of themselves as masculine or free to choose not to care if they conceive of themselves as feminine. Thus the insistence that *all* students learn caring is jeopardized as long as some, or many of, the students themselves perceive such acquisition as a violation of their gender identity. Noddings judiciously sidesteps this whole issue of gender constraints even though her own analysis provides an able explication of the prevailing norms.

If caring is as genderized as Noddings herself indicates, then this phenomenon would seem to call for what Jane Roland Martin (1981b, 1985b) has termed a *gender-sensitive* approach to education, where one recognizes the likelihood of crucial gender differences, watches for these, notices their effects, and adapts educational practices accordingly.[9] Although the first step of recognizing a critical gender difference is central to Noddings's thesis of a feminine ethic, she either ignores or discounts the serious implications for education that Martin notes: The same education will have a vastly different impact, depending upon one's gender.

At present in our society, many girls and young women are directed and helped to consider the cared-for—his needs and wants, the meaning of his actions. So that gradually through encouragement, assistance, and insistence, women come to engage in this engrossment and motivational displacement on their own. Thus they learn caring in Noddings's sense.

It would be misleading as well as mistaken to assume that men and boys do not learn caring at all in our society. But there are at least two significant gender differences. First, conventional masculine caring seems most often to take the form Noddings calls *indirect* caring, such as the ways we "care for people indirectly through maintenance of the environment" (p. 187). These indirect forms of caring are certainly valuable and worthwhile, but they are not equivalent practices in Noddings's sense.

In the second place, many boys will have acquired early on a sense that their major role as a male is to pursue their own projects successfully, which is, on Noddings's analysis, one appropriate way for the cared-for to receive caring and thus complete the relationship. But attention to the maintenance and enhancement of relationships is, then, at best a secondary, if not "feminine," responsibility.

Again we must be careful that we do not confuse sex with gender. For most purposes we can think of two biological sexes, male and female. But gender is plural; there are numerous versions of what it means to be a *woman* or a *man*.

And in our contemporary society students could have access to a wide range of gender meanings, including nurturant men and single-minded women who successfully pursue their own projects. But it may require a conscious, explicit gender-sensitive educational effort to make these gender options available to most students; and without such efforts, Noddings's ethics of care may well remain no more than a feminine ethic.

In the closing pages of *Caring*, right after her suggestions for the changes that could establish better support structures for a community of caring within schools, Noddings asks this poignant question: "Why is it likely that the kind of thinking I am engaged in will lead nowhere?" (p. 199). She observes then that this is not due to a failure of practicality or economics, both of which should realistically be on her side. She also recognizes the issue of *power*; but she mentions it only in passing and treats it as if it were primarily an individualistic matter of those who have "succeeded in the traditional masculine structure" not wanting to give up their "hard-won power" (p. 200).

Noddings then comes close to resignation about this unchanging power structure when she observes, as if it were a necessary unalterable fact (perhaps also desirable), that "women, by our very nature, are unlikely to seek domination in education; our circles will be circles of support and not of power" (p. 200).

Then, with only one more page to go, Noddings moves on to another topic and seems to leave us precisely where the dangerous position would predict—with no recourse but to go on caring as well as we can under a set of antithetical conditions, while the larger structures remain beyond our power to change as long as we adhere to this morally admirable *and* politically powerless ethics of care.

It is here that those of us whose work, responsibilities, and morality fits an ethics of care must face what Marilyn Frye (1983) has aptly termed the "fatal combination of responsibility and powerlessness: we are held responsible and we hold ourselves responsible for good outcomes for . . . children in almost every respect though we have in almost no case power adequate to that project" (p. 9).

If as educators we believe in our work and truly do care for our students, we are lured by three dubious but appealing temptations that avoid facing Frye's fatal combination. We can try (1) denial, (2) romanticizing, or (3) resignation. The third choice may be the most realistic but it is also the least invigorating, the hardest on morale, and one that appears ironically to give up on morality. The first two choices are not only dishonest, they also fail to confront what is really happening, including the ways in which the conditions for effective caring are themselves undermined.

On my reading of Noddings, her critical position would seem to advocate unrelenting persistence and insistence when it comes to conditions for caring. Rather than opting for any of the three temptations, Noddings would, I think, advocate withdrawal of consent and outright disobedience if caring is

threatened, and, finally, under more extreme conditions, whatever is necessary to defend and protect those for whom one cares.[10]

Meanwhile Noddings insists that "it is time for the voice of the mother to
be heard in education." And she reiterates her invitation for men and women
"to join in a dialectical conversation," a conversation that Noddings's own
work has significantly furthered.

Epilogue

My major intention in this chapter was aptly described by Marilyn Frye
(1983) when she wrote at the end of *The Politics of Reality:* "My primary goal
here has not been to state and prove some rigid thesis, but simply to *say*
something clearly enough, intelligibly enough, so that it can be understood
and thought about" (p. 173).

My preference for clarity over theses, in this matter, is due to my conviction that definitive judgments on an ethics of care are premature. I believe
that the systematic exposition of an ethics of care, its implications and its
range of applications, although well begun, is still in a fledgling stage. In the
first place, almost all the discussions of contemporary versions have been
available in the public domain for less than twenty years. The opportunity for
development and elaboration through widespread public exchanges and critiques has occurred mostly within the last two decades of the twentieth century.[11]

In the second place, discussions of an ethics of care often focus primarily
on the gender connection, on the ways in which caring is associated with
women or with the feminine. But when I take the perspective of an educational theorist, it seems to me that although the gender connection is of
tremendous importance, the ethics of care also may represent native ground
for numerous teachers and educators, regardless of sex. A still largely unexplored question is whether an ethics of care does reveal certain "deep structures" for many educational practitioners. And if it does, what interesting
similarities and divergences might there be between an educational version
and a feminine version of this ethic?

In the third place, I believe we must be more careful to distinguish between our assessment of the accuracy of descriptive accounts of the tacit
structures of inferable directives for caring and our assessment of their ethical desirability.

The failure to maintain this distinction leads, I think, to the extremes of
both oversimplified advocacy and oversimplified rejection. Both advocates
and opponents of an ethics of care seem at times to base their ethical assessment directly on their belief in its descriptive accuracy. The logic seems to be
that if we do have an accurate account of women's own morality here, then by
implication the evaluative assessment follows without question from this fact.

In one case, if it is women's morality, then it is good (life-affirming, nurturant, peaceful, nonviolent, generous, helpful, etc.). In the other case, if it is traditionally women's, then it is bad (oppressive, exploitive, servile, imposed by men, sexist, etc.). In neither case does one slow down enough to separate descriptive power from ethical value.

On the level of phenomenological description and systematic exposition, I believe Noddings's work, as well as Gilligan's (1982), Ruddick's (1983, 1984), and others, provides rich, perceptive, and much needed articulations of our moral experience and care-based traditions. The power of these accounts is borne out by the widespread recognition, attention, and affirmation the ethics of care has received. Nevertheless, there is also considerable room for further descriptive efforts, as for example in the educational realm we already noted.

When it comes to questions of ethical assessment, I think there is enormous work yet to be done. This includes not only the questions of moral desirability within particular situations or domains but also the problems of choosing metalevel criteria for critical assessment and reconstructive efforts.[12]

In education, the curriculum should, I believe, definitely include the ethics of care within the canon of recognized ethical paradigms. To have explicit and systematic formulations of this ethics available for study and inspection provides a much needed resource for students' own critical consciousness as well as the grounds for making better informed choices about their own morality. It is a separate and further question to ask whether educators should consciously adopt caring as the ideal educational ethic.

Notes

1. All page references that are not otherwise designated refer to Noddings (1984).

2. The most widely discussed initial proponents of what I am calling *the ethics of care* are Carol Gilligan (1982), Nel Noddings (1984), and Sara Ruddick (1983, 1984a, 1984c, 1989). There are important differences among them; for example, Sara Ruddick seems more sensitive to the influence the social political culture has on the expression of a nurturant ethics and on the ways in which it can go wrong. But I think it is fair to say that these writers all share the features I have distilled as central to the ethics of care. There is now a voluminous body of literature on the topic of women and morality; much of it is concerned with the ethics of care under discussion in this paper. I cannot begin to give an exhaustive, or indeed even a very representative, listing of the works on this topic. However, I will here indicate those writers whose contribution to the critical analysis of the ethics of care I have in mind when I later turn to an assessment of the ethics: Virginia Held (1984, 1986), Jean Grimshaw (1986), Barbara Houston (1985, 1987, 1988a, 1988b), Claudia Card (1985), Marilyn Frye (1983), Sara Hoagland (1986, 1988), Jeffner Allen (1986), Joan Ringelheim (1985), Judy Auerbach et al. (1985), and Larry Blum et al. (1984).

3. Many standard moral theories seem to presuppose what Selya Benhabib has called "the mushroom view of the origin of man," a view she finds clearly expressed in

Hobbes: that men sprang from the ground like mushrooms, fully formed, rational, autonomous, independent, and self-interested creatures. For her intriguing comments on this view, see her paper given to the Stony Brook Conference on Women and Moral Theory, Long Island, Spring 1984, now published in Kittay and Meyers (1987).

4. Annette Baier (1985, 1986) elaborates on this point in the course of developing her own ideas for a women's ethic that focuses more on the issues of appropriate trust and distrust than on those of nurturance; but she also insists that relatedness is basic to an authentic human ethic.

5. Lawrence Kohlberg (Kohlberg, Levine, and Hewar 1983, pp. 22–27 and p. 141) has argued this view. See also Gertrude Nunner-Winkler (1984, p. 358). John Broughton (1983) also adopts this interpretation of Gilligan's account of the "different" morality.

6. Those who hold the dangerous ethics view include Allen (1986), Blum et al. (1976), Card (1985), Daly (1973), Frye (1983), Hoagland (1986, 1988), Houston (1987, 1989), and Ringelheim (1985). It seems to me that Card, Allen, Houston, and Ringelheim hold the view that the ethics of care is contingently dangerous. Sara Hoagland, in her paper entitled "Vulnerability and Power," makes a strong case for claiming that the "virtue" of vulnerability, frequently associated with women's nurturant ethic, is *necessarily* dangerous.

7. For a series of interesting cases that illustrate the exploitation and deforming of women's caring, see Blum et al. (1976).

8. Since my earlier publication of the original version of this chapter, Noddings has continued to write about applying an ethics of care to questions of educational practice and school reform, most extensively in her book *The Challenge to Care in Schools* (1992), which provides a helpful detailed model to follow. Nevertheless, we still face the same questions that I raise at the end of this chapter. Chapters 9, 10, and 11, address some of these dilemmas.

9. As far as I know Martin first introduced the idea of a gender-sensitive education in her 1981 Presidential Address to the Philosophy of Education Society (Martin 1981b). For her more recent thinking see Martin (1984, 1985a, 1985b, 1986, 1990, 1992, 1994). For a further discussion on the potential problems of *overgenderization*, see Diller (1984).

10. For Noddings's (1984) remarkably honest wrestling with the issues of violence and the need to protect those for whom we care, see especially pp. 108–120. Noddings summarizes her position when she says "she will neither initiate violence nor leave her inner circle unprotected" (1984, p. 111).

11. Compare this time span with the ethics of Plato and Aristotle, which have been discussed for more than two thousand years; or with the more recent Kantian and Utilitarian ethical systems, which both exceed a hundred years.

12. I have addressed some pieces of these questions elsewhere; see, for example, Houston and Diller, "Trusting Ourselves to Care" (1987).

8

Describing the Emperor's New Clothes: Three Myths of Educational (In-)Equity

KATHRYN PAULY MORGAN

I am a white, southern, female sociologist who teaches about race to a racially and eth-nically mixed population of students in the city where Martin Luther King Jr. was killed. . . . How was I going to challenge racism? . . . When I started teaching I was reluctant to address the emotionally laden content of the classroom, but over time I gave more and more attention to classroom interaction, which, like all group interac-tions is structured by inequalities of power among the participants. They are not ran-dom, haphazard, or out of the control of the teacher. Our behavior as faculty members and the way we structure our courses play major roles in the nature of classroom in-teractions as they unfold throughout the semester: they mimic, reproduce, and with creative management can interrupt, the normal hierarchies of society. (L. W. *Cannon,* Fostering Positive Race, Class, and Gender Dynamics in the Classroom, *1990, p. 126, emphasis added.*)

These are the poignant words of Lynn Weber Cannon, a teacher in Memphis, Tennessee. These are words that resonate for me in my own uni-versity classrooms where I interact daily with First Nation's students strug-gling to deal with cultural alienation, students with disabilities whose courage takes my breath away, mature students risking the formation of new selves by coming to university, Trinidadian students of Chinese and Arab heritage be-ing pressured to identify as white Canadians, and students who have been so brutally demeaned in other classrooms that they vow never to speak again in a formal educational setting. Like Weber Cannon, I have become increas-ingly aware of a multiplicity of axes of privilege and oppression that affect all of us in educational settings. In my own personal crucible of learning, I have

had the good fortune to have been challenged, to have felt seemingly unend-
ing layers of scales drop from my eyes, and to hope that in the process I am
coming to greater—and always tentative—political lucidity regarding the
power-laden complexities of my varied roles in education. To help me sustain
a vivid sense of the dynamic and frightening ideological and material axes of
power in which we are all differentially situated in contemporary North
American culture I have developed Figure 8.1.

The center point represents a particular individual who can be seen as the
nexus or site of intersection in a larger set of personal, communal, and institutional interrelations. Domination is the horizontal axis and is deliberately
ambivalent. Privilege involves the power to dominate in systematic ways,
which are simultaneously ideological and material, institutional and personal.
Oppression involves the lived, systematic experience of being dominated by
virtue of one's position on various particular axes. Following Foucault (1977,
1980), I believe that, in North America, each of us occupies such a point of
specific juxtaposition on each of these axes (at a minimum) and that this point
is simultaneously a locus of our agency, power, disempowerment, oppression,
and resistance. The antipodes represent maximum privilege or extreme oppression with respect to a particular axis.

In order for each of us to become fully aware of the power hierarchies in
which we participate, we must strive for both awareness and honesty with respect to our own positioning on the various axes of this grid. Only in this way
can we avoid mimicking and reproducing in our own pedagogical behavior
and in our theorizing precisely those hierarchies that undermine any attempts to create genuine educational equity (*Canadian Women's Studies* 1992;
Eichler 1988b; MacKinnon 1987, 1989).[1]

In this chapter, I propose to examine only one of these axes, that of gender.
By focusing on gender, I do not intend to privilege it above all other axes for
investigation. I recognize that, for very many participants in the educational
community, an axis such as race or class may have greater priority and that
sustained analyses of the dynamic interaction and resonance of various axes
are necessary. I recognize, too, that very often the axes of privilege and oppression are not as separate as the diagram would suggest and are systematically and politically bound up with each other in a way that confounds any
simplistic attempt at isomorphic analysis based on privileging one axis
(Anzaldua 1990; Lugones 1991; Majaj 1994; Moraga and Anzaldua 1981;
Spelman 1988).[2] But gender is one place to begin as I analyze various myths
that camouflage the naked facts of educational inequity. It is also one place to
begin in searching for equitable gender-liberatory models of education that
must always be seen as addressing only one dimension of a multidimensional
theory of emancipatory education.[3]

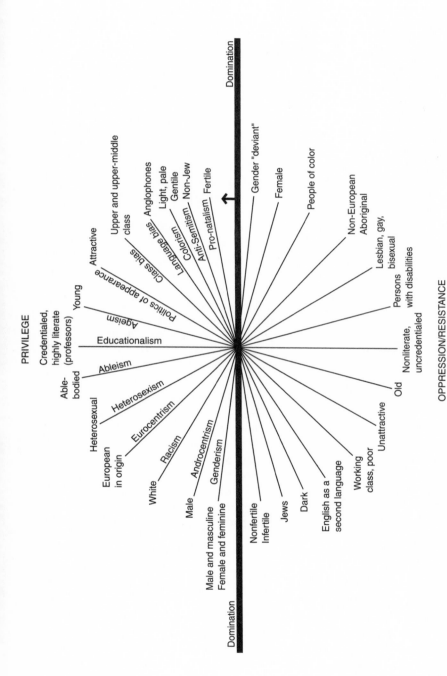

Figure 8.1 Intersecting Axes of Privilege, Domination, and Oppression

Why We See the Emperor as Fully Clothed, or The Colonization of Girls' and Women's Educational Sensibility

Power in education is operationalized by creating, defining, encoding, transmitting, and evaluating claims to knowledge. In Esland's (1971) words, "Through their control of the transformation of the child's consciousness, its exponents (i.e., of the curriculum) engineer theoretical world views which are thought to be valid currency in their society" (p. 84). Often the cultural specificity of this process—signaled by use of the pronoun *their*—is ideologically mystified by such phrases as "understanding and being committed to the ultimate goals of education" or "striving to develop the educated man."[4] To be seen as educated in this context means that one's consciousness has been transformed through the acquisition of conceptual schemes, the knowledge and acceptance of certain canons, and the internationalization of particular norms of reasonableness and evidence. Proof of one's educated sensibility is provided through private reflections, informal conversations, and public performances such as tests, papers, dissertations, and publications that validate one as a member of the educated community.

Encoding power includes control over the educational curriculum and control over educational discourse which determines both the actual language of the classroom and what are going to count as educationally relevant contributions to the conversations of education (Bernstein 1971, 1977; Bourdieu 1973; hooks 1989, 1992). Power over transmission entails control over the conferring of pedagogical legitimacy on some forms of cognition, patterns of thought, and sets of values and ignoring or devaluing others. Finally, mastery of the curriculum and demonstrated competence in the admissible forms of articulation are inextricably tied to control over the definitions of achievement (Bowles and Gintis 1976; Nicholson 1983).

But plainly, the people who encode, transmit, and define what will count as knowledge, the people who establish the rules of educational play in the classroom, and the people who define and reward the winners have the educational power.

Ideally, from the point of view of the winners, this educational event should be experienced in a non-alienated way in an educational community committed to educational equity. Realization of this ideal would mean that when each of us speaks, we would feel—partially because of our education—a sense of authenticity. We would experience a sense of personal integrity because when we come to situate ourselves culturally, historically, intellectually, racially, and sexually, we feel that we educate and are being educated in a community where each of us, in our situated particular subjectivity, has been fully recognized as a valued legitimate participant (Aisenberg and Harrington 1988; Anzaldua 1987; Carty 1991; Lugones 1989; Martin 1985a; Ng 1994).

Educational power seldom resides, however, in the entire cultural and political community. As Michael Young (1971) remarks, "Particular classes maintain their dominance by being able to confer cultural legitimacy on certain styles of thought and therefore on certain aspects of reality" (p. 12). Various groups, classes, and races often use the institution of public education to confer legitimacy on particular styles of thought and particular models of reality, which serve to perpetuate particular forms of hegemony. In Great Britain, Canada, the United States and in various former European colonies in Africa, the Caribbean, and the Far East, hegemonic educational power has traditionally resided—and continues to reside—with white, middle- and upper-class males (Spender 1982; Gaskell, McLaren, and Novogrodsky 1989). In 1989, Pearson, Shavlik, and Touchton noted that "if all women administrators at the dean's level and above [in the United States] were equally distributed among all the institutions, there would be only 1.1 per institution."

In the area of curriculum content, little needs to be said about the continuing preponderance of white male authors and the overwhelming masculine imagery. Although some of the most vulgar manifestations of racist and sexist symbolism have been muted as a result of the critiques of sexism, racism, and ethnic bias in the 1970s and 1980s, fully inclusive respectful valorization of the images and voices of any group other than privileged white males as originators of *human* knowledge remains mystic rather than real (Collins 1990; Eichler 1988b; hooks 1989; McIntosh 1987; Minnich 1990; Sadker and Sadker 1994; Spelman 1988; Spender 1982; West 1993).

In the classroom and more informal educational settings, the use of dominant metaphors and preferred modes of cognition continue to carry political gender messages. Consider the physical sciences. In the seventeenth century, Francis Bacon celebrated the new science, describing it as inaugurating the "truly masculine birth of time," which required a new conceptualization of nature that involved conquering and subduing Nature in her "inner Chambers" (Easlea 1981, p. 84).

Contemporary scientists often continue with the same masculine rhetoric. For example, Jacob Bronowski, author of the influential series and book, *The Ascent of Man* (!) (1968), maintains that every good scientific experiment is a "challenge to nature," a challenge that compels nature "to declare herself for or against our model of her." Such a test is carried out in a laboratory or field setting where "we try to strip the test to its naked essentials." Bronowski continues, "We command nature as no animal does . . . because we are able to see her objectively, that is to analyse her into objects." Similarly, Willard Libby claims that "the experienced scientist knows that nature yields her secrets with great reluctance and only *to proper suitors*" (emphasis added). Even more strikingly, the biologist Richard Lewontin proclaims, "Science is a form of competitive and aggressive activity, a *contest of man against man that provides knowledge as a side product*" (emphasis added, Easlea 1985, p. 170).

The competitive, domination-saturated rhetoric of a "contest of man against man" sends a message that is not lost on aspiring girls and women science students who feel a sense of gendered alienation from the invasive voice. Scientifically talented girls and women sense a threat generated by the competitive practices and discourses of largely white male scientists, a threat to some of their deepest values regarding the importance of supportive relations, nurturance, and caring (Surrey 1991). Often girls and women who achieve in the domains of science do so only by becoming gender-neutered or by becoming "one of the guys" (a more profound form of gender alienation) in both their social *and their cognitive/linguistic behavior*. The more self-reflective and political among them report a feeling of gender schism and womanly mutilation as well as a sense of discipline-based censorship (Hrdy 1986).

A second instructive example comes from philosophy, the one theoretical discipline that tries to maintain a monopoly over definitions of *reason, reasonable*, and *the rational man* (Lloyd 1984). Informal philosophical discourse is saturated with competitive, violent, militaristic metaphors (Ayim 1986, 1988). The highly ranked, promising philosophy student is not the one who demonstrates a quiet, hesitant profundity but, rather, one who engages in the abrasive and adversarial interactions that are virtually definitional of philosophical debate in the English-speaking world. In philosophy, women students are expected to engage in detached, unemotional, transcendently appreciative study of various philosophical theories whose aim is to produce sound arguments to discredit women's rationality and capacity for theoretical study and discourse (Agonito 1977; Mahowald 1983). Whether reading passages from the *Malleus Maleficarum* (a book from 1484 that was the detailed canonical source used by witch persecutors and legal prosecutors to identify, try, torture, and sentence alleged participants in witchcraft), which say "Women are intellectually like children. . . . She always deceives. . . . Women also have weak memories. . . . She is a liar by nature" (Kramer and Sprenger 1971) or studying the gender-discrediting motivations of crainiologists in the nineteenth century, women are expected to remain calm, and to decontextualize from the lived pain, torture, incarceration, and killing of women for the exercise of their rational intelligence (Lowe 1982).

As in the sciences, women are expected to internalize masculine models of interaction to show that, unlike the women described in the philosophical theories, they are exceptions to the rule that assigns noncognitive, emotionally intuitive processes to virtually all women and members of other groups whose intelligence is seen as far inferior to that of white males. Today, a woman in philosophy receives a compliment when, *per impossibile* given the theories, she is told that "she thinks like a man"; analogously, both a man and a woman philosophy student feel insulted when they are told, "You think like a (typical) woman." Women students and women philosophers are continually being socialized into contemporary masculine patterns of philosophical discourse and are being asked to declare allegiance to a definition of the philosophical canon determined almost exclusively by "Great White Male Thinkers." Being regarded and respected as a good student and practitioner of philosophy means being able to think rationally and theoretically like a (white) man. This exacts a high price at the level of personal womanly integrity and womanly self-esteem (Beauvoir 1952; Finn 1982; Ruth 1981; Martin 1994).

Even explicit radical critiques of education have been carried out within communities of male thinkers. In the moving essays of Martin Buber (1947), aptly entitled *Between Man and Man,* he addresses the teacher and boy who encounters him. In the spirited and sustained criticisms of education produced by Paulo Freire, it is still clear that the most significant community of learners is expected to be made up of boys and men (Freire 1968, 1973; Kenway and Modra 1989).[5]

In education, although girls and women now make up the majority of those being educated in North America, girls and women are a colonized population (Mies, Bennholdt-Thomsen, and Von Werlhof 1988). Girls' and women's curiosity, our search for intellectual power, our desires to speak, our sense of intellectual competence, our interests, our questions, and our needs are often disproved, demeaned, dismissed, and punished (Hall and Sandler 1982, 1986; Backhouse, Harris, Michell, and Wylie 1989; Smith n.d.). At best, our "primitive," not fully rational, not fully universal views and capacities for understanding are exploited and appropriated by men. Servants and handmaidens in the masculine domains of knowledge creation and dissemination, good, heterosexually approved girls and women serve as supportive companions to the men who create, define, encode, and transmit human knowledge especially at what are described, in masculine rhetoric, as the frontiers of human knowledge.

Women who display their own curiosity and speak in their own voices have long been found dangerous or suspect. In the context of Western European symbolic imagery, women's curiosity has been indicted as responsible for the ills of the world. Whether one looks at patriarchal constructions of Eve's search for the Tree of Knowledge of Good and Evil or the probings of Pandora, the message is the same: A woman's curiosity is a dangerous vice; it must be constrained and directed to the agendas of men in order to avoid generating evil.

The educational implications of assumptions of intellectual inferiority are clear: Since girls and women cannot excel, educators should not expect that girls and women will excel. Nor should we impose unreasonable educational demands on girls and women or hold them to the rigorous expectations directed to white boys and men. Nor should we give any real importance to the voices of girls and women when those voices arise out of their own experiences (Lewis and Simon 1986). In short, education is, ideally, an androcentric institution created, maintained, dominated by, and directed toward privileged white boys and men. Girls and women should appreciate being able to participate in that institution in the name of educational equity.

Androcentric educational settings (whether single-sex or coeducational) take a severe toll on girls and women. When girls and women try to break through these gender constraints by being more intellectually assertive, by challenging received authority, by speaking forcefully, they are labeled unfeminine, unladylike, aggressive, uppity, shrill, castrating, or more subtly said to be suffering from penis envy. In boys and men, the identical behavior is praised, reinforced, and welcomed as the mark of the developing, autonomous, inquiring—and masculine—mind.[6]

Fearing such labels, girls and women respond powerfully to the queries captured in Marge Piercy's poem "For Strong Women" (1982, p. 252):

why aren't you feminine?,
why aren't you soft?,
why aren't you quiet?,
why aren't you dead?

Often we respond by silencing ourselves as our repeated attempts to participate actively in the intellectual, political, and moral dialogues at the heart of education are ignored, dismissed, or demeaned.

Furthermore, because of gender dissonance at the heart of education, publicly credentialed advanced education per se comes to be seen as an impediment to the fulfillment of other relational roles into which girls and women are heavily socialized as heterosexual wife and mother. Contemporary studies in North America, Europe, and Australia continue to demonstrate tension between women's achievement of public forms of educational power (with an accompanying sense of intellectual empowerment and entitlement) and the interpersonal achievement goals of girls and women who have been being socialized into heterosexist "Culture(s) of Romance," powerful cultures that transcend differences of class and race (Holland and Eisenhart 1990; MacDonald 1980; Weiler 1988).

One available strategy for girls and women to mediate these gender tensions and gender dissonances involves a kind of colonized assimilation of our educational sensibilities to ideal norms of racialized male identification. We accept and live out male-focused definitions of what it means for us to be educated. As these definitions become internalized, we become increasingly comfortable seeing primarily images of white boys and men active in the world and in positions of authority and dominance. We come to find it normal to read primarily the writings of white male authors and we inordinately appreciate those teachers, professors, and colleagues who make even modest attempts to be more inclusive of women in their defining of the canon. Through the process of colonization we internalize a misogynistic censor. This process is complete when we believe and feel that, yes, our concerns, our ideas, our feelings, and our life experiences are educationally irrelevant, secondary, limited, and inappropriately particularistic.

Under colonization, women's voices—when we speak at all—are marked by hesitancy, timidity, self-denial, and self-depreciation. We are encouraged to see the emperor as *fully* clothed wearing only the raiment of white masculine intellectual paradigms, modes of cognition, standards of achievement, research methodologies, and agendas of curiosity and interests. We come to feel honored by being admitted to the inner circles of his educational court, granted presence and legitimacy as—and only as—good colonized subjects who can aspire only to be faint approximations of the educated man.

Girls' and women's colonized educational behavior is then taken as (circular) proof of the patriarchal assumptions about woman's nature and limited potential, thereby reenforcing those very assumptions. The ultimate misogynistic twist occurs when women themselves are held responsible for this situation. Simone de Beauvoir (1952) bluntly dismisses this misogynistic analysis by remarking, "Her wings are clipped, and it is found deplorable that she cannot fly."

Looking Again: Exposing the Emperor's Mythic Camouflage

Educational critics who fight against colonization of girls and women in education often invoke an ideal of gender-sensitive educational equity as an alternative to patriarchal and Eurocentric patterns of domination (Diller and Houston Chapter 14, this volume; Houston Chapter 4, this volume; Martin 1994). For us to arrive at this goal, however, it is crucial to expose three myths that camouflage a state of educational inequity and that perpetuate the gender axis as an axis of privilege and oppression: (1) The Universality Myth, (2) The Coeducation Myth, and (3) The Equal Opportunity Myth.

The Universality Myth (Or, Why Does Everything [Still] Seem to Be Mostly [White] Men's Studies?)

Challenging the universality myth requires several steps. The first important step is unmasking the assumption of white male supremacy in its educational manifestations (Bannerji, Carty, Dehli, Heald, and McKenna 1991; Collins 1990; hooks 1989; Hull, Scott, and Smith 1982). Stated straightforwardly, the assumption of white male supremacy states that men are superior and important because they are men and because they are white. Translated into an educational context, it means that insofar as education crucially involves the creation, transmission, and personal assimilation of culture, it is important to focus on the experiences, achievements, thoughts, writings, and experiments of white men as the most exemplary of human achievement (Bennett 1988; Bloom 1987; Gaskell, McLaren, and Novogrodsky 1989; Pearson, Shavlik, and Touchton 1989; Smith 1987).

The second step involves identifying and naming the resulting androcentric solipsism of the learning enterprise with respect to curriculum, pedagogy, and goals. I use the term *solipsism* here as a kind of metaphor to suggest a view with such powerful blinders that it maintains that all and only what it sees is real. Worse than simple male intellectual chauvinism or more straightforward androcentrism (which at least implies a periphery and approximations to a center) this solipsism is often masked by the title of universal knowledge (MacKinnon 1982). It comes in two varieties. *Factual solipsism* maintains that this alleged universal knowledge simply is all there is to know; *normative solipsism*—expressed in the axiom "Man is the measure of all things"—maintains that this alleged universal knowledge is all that is *most worthy* of knowing (Black 1989; Eichler 1980, 1988a, 1988b; Minnich 1990; Thiele 1987). In either case, the educational upshot is the same: The worthy content of education is defined by the interests of men, the suitably worthy recipients of educational effort are boys and men, the advanced students most worthy of mentoring are men, and the primary ·creators, exemplars, and transmitters—particularly of advanced knowledge—are expected to be men, preferably white, highly articulate, and Eurocentric in intellectual allegiance. That this androcentric solipsism has constituted the main focus of postsecondary curricula is, by now, a widely documented—and continuing—phenomenon. Hence, the unnamed ubiquitousness of Men's Studies. This is one of the main reasons given for the continuing need for programs explicitly designated "Women's Studies" at the college and university level.[7]

To see how androcentric solipsism operates, consider the hypothetical example of an English department of any large, prestigious North American university. Although it is true that many English departments are now in the forefront of apparent curricular transformation in the sense that the syllabi no longer consist completely of European white males, at this hypothetical university androcentrism is being entrenched at deeper levels of canonical and disciplinary legitimacy. For example, students read only white male authors as the required reading but are referred to women authors and women-authored feminist criticism as additional or optional reading. Instructors construct essay topics and examinations in such a way that only white male authors are included as worthy of serious, intense consideration so that the syllabus itself appears more inclusive but the normative androcentrism continues. Similarly, in the undergraduate course offerings, there may be a course on Virginia Woolf or a survey course on "Women Writers," but the proportion of such courses is minuscule compared with the detailed attention given to Chaucer, Wordsworth, Yeats, or Tennessee Williams. In this department, it would appear decidedly odd to offer a survey course on "Men Writers."

Students who want to study, for example, the epistolary tradition of nineteenth century female suffragists or the poetry of Audre Lorde are hard pressed to find courses in which to do this and, if they persist, are referred to the university's Women's Studies program as "the place where you study 'that sort of thing.'" If these same students argue that, for example, Alice Walker, Joy Kogawa, M. Norbese Phillips, Toni Morrison, and Maxine Hong Kingston ought to be included in courses called "Major Writers of the 20th Century," they are told to take *the* (only) "Women Writers" course or that "these are not major writers" or that "their material is of inferior quality" or that "we do not intend to commit extensive curriculum and staff resources to these figures because these authors only appeal to women—or to blacks—or to readers of 'diaspora literature.'" And where such universities send their graduates to staff other colleges and universities in the English-speaking world and to train future teachers of English in the primary and secondary school system, androcentric Eurocentric definitions and values are perpetuated in and by the authoritative communities of scholars who continue to be white men despite affirmative action hiring policies.

What we have here is no longer mere omission or oversight because some women writers are included in the syllabus. Here a deeper structural normative androcentrism is at work.

The third step in unmasking pseudo-universalism involves identifying the deeply Platonic bias of traditional accounts of learning and educational achievement. Apart from those disciplines whose mandate is concern with the particular (e.g., astronomy and history), much of education is under the sway of the model of learning represented in Plato's dialogues, the *Republic* and the *Symposium*. Platonic universalism maintains that truly human learning reaches its most valued stage in the production of universal, transcendent, impersonal, detached, abstract, theoretical reasoning. Such learning comes to be labeled "pure" and that which "fails" to achieve such transcendence is accorded a label of lesser status, namely "applied" knowledge. Whatever is particular, concrete, personal, felt, and individual, anchored in space and time, is seen at best as a stepping stone to greater universality. At worst, it is seen as irrelevant to and interfering with the educational enterprise—particularly at the university level.

According to many theologians, philosophers, psychologists, social scientists, administrators, and educators, girls and women are seen as the experts of feeling, as experts in attending to the concrete and the particular.[8] This leads to a second pernicious exercise of a double standard. When boys and men offer particular, individuated perspectives in the classroom, their behavior is welcomed as a stepping stone onto the ladder of transcendence. When girls and women do the same, the behavior is often seen as the most they are capable of contributing and, more often, as inappropriately personal and as an impediment to the major thrust, so to speak, of education. Thus, the particular knowledge that arises out of girls' and women's experience is used simultaneously to define and limit the capabilities of girls and women—and to dismiss them in the light of the Platonic norm of universalism. In theory and in practice, girls and women are defined, devalued, and dismissed—and so present no challenge to normative androcentric solipsism. The privileging of men and the prioritizing of Men's Studies are safe.

The Coeducation Myth

The myth of coeducation pretends that since girls and boys, women and men, have equal access to all the educational facilities in public education, genuine coeducation is taking place. It pretends that this alleged equal access gives girls and boys the *same* education. This myth is undermined by first unveiling the myth of universality with respect to the curriculum and the canon and then stating, openly, that what girls and women are being invited to participate in is the androcentric education of boys and men (Thompson 1983).

In a moving passage in *Three Guineas*, Virginia Woolf (1938) perceptively remarks,

> The questions that we have to ask and to answer about that [academic] procession during this moment of transition are so important that they may well change the lives of all men and women forever. For we have to ask ourselves, here and now, *do we wish to join that procession*, or don't we? . . . Let us never cease from thinking—what is this "civilization" in which we find ourselves? . . . Where is it leading us, the procession of the sons of educated men? (Quoted in Rich 1979b, pp. 131–132; and Gaskell, McLaren, and Novogrodsky 1989. Emphasis added.)

Who are the sons of educated men? Look at the processions in your academic setting. Apart from in those schools, colleges, and universities primarily committed to the education of black students or, exclusively, to girls and women, those in power in the processions are predominantly able-bodied white and middle- or upper-class men. This was true in Woolf's time; this is true in our time.

What does this mean for boys, particularly if they are white and middle or upper class? It means that they can claim the study of white history as their own subject; they can claim the male writers as their models and forefathers; they can identify wholeheartedly with the valued writers of radical Western revolutionary political documents; they can celebrate the Renaissance as their renaissance; they can applaud the founding of the Royal Society and the achievements of the vast majority of Nobel Prize winners as something that their community of men has accomplished—and see all of this as objective proof of the superiority of white males. They can feel comfortable being educated into that tradition and can meaningfully aspire to take their place in it, especially if they are articulate and highly credentialed. Their intellectual power is prized and nourished, and it is not surprising that it flourishes in this educational context.

In this supportive milieu, white boys and men can become strengthened by surviving the crucible of critical, challenging, educational discourse with educational authorities who are white men like themselves. Here white boys and men can experience a comforting congruence between achieved power, achieved masculinity, and developing autonomy (Martin 1981b, 1990). Becoming educated can confer upon them a lived sense of valued personal integrity. This is what it means for co-education to be a racialized male-identified institution.

What does it mean for girls? If you are a girl or a woman, being invited to enter the "locker rooms of the mind" where boys and men are encouraged to develop their intellectual muscles and postures of domination in the wrestling rings of the classrooms, the seminar, and the public forum," "what you are being offered is *not* genuine education. As Gaskell, McLaren, and Novogrodsky (1989), Rich (1979a), Martin (1981, 1990), and many others have pointed out, real coeducation would involve a radical transformation of the academy in such a way that girls' and women's voices, girls' and women's achievements, and girls' and women's questions would be seen and felt to be of equal merit and equally worthy of study and emulation. And this means girls and women in all our diversity—not just the voices, achievements, and questions of white, middle- and upper-class girls and women who are northern European in origin. As Emily Pauline Johnson, the Mohawk writer and actor says, "There are those who think they pay me a compliment in saying I am just like a white woman. My aim, my joy, my pride is to sing the glories of my own people" (Brant 1993).

We have some distance to go before we achieve the real goal of coeducation. For girls and women, participating in what is called coeducation often leads to devastating experiences of mutilation, gender neutering, schism, and internalized misogyny. Achievement for a woman, particularly at advanced levels, can only come if she pays the price of male identification. The price is high—it is the price of a permanently and multiply alienated conscience (Mahtani 1994; Majaj 1994; McIntosh 1992; Williams 1991). This is not fun. This is not real coeducation. This is not educational equity.

The Myth of Educational Equality of Opportunity

The myth of coeducation is often interwoven with the myth of equal opportunity in public education. It maintains that girls and boys, women and men, now experience equal opportunity in terms of access, response, privileges, and rewards in public educational settings. But contemporary educational settings are not ones of genuinely equal opportunity. In her book *Schools for the Boys? Co-Education Reassessed*, Pat Mahoney (1985) remonstrates that in Britain, coeducational schools continue to be, in essence, male monopolies. She documents how boys monopolize physical space, linguistic space, and teacher attention and demonstrates how boys are regarded as more capable than girls and cited as model pupils. Similar large-scale studies such as the now well-known "Chilly Climate" studies continue to demonstrate the pervasiveness of formal and informal negative discriminatory practices directed at girls and women at the college and university level in the United States and Canada (Hall and Sandler 1982, 1986; Backhouse, Harris, Michell, and Wylie 1989; Sadker and Sadker 1994). Relatively speaking, for white boys and men, the climate is warm, nurturing, and strengthening; for virtually all girls and women, the climate is chilly, often leading to intellectual frostbite, numbness of spirit, and amputation.

Educational settings are often ones of sexual terrorism as male monopolies are held in place through threat, intimidation, coercion, and violence. Mahoney (1985) found that the usual experience of girls is that they will be sexually harassed by boys on the playground, in the corridors, and even in girls' washrooms. Girls were frequently verbally abused and "put down" by boys while being expected to provide services for them. All major players in the educational setting—children, teachers, and administrators—regarded these experiences as normal, as boys "simply being boys." Other recent research demonstrates similar pervasiveness of harassment at the secondary school level, the college and university level, and in the professional schools (Cammaert 1985; Clark et al. 1989; Dagg and Thompson 1988; Day 1990; Dziech, Wright, and Weiner 1990; Fitzgerald, Weitzman, Gold, and Ormerod 1988; Larkin 1994; Morris 1989; Moscarello, Katalin, Margittai, and Rossi 1994).[9]

We need to take into account the extent to which those in power in U.S. and Canadian colleges and universities have come, albeit reluctantly, to acknowledge the need for formal grievance procedures to curb sexual, gender, heterosexual, anti-Semitic, racial, and ethnic physical and verbal harassment. We need to acknowledge how busy our harassment and safety officers are and to register how vociferously males in power fight to protect their "right to harass" in the name of academic freedom.

The problem of harassment is, however, linked systemically to other patterns of discrimination and oppression. At the University of Toronto, the following sobering poster is displayed:

OF THE 30,943 WOMEN STUDENTS AT THE UNIVERSITY OF TORONTO 10,314 WILL BE SEXUALLY ASSAULTED IN THEIR LIFETIME—8,664 OF THESE WOMEN WILL KNOW THEIR ATTACKER—3,868 WILL BE RAPED BY AN ACQUAINTANCE WHILE THEY ARE AT THE UNIVERSITY OF TORONTO.

Systemic sexist discrimination goes very deep. Consider the University of Toronto. Approximately 100 years ago—despite powerful opposition—

women were admitted to the University of Toronto in the name of equal opportunity. One hundred years later, an official ad hoc committee reporting to the president published a strong forthright document entitled "A Future for Women at the University of Toronto" (Smith n.d.). The authors cited and documented the following practices as interfering with the university's claim to be an institution providing equal opportunity for women and men:

1. sexist biases and practices demeaning to women, for example, an entertainment event for students and faculty in a social science department depicting naked women weighing their breasts and graphs of data presented in the shape of a female breast;
2. male bias in the language of official university business and the explicit ridicule or punishment of administrators, faculty, and students who attempted to use nonsexist or gender-inclusive language;
3. inadequate child-care facilities;
4. sexual and gender harassment;
5. differential evaluation and status with respect to varsity athletics;
6. recruiting, selecting, rewarding, and promoting men over well-qualified women in the professorial and administrative staff;
7. double standards of expectation for women and men, whether students or faculty;
8. devaluation of academic work done by women on women, whether students or faculty; evaluation and ridicule of men doing academic work on women;[10]
9. sexist language and humor in the classroom; for example, the remark of a philosophy professor who, having lectured on Aristotle's views on women [thereby incorporating women into the curriculum?!], followed his comments with a joke for the heterosexual male students present: "We all know one thing that women are good for";
10. gender bias in and male monopoly of the curriculum.

I do not believe that this university is unique. In fact, I think it would be almost impossible to identify this specific North American university from the practices described on this list. Often North American schools portray themselves as committed to equal educational opportunity with respect to access, response, support, rewards, and privileges. This is an ideological myth that hides systemic, gender-specific practices of violence and that supports permissive definitions of sexual and verbal harassment, demeaning practices that generate fear and feelings of intimidation, deliberate exclusion from crucial experiences of role modeling and mentoring, and biased, dismissive, and trivializing formal and informal treatment of girls' and women's needs, desires, goals, and accomplishments. In these kinds of settings of "equal opportunity" girls and women often count themselves lucky if they experience the less invasive forms of physical, emotional, psychological, and political violence (Kelly 1987; Ramazanoglu 1987).

We have already called into question descriptions of privileged, allegedly meritorious boys of the Victorian nineteenth century attaining their meritorious status as "independent" and "autonomous" students because we can now see the safety and security of their world and see hitherto "invisible" support of family structure, social class, the work world, courtship, and marriage complete with servants and women family members attending to all other dimensions of their lives. We must now question educational institutions that practice—and institutionalize—affirmative action for privileged white boys and men on a spectacular scale despite official rhetoric to the contrary (Trofimenkoff 1989).

Conclusion

It is not surprising that North American public educational institutions replicate, generate, and strengthen the patriarchal domination of women through androcentric intellectual canons and paradigms, devaluation, harassment, and violence. The axis of gender as an axis of domination and subordination, privilege and oppression is a central principle of societal organization in the dominant culture. What *is* inadmissible is that they characterize themselves as liberal, progressive institutions led by emperors/presidents clothed in mythic vestments of freedom, openness, and equal opportunity. We need to reject the camouflaging myths and expose the nakedness of inequities and social injustice for what they are. Educational equity for girls and women and for the members of virtually all institutionally oppressed groups in North America needs to be fought for with lucidity, energy, and passion; it does not exist now.

Notes

1. I am defining the term *educational equity* as involving the identification and removal of systemic barriers to educational opportunities that discriminate against women, visible minorities, aboriginal peoples, persons with disabilities, people living in poverty, or members of other groups that have been identified as being underserved with respect to their needs for education. The advantage of working with equity language rather than equality language is that it increases flexibility in working with both formal and substantive definitions of equality. See *Canadian Women's Studies* (1992), Eichler (1988a), and MacKinnon (1987, 1989).

2. For powerful, deeply persuasive arguments claiming that even for analytic purposes it is impossible to separate various axes, see Anzaldua (1990), Lugones (1991), Majaj (1994), Moraga and Anzaldua (1981), and Spelman (1988).

3. The importance of explicitly addressing gender analysis and gender oppression in emancipatory pedagogical theory is underscored by feminist theorists who, rightly, criticize the shortcomings of the critical pedagogy movement. See Carmen Luke and

Jennifer Gore (1992), especially the pieces by Elizabeth Ellsworth and Jane Kenway and Helen Modra.

4. For a clear statement of the importance of producing educated men, see R. S. Peters (1972). Jane Roland Martin's brilliantly nuanced, insightful entire volume of work is the most sustained and creative critique of the long, depressing European tradition of "the educated man." For more indirect approaches, which promote the role of education in maintaining the dominant patriarchal U.S. culture, see the work of William Bennett (1988) and Allan Bloom (1987).

5. It is difficult to give a gender-neutral reading to Freire (1968). For example, he discusses the desire of the oppressed men to become like their oppressor, "the eminent men" of the upper class (p. 49). This is problematic because for women in patriarchal cultures, the question of male identification is far more complex. So, too, is the question of identification with (which?) "eminent women" of the upper class since upper-class women can be seen to exist in a state of class-specific oppression and bear a very different and precarious relation to class status than do men of wealth and power. Similarly, when discussing the oppression of peasants, Freire (1968) cites an illustrative passage showing how "the oppressed" are emotionally dependent. He says, "The peasant is a dependent. He can't say what he wants. Before he discovers his dependence, he suffers, he lets off steam at home, where he shouts at his children, beats them, and despairs. He complains about his wife and thinks everything is dreadful" (p. 51). Given asymmetric cultural assumptions and practices regarding wife and child abuse, it is difficult to give this passage a plausible gender-reversed reading. It is clear that it is oppressed males for whom Freire is creating liberatory pedagogical theory.

6. The experience and application of double standards of cognitive, emotional, and moral assessment based on what would appear to be identical behaviors is part of a much larger set of ideological maneuvers directed, in this instance, at girls and women to induce a sense of inconsistency, unintelligibility, craziness, and experiential madness. I have explored the implications of this dynamic in the area of moral assessment in Morgan (1987b). For a breathtakingly subtle analysis of the double standard principle at work in research, see Eichler (1980).

7. Clearly androcentrism can cross ethnic and racial boundaries. For example, in a large North American university, in a full year course on the African novel, the black male African Studies professor put only male authors on the syllabus. When the androcentricity was challenged, particularly by Women's Studies students, his response was, "There are no African novels of quality written by African women," a characteristic retreat of normative solipsism. When further pressed by fearful but courageous students, he put a mediocre novel by a relatively unknown African woman on the syllabus. The novel came complete with teaching notes at the beginning and resembled a Harlequin Romance in plot and prose. When the students objected to the text, he once again used it as proof of the inferiority of writing by African women, thereby sustaining the normative androcentrism.

8. Even as progressive a thinker as John Stuart Mill falls prey to this stereotyping. In *The Subjection of Women* he recommends an ideal, complementary, necessarily heterosexual model of marriage based precisely on this cognitive double standard. He views the male husband as the exemplar of abstract theorizing effective in the public world but pitifully inept in the lived domestic world without the illumination of the female wife whose excellence consists in attention to the concrete, the particular, the

individual, and the important little details. See Mill (1970). This cognitive double standard has frequently been invoked in support of training women to be the teachers of young children and reserving educational dominance positions directed to advanced—presumably more theoretical—education, for males (who are almost always white). This is one of the reasons why qualitative research is regularly denigrated by theoretically or quantitatively oriented male (and male-identified) researchers who regard what they do as *hard* research in contrast to *soft* or feminine research.

9. What is profoundly disturbing—but not surprising—about this research is the extent to which the harassment intensifies the closer women come to structurally challenging the dominant males, for example, in the women's last years in professional schools or late in their doctoral programs. I do not believe this is mere coincidence.

10. For an extremely perceptive analysis of this phenomenon, see McCormack (1987).

FEMINIST PEDAGOGY AND
THE ETHICS OF CARE

Chapters 9, 10, and 11 are written as a connected discussion on two paradoxes in feminist pedagogy. Chapter 9 describes the paradox of critical nurturance and the role model paradox. Chapter 10 takes up the problems associated with critical nurturance, and Chapter 11 delves into the details of the role model paradox. Since Chapters 10 and 11 both respond to Chapter 9, we recommend reading Chapter 9 before Chapter 10 or 11.

9

The Perils and Paradoxes

of the Bearded Mothers

KATHRYN PAULY MORGAN

Feminist classrooms aspire to be gender-sensitive educational settings committed to principles of participatory democracy. In the words of Nancy Schniedewind (1983), "Feminist pedagogy demands the integration of egalitarian context and process" (p. 262). In their most idealistic moments, teachers of feminist classes describe their rhapsodic participation in a collaborative community of learners engaged in critical and collective gender equitable world-world building. Their task involves providing nonoppressive leadership in a way that facilitates the building of this democratic educational community (Gutmann 1987). But how?

Often, as teachers, we are faced with classrooms of recalcitrant democrats who, collectively, decide that they want to listen to us qua authority figures and not to their fellow classmates (regardless of the emphasis you place on the validity of diverse, personal/political experience). We need to ask ourselves, as we teach in such classrooms, whether we, in concert with our students, paradoxically, replicate the very power asymmetries that parallel those in patriarchal classrooms. By virtue of acknowledging and using the authority that we personally and institutionally bring to our classrooms, are we once again consigning our students to silence? (Lather 1991; Walkerdine 1983) How should we think about that authority?

If I look at metaphors that give some promise of equality such as sister, peer, friend, or translator, it seems to me that the teacher, as teacher, vanishes altogether. What place is there for the knowledge, the methodologies, the insight, the syntheses, and the critical evaluative standards that the teacher brings to any classroom? Are these forms of power not the very basis for her entitlement as a teacher?

What if she abandons them? I foresee the following dire consequences:

124

1. she abdicates her important modeling responsibilities as a woman publicly authorized to exercise various forms of power;
2. her behavior reenforces the perception that women can only exercise explicit public forms of power with ambivalence; and
3. she suffers personal mutilation insofar as she engages in the denial of important dimensions of her own subjectivity[1].

For many women, this litany of consequences is all too familiar because they, once again, identify aspects of woman-destructive altruistic invisibility. What is dangerous in the setting of the feminist classroom is that it is precisely these identity-destroying forms of denials that appear to be called for in the name of pedagogical liberation.

Surely this can't be right. Will every conceivable exercise of authority in a feminist classroom lead to such painful and paradoxical consequences? Maybe we need to search for another metaphor. Maybe feminist teachers need to think of themselves as bearded mothers.[2]

Exploring the Metaphor

"The content of woman's great science . . . is humankind and among humanity, men. Her philosophy is not to reason, but to sense. A woman who has a head full of Greek . . . or carries on fundamental controversies about mechanics . . . might as well even have a beard; for perhaps that would express more obviously the mien of profundity for which she strives" (Kant 1764/1960).

Can you imagine yourself behaving not simply as a bearded woman, problematic as that would be, but as a bearded mother? How would you know what to do? It is not easy. Often it feels like a contradictory enterprise.[3]

Feminist teachers are expected to be *bearded* in the sense that we are expected to claim for ourselves the forms of rationality, the modes of cognition, and the critical lucidity that has been seen to be the monopoly of bearded men with fully developed rational souls. (See, for example, Aristotle 1885; Aquinas [thirteenth century]/1973; Hegel 1896; Kant 1764; Darwin 1874.) But teaching itself has been characterized as one of the preeminent "caring professions" and feminist teachers, above all others, are expected to be nurturers explicitly committed to an ethics of care (Gilligan 1982; Noddings 1984; Weiler 1988). We are expected to offer support in an unconditional, trustworthy way in response to students' legitimate needs for growth and reassurance. In short, we are expected to be mothers—bearded mothers.

One way to resolve a contradiction is to abandon one of its components. I do not want to do that. As the particular woman I have become, I bring power to various educational settings, including my classroom (Bernstein 1977; Bourdieu 1973; Burbules 1986; Esland 1971; Foucault 1977; Gore 1990; Johnson 1978; McLaren 1989; Smith 1987). As a scholar in the field, I bring *expert power* to bear on the subject matter. As a trained philosopher, I bring *informational power* to bear insofar as I am prepared to set forth evidence and arguments as part of a reasoned debate. I have access to *legitimate power* because I have access to the lectern and several hours of the class's attention. Insofar as I am connected with a variety of other power structures, for example, registrars, scholarship committees, other instructors, I have access to various forms of *reward and coercion power* vis-à-vis my students. Finally, insofar as we might be joined together by a common interest in exploring the role of women and power in feminist education, my students may come to perceive me as someone similar to themselves. If found relatively likable, I may have access to *referent power* as well.

Aisenberg and Harrington (1988) describe the process and exhilaration involved in women integrating these forms of power:

> Through learning, a woman whose social identity is essentially sexual, and whose social role is essentially supportive, develops another dimension of personhood. Her intellectual abilities grow and she acquires methodological tools for acquiring further knowledge and assessing it, for creating inquiries of her own, for offering new findings and interpretations to colleagues and to the public. *She gains the power of initiation and the authority, the inner authority, that is, to speak definitively about what she knows. An active self, an intellectual self, extends the sexual and relational self already fostered by social encouragement, and the result is the exhilarating sense of wholeness, of new life.* . . . This personal coming-to-life instills in many a strong interest in replicating that experience in others through teaching and seeking institutional change (pp. 136–137, emphasis added).

These forms of power, these personally fulfilling forms of growth into inner authority have traditionally been preempted by white men—both as practitioners and in the eyes of the beholders. Cognizant of this racialized masculine preempting of rationality and public power, I believe that the taking on of these public forms of power by women who are feminist educators is an important personal and political task in which to engage. I am not about to shave.

I am not about to abandon the other side of the contradiction either. Along with other feminist educators I choose to participate in an educational process of radical egalitarian nurturance. We try to care, to provide support, and to respond to students' legitimate needs and demands for growth and reassurance. In a sense, one way of characterizing our educational role is to say that we are involved in exploring the full radical public potential of a maternal educational paradigm (Gilman [1915] 1979; Held 1986; hooks 1989; James 1993; McClung [1915] 1972; Ruddick 1983).[4]

But the pedagogical practices of bearded mothers are fraught with their own perils and paradoxes. In this chapter, I describe two.

Two Poignant Paradoxes of Bearded Mothers

The Paradox of Critical Nurturance

Feminist educators are often expected to have a large wardrobe of hats: that of mother, sister, peer, mentor, translator, friend. Sometimes, like Dr. Seuss's character Bartholomew Cubbins, we are expected to wear them all at once. It is not surprising that they should topple when various paradoxes and tensions destabilize them. I have entitled this situation the "paradox of critical nurturance" because feminist teachers who are women are expected to be critical and nurturing at the same time.

The centrality of critique is undeniable. In her influential essay "Taking Women Students Seriously," Adrienne Rich (1985) stresses the importance of insisting upon critical thinking:

> We can refuse to accept passive, obedient learning. . . . We can become harder on our women students. . . . Most young women need to have their intellectual lives, their work, legitimized against the claims of family, relationships, the old message that a woman is always available for service to others. We need to keep our standards very high, not accept a woman's preconceived sense of her limitations; we need to be hard to please, while supportive of risk-taking, because self-respect often comes only when exacting standards have been met. . . . Nor does this mean we should be training women students to "think like men." Men in general think badly: in disjuncture from their personal lives, claiming objectivity where the most irrational passions seethe (pp. 27–28).

Women's engaging in public rational critique has been systematically emphasized by Wollstonecraft (1792) and later Enlightenment feminists (Taylor [1851] 1970; Beauvoir 1952) as evidence of women's capacity to reason. Such public displays undercut any lingering claims that regard excellence in reasoning as a male-specific form of power. In addition, feminist scholars engage in constructing new forms of knowledge and new critical methodologies, practices that demand the display of rigorous intellectual excellence, authority, and the capacity to use new standards in a critical fashion. For many women, their public flexing of rational authority and power is still often *felt*—and perceived—to be a gender contradiction, a kind of metaphysical impropriety (Aisenberg and Harrington 1988). Thus, it is all the more important that women who feel like women and who are publicly acknowledged and respected as women personally claim and feel a sense of personal integrity in the intellectual and political role of active critic and rigorous creator of knowledge.

But the substantive word in the phrase is *nurturance*. Feminist educators are expected to provide educational settings and engage in pedagogical activities that are supportive both of girls' and women's vulnerabilities and of their strengths (Schweickart 1990). Such education has the potential to generate powerful emotions; and it does. Feminist classrooms are expected to be safe places where women's anger can be expressed—and students feel enormous betrayal and fear when that expectation is not met (Ellsworth 1989). Feminist classrooms are often places of pain, of joy, of support, of rage, of rejoicing as the collective search to create truthful women-centered knowledge takes place in an atmosphere of mutual trust and respect.

Ideally, in a context of trust created through reciprocated nurturance, teachers and students risk exploring the intellectual and political significance of the most intimate dimensions of their lives such as their sexuality, their sense of their own bodies, their feelings, their experience of childbirth and child raising, their lived experience of being of a particular color in a white supremacist society, their sense of personal strengths and horizons, and their experience and political understanding of the roles of love and caring and hatred and violence in their lives. Through active nurturing by feminist educators, students can come to see how the personal is epistemically significant and become willing to risk placing their own lived experiences of oppression and resistance in the public educational domain. As a consequence, they can begin to see how taking women's experience and women's diverse expressions of agency and resistance seriously challenges deeply held assumptions in virtually all the humanities and in the social and behavioral sciences (Anzaldua 1990; Brewer 1993; Collins 1990; Eichler 1988a, 1988b; Fiol-Matta and Chamberlain 1994; Fowlkes and McClure 1984; Hartman and Messer-Davidow 1991; James 1993; Kramarae and Spender 1992; Minnich 1990; Mohanty, Russo, and Torres 1991; Rose 1994).

Feminist educators are not only expected to validate the pedagogical significance of feelings and individual personal experience, we are expected to deal more directly with feelings such as anger, fear, vulnerability, rage, ambivalence, joy, and rejection. We are also expected to implement an ethics of care, to be available to listen, to offer counsel, and to give support and encouragement such that genuinely autonomous growth occurs through these private and collective experiences of nurturance. Moreover, this support is expected to be there in an unconditional form.

But is supportive nurturance compatible with critical theorizing? I believe there is a deep paradox in thinking of pedagogical nurturers criticizing, challenging, calling into question, posing contrary evidence, developing counterexamples, and detecting contradictions and other forms of inconsistency and inadequacy in the students they are nurturing. And it is even more paradoxical, I submit, to see this very process of criticism as the nurturing. This sounds much more like the behavior of the symbolic father whose approval is conditional (Culley and Portuges 1985; Chodorow 1978; Dinnerstein 1978).

Here, then, is the first paradox: Feminist teachers are committed to both developing a complex critique of androcentric paradigms, patriarchal traditions, and gender inequitable educational practices and generating new sets of critical standards of excellence in women-centered methodologies. Feminist teachers are expected to display and use the critical standards and skills in question. Feminist education, however, is also deeply committed to the creation of bonds of "political maternal nurturance," which would seem to preclude such criticism. Thus, it would appear that either the practice of critical evaluation or the maternal nurturance of one's students must go. But how can either one be abandoned and the resulting process still be called *feminist education?*

The Role Model Paradox

Feminist classrooms are expected to be subversive pedagogical settings that overthrow deeply entrenched patriarchal beliefs. Central to this process is the feminist teacher who, in an atmosphere of social trust, facilitates socialization into and personal internalization of new forms of individual and collective empowerment in a politicized community of learners. In short, the feminist teacher is expected to function as a role model (Bandura and Walters 1963; Bernstein 1971, 1977; Bourdieu 1971, 1973, 1977; Clausen 1968; Young 1971).[5]

For many women, role models are crucial.[6] In a moving passage, bell hooks (1989) says,

It was as a student in segregated black schools called Booker T. Washington and Crispus Attucks that I witnessed the transformative power of teaching, of pedagogy. In particular, those teachers who approached their work as though it was indeed a pedagogy, a science of teaching, requiring diverse strategies, approaches, explorations, experimentation, and risks, demonstrated the value—the political power—of teaching. Their work was truly education for critical consciousness. In these segregated schools, the teachers were almost all black women (p. 50).

After describing various characteristics of the lives of these teachers, hooks continues:

They were the teachers who conceptualized oppositional world views, who taught us young black women to exult and glory in the power and beauty of our intellect. They offered to us a legacy of liberatory pedagogy that demanded active resistance and rebellion against sexism and racism. They embodied in their work, in their lives (for none of them appeared as tortured spinsters estranged and alienated from the world around them) a feminist spirit. They were active participants in black community, shaping our futures, mapping our intellectual terrains, sharing revolutionary fervor and vision. I write these words, this essay to express the honor and respect I have for them because they have been my pedagogical guardians. Their work has had a profound impact on my consciousness, on my development as a teacher (p. 40).[7]

What happens for women and for men in oppressed groups if those role models are not present? One woman graduate student from a large public research university said that the lack of appropriate role models for female students is the worst aspect of her experience in graduate school. Another said, "I am from the physics department, which has a large body of faculty members, but not even *one* female professor. I never felt for the department that it was an issue. It makes me a bit bitter when I see so little chances of becoming a professor one day" (Morgan et al., forthcoming). In her article "Disempowering White Working-Class Females: The Role of the High School," Lois Weis perceptively analyzes a working-class high school, showing how, despite a superficial commitment to challenge traditional gender identity through pamphlets in the guidance office, the actual behavior on the part of female teachers in relation to male teachers—the actual modeling behavior—contributes to a clear perception that "White male teachers dominate articulated voice and space in school, reinforcing an ethos of White male separateness and superiority" (Weis 1991, p. 120).

Many advocates of educational equity promote role model–mediated socialization. One of the major arguments offered in favor of affirmative action is the role model argument, which claims that it is crucial for there to be people in positions of authority and competence with whom women and members of discriminated-against groups can identify (Caplan 1992; Courtenay-Hall 1992; Laurence 1989; M. Martin 1976; Pang 1991; Rowe 1981; Sumner 1987; Wasserstrom 1977). The argument assumes that, psychologically and institutionally, "nothing demonstrates possibility more vividly than actuality." Nothing can undo the damaging stereotypes, systemic institutional discrimination and accompanying forms of internalized psychological oppression more effectively than many living, breathing, funny, strong, intelligent, loving counterexamples in positions of public recognition, power, and personal respect.

Students in feminist classrooms expect that their feminist teachers will function as exemplary counterexamples, performing as transformative intellectuals (Giroux 1989) whose pedagogical and political engagement involves demonstrating personally that a fulfilling life of joy, self-respect, challenge, and creativity can be lived in the academy and can be made possible through liberatory feminist education. Aisenberg and Harrington (1988) describe the radical distinctiveness of women in educational modeling roles as transformative intellectuals, by claiming that they add up to a deeply radical countersystem of social order that

> challenges excessive hierarchy and exclusivity in the holding of authority, one that incorporates diversity, spreads authority through processes of cooperation,

resists centrality both in the holding of political and intellectual authority and in the defining of truth and value, and protects individuality through the legitimizing of a personal component in professional life (p. 136).[8]

But is this possible? Feminist education is, preeminently, a form of existential liberation from the straitjacket of patriarchal education with its essentialist defining of *woman* as invisible other(s) and the correlative assignment of her to various worlds of supportive immanence. Merely identifying and criticizing women's education as patriarchal and confining does not yet entail full transcendence, although it may stave off total gangrene of a woman's intellectual subjectivity. However, once genuinely integrated educative "deep breathing" becomes possible, a central feminist goal emerges: developing a *self-created, self-chosen* form of educated subjectivity and personal vision situated dialectically in an educational community of similar subjects striving collectively for self-esteem and respect. The goal of autonomy is clear, and it is expected that autonomy will be facilitated through modeling and identification.

Yet the very process designed to produce autonomy must also threaten it. One of the crucial socialization goals of feminist education is the development of a norm-laden feminist sensibility through which an *educated* feminist comes to experience and evaluate the world through her feminist perspicacity, awareness, insight, and interpretive categories. In formal educational settings, this means developing an appreciation for and an ability to apply feminist methodologies. It also involves becoming sensitized to theoretical assumptions and pedagogical processes that deny or undermine a woman's full personhood and sense of legitimate place in the academy. Acquiring such a sensibility involves intense and deep processes of internalization of "lessons in perception and heuristics" best learned through identification with and emulation of a role model whose own practice provides a powerful example of the exercise of such a sensibility. Recall the words of bell hooks (1989, p. 50). "They embodied in their work, in their lives . . . a feminist spirit. They were active participants in black community, shaping our futures, mapping our intellectual terrains, sharing revolutionary fervor and vision. . . . they have been my pedagogical guardians. Their work has had a profound impact on my consciousness." The central argument is that internalization of a feminist educative sensibility is necessary for feminist education to succeed. Such internalization is mediated (at least) through identification with another woman, the feminist teacher. Adopting her as a role model, the female feminist student sees her as someone whom she can perceive as a possible ideal variant of herself. For successful socialization to take place, identification with the teacher role model is needed and such an identification is seen as both legitimate and instrumentally necessary. Students often report profound identifications with their teachers. Such identification strengthens the teacher's resulting referent power. By definition, a person who successfully identifies with her teacher and is thereby socialized will replicate various actions, attitudes, or emotional responses exhibited by her real-life (or symbolized) model. But such replication is, I believe, the replication of the identity of another, not the mark of a unique, self-created individual.

Here, then, is the second paradox: Feminist education both encourages and undermines autonomy through the role-modeling practices central to feminist pedagogy. Ironically, and sadly, feminist autonomy is compromised by the very educative process that is designed to foster it.

Conclusion

What is the cumulative force of these paradoxes? Is feminist teaching a genuinely contradictory enterprise, an educational ideal doomed to realization only to the extent that it fails its mandate to be feminist? My own sense of the situation is that the paradoxes are real and they are deep. One solution, of course, is for the feminist teacher to abandon her position as a role model committed to critical excellence. But if she dispenses with these aspects of her responsibilities, it is not clear now that what the personally situated feminist educator brings to the classroom by way of knowledge, methodology, insight, synthesis, and critical standards has any remaining relevance. Moreover, this abdication carries with it an abandonment of the politically significant role of embodied rational woman authority. Conversely, for her to abandon her commitment to nurturance, to living in a community of learners committed to an ethics of care would carry with it a renewed sense of personal alienation and the severing of important relational bonds that are central to the ideal of feminist community. At present, I see no obvious resolutions to the paradoxes I have posed.

Notes

This chapter is a significantly revised version of an article entitled "Perils and Paradoxes of Feminist Pedagogy," which appeared in *Resources for Feminist Research/Documentation Sur La Recherche Feministe*, special issue 16(3): Women and Philosophy/Femmes et Philosophie. Maureen Ford, Barbara Houston, Kathryn Morgan, Katherine Pepper-Smith (eds.). Toronto, ON: Ontario Institute for Studies in Education (1987), pp. 44–52. The original article was reprinted in *A Reader in Feminist Ethics*. Debra Shogan (ed.). Toronto, ON: Canadian Scholars Press (1992).

1. This point is made by Susan Stanford Friedman in "Authority in the Feminist Classroom: A Contradiction in Terms?" (Culley et al. 1985, pp. 203–208). I found this article along with Margo Culley's essay "Anger and Authority in the Introductory Women's Studies Classroom" (Culley et al. 1985, pp. 209–218) and Linda Briskin's work on feminist pedagogy (Briskin 1990) to be powerful catalysts in the setting of my own pedagogical practice to help me think more seriously about the role of authority and power in feminist classrooms.

2. I wish this metaphor were of my own invention, but it is not. I am grateful to Margo Culley et al., in "The Politics of Nurturance" (Culley et al. 1985, p. 15), who cite the poet Anne Halley as the source of the phrase.

3. In some ways, this is a variant on a common theme in Western philosophical thought regarding the contradictory nature of "rational woman," "the standard of the reasonable woman," "the woman on the street," the "educated woman." For elegant, scholarly, and properly impassioned analyses of these notions in relation to education, see the work of philosopher Jane Roland Martin. In particular see Martin (1985b, 1994).

4. In his theoretical work on socialization, Danziger (1971) distinguishes between positional (i.e., role-specific) and personal (individualized person-specific) role models. He argues persuasively that when the two domains overlap, there is maximum potential for influence and the exercise of multiple forms of power vis-à-vis those being socialized. I believe that feminist role models, in feminist classrooms, have the power to conflate these two domains—and are expected to do so given the pedagogical and political importance given to personal narrative on the part of the teacher as well as the students. I analyze the potential political dangers of this conflation in Morgan (1974) and return to them in relation to the role model paradox, in this chapter.

5. In the nineteenth and twentieth centuries, early maternal feminists such as Nellie McClung ([1915] 1972) advocated the moral superiority of maternal practice as defined by middle- and upper-class white Victorian women as a norm for public institutions. In the twentieth century, white feminist theorists such as Ruddick (1989) and James (1993) openly rejected a privatized domesticated model of mothering in favor of community-structured, public mothering relations. Such communal models, analogous to that proposed by Charlotte Perkins Gilman (1915) in *Herland,* collapse a public-private split that confines mothering relations to the domestic domain (whether involving wages or not). Clearly, diverse students in our classrooms will bring very different expectations regarding maternal practice deriving from their own communities and lived experiences of mothering.

6. I find much of the North American social/psychological literature on socialization deeply conservative and see it as exploring processes that replicate the dominant oppressive structures of North American society through public education and through more disciplined repressive, obedience-based motivational structures such as the U.S. military (Foucault 1977). More critical and potentially liberatory work on socialization is found in Barton et al. (1980), Bernstein (1971, 1977), Bourdieu (1973, 1977), and Young (1971).

7. Not all women feel this way about role models. In a recent interview, the acclaimed white lesbian writer Jane Rule remarks, "Bad role models . . . are useful only for telling you what not to do. And good role models only get in the way of what you should become" (Cole 1995). The very great irony here, of course, noted by the interviewer, is that Rule herself has become precisely such a good role model.

8. I do not here address the issue of who can be a role model for whom. This is a very complex issue involving many thorny and elusive questions regarding human subjectivity and the nature of situated selves (Benhabib 1992). Whether, for example, an older able-bodied Iroquois male teacher can be a significant role model for a second generation immigrant, urban, Muslim, adolescent woman in a working-class, white high school is, I believe, a very complicated question to which the answer is not at all obvious, at least to me. It is clear that avoidance of multiple cultural imperson-

ations (Pratt 1984) will be important for the teacher if she is to maintain some sense of integrity.

This issue is made all the more difficult by the general absence of serious critical programs of teacher education that address significant issues of Eurocentrism, colonialism, sexism, racism, ethnic oppression, and other forms of oppressive bias in education. See, for example, the work of Banks (1991), Butler (1985, 1989), Camper (1994), Carty (1991), Clarke (1993), Fiol-Matta and Chamberlain (1994), Martin (1994), Morris (1993), and Tatum (1992).

10

Is Rapprochement Possible Between Educational Criticism and Nurturance?

ANN DILLER

Teachers in contemporary North America are increasingly expected, by students, by colleagues, by ourselves, to be nurturant and caring educators. But when we try to combine these expectations for care and nurturance with the standard educational task of assessing and criticizing our students' work, we encounter tensions between what seem to be conflicting demands for care and criticism.

In her account of what she terms *paradoxes* in feminist pedagogy, Kathryn Morgan describes her own heightened awareness of this tension. Morgan observes that our feminist teachers are "expected to be nurturant, to be supportive, to respond to students' legitimate needs for growth and reassurance." In addition, we are "expected to implement an ethics of care, to be available to listen, to offer counsel, and to give support and encouragement" (Morgan Chapter 9, this volume). But when we try to meet these expectations and also undertake the usual pedagogical tasks of educational criticism, we encounter one of Morgan's paradoxes: "I believe there is a deep paradox in thinking of pedagogical mothers criticizing, challenging, calling into question, posing contrary evidence, developing counterexamples, and detecting contradiction and other forms of inconsistency and inadequacy in the students they are nurturing. And it is even more paradoxical, I submit, to see this very process of criticism as the nurturing" (Morgan Chapter 9, this volume).

Although our experiences with feminist pedagogy, in addition to calls for an ethics of care in education and widespread concern and controversy about the place of nurturance in schools, have all combined to accentuate these difficulties, the general tension between nurturance and criticism is not a new educational problem. Therefore, we have a number of existing responses to the problem, both traditional and contemporary. Taken together these responses provide us with opposing, indeed often contradictory advice. The range of advice does, however, help us to map the contours of the problem in its standard form.

In this chapter I explore the possibility of a rapprochement between educational criticism and nurturance. I first consider three different ways to configure the relations between nurturance and criticism. Although all three of these approaches are informative, they are also partial and problematic. I conclude, therefore, that we need to look further. Drawing upon presuppositions from feminist pedagogy and key tenets from an ethics of care, I then suggest an alternative configuration.

To Nurture Is to Criticize

When Kathryn Morgan writes "it is even more paradoxical, I submit, to see this very process of criticism as the nurturing," she calls our attention to one long-standing traditional response from what we might term the *For Your Own Good* model. A central claim here is that on a proper understanding of what nurturance is, we can see that to nurture is to critique and to critique is to nurture. The mistake we need to avoid is that of confusing indulgence, or spoiling the child, with nurturance. If we truly love and care for our children we do not spoil them or overindulge them, rather we expect, demand, require, and teach adherence to certain standards of behavior for the sakes of both the child and the community.

Whatever educational aim or metaphor one chooses—initiation, growth, development, empowerment, enhanced freedom, responsible citizenship, and so on—the teacher's job is to help the student "learn," to contribute to the student's own "progress." The teacher is not there simply to indulge the whims of students, in a willy-nilly fashion, devoid of any standards or criteria.

Not to make appropriate demands, not to expect and require adherence to standards is to confuse nurturance with neglect, to conflate care and indulgence. The tasks of teaching require us to make real demands upon students, to hold them to standards of achievement; to expect otherwise is to underrate the teaching function and to over-romanticize the teacher-student relationship.

Although we may not state our beliefs in precisely these terms, as teachers most of us do feel the pull of similar "for your own good" claims; and we accept the tasks of pedagogical criticism, whether it be with reluctance, enthusiasm, or simple matter-of-factness, as part of the teaching imperative. Furthermore, these criticisms are well-intentioned, are taken to be for the good of the student, even if we do not necessarily equate them with nurturance.

But when we turn to the experiences of students themselves, when we observe the actual effects of pedagogical criticism, we encounter a dissenting viewpoint, accompanied by an alternative account of what is happening. In brief, the recipients of criticism frequently do not equate it with nurturance, and they generally fail to perceive criticism as part of any larger nurturant configuration.

Most students and many of the rest of us experience criticism as a form of attack. For women, in particular, we find that criticism often reinforces our own self-doubts and may discourage our already tentative risk-taking efforts. For most people criticism tends to elicit defense mechanisms, to result in resentment and antagonisms, and to siphon off energy into defensive maneuvers. All of which interfere with or disrupt the advancement of any further learning. It is observations such as these that lead to the *Never Criticize* position.

Never Criticize

One of the strongest proponents of the never criticize position is William Glasser. He does not deny the good intentions of those who pursue a for your own good policy. The trouble, says Glasser (1984), is that the outcomes are not the good that is intended. Quite the contrary: "The basic flaw of criticism, therefore, is not that it isn't well intended, but that its intentions are almost never realized" (p. 166).

Glasser (1984) gives us a vivid account of the untoward consequences of being criticized:

> When we are criticized, the sudden huge difference occurring [in the brain] . . . makes it feel as if the whole brain is exploding in pure pain. . . . Nothing we encounter leads to a greater and quicker loss of control than to be criticized. And, equally, it is harder to regain control when we are criticized than in any other situation. In my opinion, it is by far the single most destructive behavior we use as we attempt to control our lives (p. 163).

His conclusion is not surprising: "We can avoid a lot of misery if we don't criticize. . . . Criticism is a luxury I believe none of us can afford" (Glasser 1984, pp. 163–164).[1]

Something very close to Glasser's never criticize position has emerged in recent years in the women's movement. An arena where this has been played out has been the reviewing of women's writings by other women. One forum for discussion has been *The Women's Review of Books*, where authors of critical reviews have, at times, been passionately attacked for their criticism of women's work. The central contention seems to be that in a culture where women's writings have so often been denigrated and trivialized, we should be careful not to treat each other in this same way, but should rather provide support and appreciation.

Suzette Elgin (1989) takes up this issue when she responds to complaints about negative reviews of women writers: "When a woman who is distressed by a review complains, she gets support and sympathy from other women—and I understand why" (p. 15). But Elgin goes on to observe that this creates a number of problems, not the least of which is the question of women's own learning. Elgin raises the specter of neglect and argues that this situation "literally holds back the progress of women writers . . . it makes reviews of their work less likely" (p. 15). And she returns us to the educational question again: "How are women ever supposed to *learn?* If they can write inferior work and receive excellent reviews from other women—all the while dismissing negative reviews by men as irrelevant because they are sexist—how are they ever to learn that they can and must do better? I don't know the answer" (p. 15). This recognition of an ongoing educational imperative brings us to our third alternative, which is an effort to do justice to the concerns and insights as well as to remedy the shortcomings of the first two approaches.

Do Both but Keep Them Separate

If we take educational criticism to include honest, candid feedback with accurate information on how well one is doing with respect to certain standards or criteria, and if we take educational nurturance to include support, care, and encouragement for the person of the student, then it would seem that both of these are pedagogically desirable although incompatible, or at least in serious tension, when found together at close quarters, being attempted by one person.

So why not keep both of these activities but make them clearly separate? For example, we already do have certain common educational practices such as those of external examinations, standardized tests, and external examiners, wherein the teacher supports, coaches, and nurtures the students as they prepare together for the external critic often in the form of an examination. In fact just such an explicit separation is recommended by the authors of *Women's Ways of Knowing* (Belenky et al. 1986) as a particularly appropriate method for problems women students encounter in the tensions between nurturance and criticism.

Such a separation not only seems plausible, it also fits our existing genderized expectations—indeed, if external critics are male and internal teachers are female, it could fit all too well, dangerously so, by perpetuating genderized stereotypes. For example, when Canadian researcher Aniko Varpolatti (1986, personal communication) interviewed a group of adolescent girls training to be coaches about their vision of the ideal coach, one striking reply was that the ideal coach would be two persons, one woman and one man. The woman coach would be supportive, encouraging, helpful, there to care for them if they were injured and the male coach would challenge them, push them, make them work hard and keep trying to do better. Suddenly we are back in the world of separate spheres, one construed as masculine and the other as feminine.

The perpetuation of genderized stereotypes is not the only danger with this division of labor. Such a division lends itself to a misleading, if not disempowering, epistemology—a view of knowledge and truth as "out there" somewhere, having an independent existence of its own, rather than recognizing that knowing and the known are bound up together in an ongoing process of human inquiry done by persons like ourselves. If one task of education is to increase our understanding, skills, and capabilities for participation in a community of inquirers, then membership, at least on the level of a practicing novice, needs to be readily available to students as well as to their teachers and should be neither perceived nor held as the exclusive property of external examiners.[2]

Do Both Together—But How?

If we reject the conflation of nurturance and criticism, the never criticize position, and the separatist answer as all three inadequate solutions, we will have come full circle back to our initial tension and Kathryn Morgan's paradox. At this point it is worth reminding ourselves that Morgan sets her paradox within the context of feminist pedagogy and of an ethics of care, for it is here that this tension, which runs throughout contemporary education, is brought into full relief and highlighted. It is here that the latent and often tacit expectations for nurturance become explicit demands, while at the same time the destructive effects of criticism are also expressed outright and laid bare, enumerated, and taken as a cause for serious concern, so much so that the never criticize position is sometimes perceived as a viable alternative, whereas the option to relegate nurturance to some other non-pedagogical domain is not entertained, even though such a move is one version of a traditional educational stance.

Just as the context of feminist pedagogy presses the paradox upon us in its most unrelenting form, so also, I believe, this same context gives us the elements for generating new possibilities. To answer the How question I believe we must turn to some of the basic presuppositions in feminist pedagogy and to some key tenets of an ethics of care. In the first place we can make use of the strong emphasis placed on a relational ontology—the recurrent insistence on the observation that we are relational beings: We are born and raised enmeshed in a network of relationships; our existence, survival, and well-being are all irrevocably interconnected.

Once we turn our attention to our relational connections with each other, we are in a position to make two closely related ethical shifts: (1) we remember to give an explicit non-subordinate place to the work of nurturance itself; we insist that relational tasks carry primary value in and of themselves, that they do not get relegated to the status of mere instrumental necessities, or ways to "improve working conditions," done only in order to enable pursuit of other non-relational endeavors; and (2) we provide support for each other as persons, as ends-in-ourselves who are more than (not coextensive with) ourselves as learners, students, teachers, more than bearers of knowledge, ignorance, or expertise. In sum, a full-fledged, non-subordinate status is restored to, or bestowed upon, both the work of nurturance and the status of persons as more than, and not reducible to, the purposes and practices of teaching and learning. We might say: "One should always treat students as persons who are ends-in-themselves and not merely as means to their own learning."

At first glance these ethical shifts may seem only to strengthen the case for nurturance and to leave criticism in an even more problematic spot than before; one may wonder whether we have returned to the never criticize position by a circuitous route. But there are two more important shifts yet to be made here—an epistemological shift and a pedagogical one.

Our epistemological and pedagogical points are accurately reflected in Kathryn Morgan's (1991) statement that:

> Successful pedagogy involves creating educational experiences which foster the collective development of girls' and women's awareness of themselves as legitimate and critical participants in the creation of human knowledge. This sense of self is based on women experiencing the legitimacy of their own experience as relevant both to their own education and the education of others.

Morgan's articulation of these aims for girls and women should remind us that we want just such awareness, legitimacy, and critical participation for all our students.

Notice that once we start to pay attention to our relational interdependence and to the ways in which we learn from each other, the unidirectional focus on the teacher-student relationship can become multidirectional, the classroom scene turns into a complex sociogram with lines going every which way from student to student to teacher back to groups of students. And, yes, we may have a *community*. But it is not enough just to say "community," because our issue is still what sort of community is this? Is it nurturant or critical?

A Jointly Constituted Community

So our question has become: How is this educational community to be constituted? Here is where our conjunction of both nurturance and criticism should not be lost. This community must, therefore, be jointly constituted as both: (1) a community of support; and (2) a community of inquiry. The term *jointly* is a pivotal word here for it carries two senses of *joint*. One sense is that of joining the support function and the inquiry function without submerging either. The second sense in which these communities are jointly constituted is that students and teachers alike join together to create and recreate their own ongoing communities.

To be constituted as a *community of support* a group must provide a "safe space" where members can come together as persons who care about each other as people, "without masks, pretenses, [or] badges of office" (Greene 1988, pp. 16–17). All members assume some responsibility (not necessarily equal responsibility) for mutual well-being.

My concept of *communities of inquiry* follows from William James's ([1899] 1958) premise that "the truth is too great for any one actual mind . . . to know the whole of it. The facts and worths of life need many cognizers to take them in" (p. 19). Every participant acts as a "cognizer" who brings their own partial perspective to bear on the common inquiries of the group.

Ideally all members of the jointly constituted community of inquiry and support take part as co-explorers (see Chapter 12 this volume). Each co-explorer tries to satisfy what Maria Lugones (Lugones and Spelman [1983] 1986) calls "the need for reciprocity of understanding." This means that each person makes a methodological commitment not only to listen to others but to endeavor to understand them on their own terms, and each expects, in turn, to have an equivalent effort directed toward understanding their experiences.

Inevitably some persons will be more able, experienced, and skillful members. In educational settings asymmetry not only flows from the institutional structures themselves (e.g., the power of the teacher as the constituted authority, the giver of grades, the arbiter of pass or fail) but also arises out of differing degrees of knowledge, expertise, command over the tools, ability of articulation, acquaintance with the relevant canons, and so on. Still, lines of asymmetry are fluid and territorial, not absolute. Just as no one person possesses the whole of truth, neither is anyone the bearer of absolute ignorance. Knowledge and ignorance are questions of degree, of territory, not matters of absoluteness.

Have We Resolved the Paradox?

It is time to ask the question whether these "jointly constituted" communities can resolve the paradox or at least ameliorate the difficulties we encountered with our three proposed solutions. We saw that criticism not only often fails to accomplish its well-intentioned aims but also is frequently miseducative in its effects, and nurturance without criticism is generally non-educative. We

also determined that the attempt to do each separately, for educational purposes, can be misleading and disempowering. What happens when we shift
to a jointly constituted community of support and inquiry, to an explicitly relational community where criticism and nurturance are practiced by everyone? Within this expanded context of an interdependent community, I believe we can bring these two activities, nurturance and criticism, together in
such a way that each can enhance, as well as correct for, the other.

First, because the community practices and values support for students as
persons who are cared for and appreciated as constitutive members, students
can be given a ground of personal worth apart from, and separable from,
their achievements or shortcomings, as academic learners. This may help us
to short-circuit tendencies toward a confused merger of being and doing, in
which self-worth becomes based on performance and mistakes become indi-
cators for flaws or deficiencies in one's very being as a person. When criticism is not experienced as undermining one's whole sense of self, we open up
the possibility for *hearing* criticism without being personally devastated by it,
which then means one is more likely to be able to acknowledge mistakes and
thereby learn from them.

In the second place, criticism can be transformed into mutual helping activities when done among students and peers themselves within a community
of inquiry. By participating together in trial and error procedures, making
corrections along the way, and learning from each other, students can experience criticism as an inherent part of their own progress, as ways to accomplish group ends, to become better players in the game of inquiry, or to pursue their own learning.

Another advantage is that the sources of critique are now multiple, numerous, more mutual, less asymmetrical, less imperious, and less threatening
than when they come from an authoritative teacher or professor. A critical
question or suggestive critique from a peer can be handled in a "take it or
leave it" manner. Corrections from peers are easier to challenge and easier to
reject; they are thus easier to accept. They are also less likely to cause what
Glasser so aptly describes as an "explosion in the brain."

What does this shift to a jointly constituted community mean for teachers?
Teachers' responsibilities are not diminished, but they are altered. Teachers
are no longer the sole source of either nurturance or criticism. Teachers still
provide initial conditions and a sense of direction and continue to work with
students (and other teachers) in order to negotiate purpose and procedures.
With respect to criticism, teachers are more likely to serve as "last resort" resources, the experts who are turned to when students have taken their work
as far as they can go with each other. By the time this point is reached, the
critiques and corrections can sometimes be directed to the group rather than
to individuals. The larger task for teachers becomes the sophisticated orches-
tration of a community of support and inquiry.

Finally, if we are to succeed, we must make the tasks of support and nurturance themselves the subject of inquiry. To nurture well and to care wisely depend upon inquiry, study, investigation, and yes, critique and criticism. Thus the work of nurturance brings us back to criticism. But in the last analysis, I believe it is only this larger framework of participation in a community of both support and inquiry that allows for, indeed, creates, the enabling conditions for a true rapprochement between nurturance and criticism.[3]

Notes

1. Glasser does make two further distinctions in his anti-criticism discussion. He makes note of the importance of an acknowledged teaching relationship and he differentiates between working with children under the age of twelve or thirteen and those who are older. But he still eschews using any criticism per se. He observes that young children "know they need guidance, and they are not yet engaged in the power struggle that they will join shortly. All I need to do is tell or show them a better way and pay little attention to what they had been doing that was wrong. I can also use this constructive approach with adults if they view me as a teacher or are not in competition with me" (p.165).

2. To argue against using a strict separation of tasks, persons, and spheres here should not be confused with a rejection of all forms of separation—such as alternating times for creation and discovery on the one hand, and for correction and justification on the other hand, or making use of the standard distinctions between *formative* and *summative* evaluations. And there is much to be said in favor of teachers and students working together to prepare for something—a sporting event, an art exhibit, a science fair, a play production, or a concert—that is public or external to them all, but we cannot rely solely upon such external measures to resolve or reconcile all the issues surrounding pedagogical criticism.

3. I wish to thank Barbara Houston, Jane Roland Martin, Kathryn Morgan, Beatrice Nelson, Jennifer Radden, Janet Farrell Smith, Audrey Thompson, and the members of the 1993 PES Program Committee for helpful comments on earlier drafts of this chapter.

11

Role Models: Help or Hindrance in the Pursuit of Autonomy?

BARBARA HOUSTON

I understand women's studies to be, in large part, an enterprise devoted to helping women students say, "I am not wrong." What I mean by this claim can be made clearer if we consider the poem by June Jordan (1980, pp. 86–89) from which the line "I am not wrong" is taken. What follows are additional excerpts from Jordan's poem, which is entitled "Poem About My Rights."

> *Even tonight and I need to take a walk and clear*
> *my head about this poem about why I can't*
> *go out without changing my clothes my shoes*
> *my body posture my gender my identity my age*
> *my status as a woman alone in the evening*
> *alone on the streets/alone not being the point/*
> *the point being that I can't do what I want*
> *to do with my own body because I am the wrong*
> *sex the wrong age the wrong skin and*
> *suppose it was not here in the city but down on the beach/*
> *or far into the woods and I wanted to go*
> *there by myself thinking about God/or thinking*
> *about children or thinking about the world/all of it*
> *disclosed by the stars and the silence*
> *I could not go and I could not think*
> *and I could not*
> *stay there*
> *alone*
> *as I need to be*

alone because I can't do what I want to do with my own
body and
who in the hell set things up
like this

. . .

before that
it was my father saying I was wrong saying that
I should have been a boy because he wanted one/a
boy and that I should have been lighter skinned and
that I should have had straighter hair and that
I should not be so boy crazy but instead I should
just be one/a boy and before that
it was mother pleading plastic surgery for
my nose and braces for my teeth and telling me
to let the books loose to let them loose

. . .

I am the history of the rejection of who I am
I am the history of the terrorized incarceration of
my self
I am the history of battery assault and limitless
armies against whatever I want to do with my mind
and my body and my soul and
whether it's about walking out at night
or whether it's about the love I feel or
whether it's about the sanctity of my vagina or
the sanctity of my national boundaries
or the sanctity of my leaders or the sanctity
of each and every desire
that I know from my personal and idiosyncratic
and indisputably single and singular heart
I have been raped
be-
cause I have been wrong the wrong sex the wrong age
the wrong skin the wrong nose the wrong hair the
wrong need the wrong dream the wrong geographic
the wrong sartorial I

. . .

but let this be unmistakable this poem
is not consent I do not consent

. . .

I am not wrong: Wrong is not my name
My name is my own my own my own

. . .

This poem captures what it is like to feel wrong, wrong in one's very female being. Interestingly, we find this theme echoed when feminists talk about education. In *Amazons, Bluestockings and Crones* (Kramarae and Treichler 1992), a feminist dictionary, under the heading "Education," we find "what formal education means to women" and the following quotation from Dale Spender (1982). "*Every day* of our lives we are informed that women do not count, that we are wrong, that our different descriptions and explanations are ridiculous or unreal ... we learn that we are wrong: we become educated" (p. 34).

In contrast, women's studies, *feminist* education, is seen as a form of existential liberation. However, that liberation is not an easy one. Feeling wrong is a terrible dimension to have as part of one's *being*. But as Sandra Bartky (1990) points out, confronting gender issues and seriously thinking about their implications for one's own life is traumatic work. Women students who undertake to learn about the situations of women, who thoughtfully consider the critiques of femininity, face a terrible prospect: *They face a loss of identity*. They face a kind of deskilling that threatens any sense of mastery and competence they might have *as women*; it threatens most fundamentally their sense of *who they are*. Given that we have only two genders, given that they know they are not men, and given their need to reject the status of women as *the Other*, feminist students effectively face the specter of *annihilation*.

In the process of undoing the damaging stereotypes and self-hatred resulting from internalized psychological oppression, and in undoing them in such a way as to remove the specter of annihilation, we think nothing is more effective than a role model. In the words of Kathryn Morgan, "nothing demonstrates possibility more vividly than actuality ... [A] living, breathing, strong, intelligent, loving counterexample in a position of public recognition and respect" (Morgan Chapter 9, this volume).

Some writers on feminist pedagogy share Morgan's view that role-modeling is a very powerful pedagogical device. When the educational goal is "to replace self-hatred with self-love, incapacity with capacity, unfreedom with freedom, blindness with knowledge" (Culley 1985), then Margo Culley claims:

> The most complex and intriguing aspects of what goes on in feminist classrooms derive from the fact that the instructor who is female shares the stigma of her female students. Indeed, only in the classroom where instructor and students share the same stigma—whether it be femaleness or blackness or both—is the potential present for the most radical transformation: the transformation to wholeness, to strength, to freedom (1985, p. 211).

However, not all feminist teachers are as wholly enthusiastic about role models or role-modeling as Margo Culley. In the same feminist dictionary under "Role Model" you will find the following comment by Margaret

Atwood, one that stands in sharp contrast to the seriousness of Culley's remarks about role models.

> I dislike the term "role model" partly because of the context in which I first heard it (1982, p. 217).
>
> It was explained to me that, for whole modelhood, even at a university, scholarship was not the only requirement. One also had to be punctual, clean behind the ears, a good mother, well-dressed and socially presentable. I'm afraid I'm a bad role model, but then long ago I decided that I could be either a good role model or a writer, and for better or worse I chose writing (1982, p. 330).

Echoing Atwood's cynicism and considering the matter a little more seriously, Nancy Miller (1985) wonders: "Perhaps this peculiar form of female narcissism—a term more apt, I think, than the cooler sociological notion of role-modeling to describe the psychic miming at the heart of this doubling—is not only irresponsible but wrong" (p. 196).

In addition to these doubts, Bernice Fisher (1988) articulates the two common political criticisms of the centrality of the concept role models play in feminist education. She allows that it is a powerful notion that does have an intensity of meaning; nevertheless, or perhaps because of this, she claims that:

1. The notion has directed attention away from a realistic view of the political and economic conditions of success. The notion has been idealized such that it is implied that "if every woman merely follows the lead of so-called role-models, we all, every one of us can succeed" (p. 212). But as Fisher reminds us, the fact is that not everyone can succeed. Success in this society depends upon our access to social, political, and economic resources. Further, success may still involve hardships—sexual harassment, a constant wearing battle for credibility, and so forth.

2. Role-modeling, despite the rhetoric, masks its own subtle form of domination. The advocacy of role models encourages and perpetuates in subtle ways an unarticulated theory of leadership that still supports a kind of domination. As Fisher says, "It encourages us to *look up* to special women rather than to *look around* for the women with whom we *might act*" (p. 212). She wryly notes that feminists inconsistently criticize current political authority and yet seem to unquestionably accept the social authority of models.

There is another political criticism that can be made consequent upon our increasing awareness of how important and significant are the differences in girls' and women's experiences. It is now no secret that gender identity is intermingled with and shaped by other things such as race, class, ethnicity, religion, sexual orientation, able-bodiedness, and so forth. Further, how we see ourselves, our identity, what we take to be our situation, is a function of many factors other than gender. Further, there are many oppressions, subordinations, and lost opportunities to be addressed.

Recognition of these political realities appears to undermine the role model argument or, at least, tends to render the idea anachronistic. Along with our increasing concern about who can speak for whom about what, we may be prompted to ask, who is to be a role model for whom with respect to what? The answer is not so obvious any more. It appears as though the more we understand these matters the more the liberatory power of a role model is diminished. Or is it? We may denounce the trivialities some would associate with role models and we may feel dismay at the complexities involved in worrying about who should be a role model for whom about what, but still many become more and more committed to seeing to it that minorities within minorities have their role models too. Let me remind you again of the passionate convictions of Margo Culley (1985):

> No amount of knowledge, insight and sensitivity on the part of a male instructor can alter the deep structures of privilege mirrored in the male as teacher, female as student model. . . . One would not want to deny that many positive things can happen when a male is the instructor of female students. And the white teacher can create an authentically anti-racist classroom. But these teachers cannot be the agents of the deepest transformations in a culture where women have been schooled to look to male authority and to search for male approval as the basis of self-worth. Just so, white instructors cannot be the agents of the deepest transformations for their black students in a culture where the dominant values are white (p. 211).

Thus, despite some dissenters and whatever the political criticisms, there obviously still remains, for many feminist educators, an intense commitment to role models and their liberatory promise. Further, there is a climate of expectation. Certainly some women's studies students expect their feminist teachers to be exemplary role models. This presses on us the question of whether feminist teachers *should* function as role models.

In considering this query, Morgan (Chapter 9, this volume) raises some disturbing questions about the paradoxes associated with feminist pedagogical practices. Mirroring some of the political worries, she argues that, contrary to our hopes, expectations, and ambitions, the reliance on psychological processes of identification with role models jeopardizes the autonomy of our students.

In brief, Morgan's argument is that in order for feminist education to take place we need to develop feminist sensibility in the student. This simply means that we need to cultivate a feminist perceptiveness and set of categories of interpretation through which the student experiences and evaluates the world. To Morgan, this means, for example, developing an appreciation for and an ability to ask feminist questions and an alertness to theoretical assumptions and/or pedagogical processes that deny or undermine a woman's full personhood and sense of legitimate place in the academy.

To be more specific, developing a feminist sensibility may involve: noticing that the instructor lets males dominate the classroom conversation; seeing that women instructors who complain about sexual harassment in their faculty are ridiculed by the administration; asking why there are no women writers included in their literature course; wondering why Rousseau's views on women did not pose a serious problem for his social contract doctrine; hearing the patronizing tone in an instructor's voice as he rejects some students' requests for more material on women abstract painters; being astonished that a major text on Canadian history should have no more than eleven pages devoted to women.

According to Morgan (Chapter 9, this volume), this internalization of a feminist sensibility is mediated (at least) through identification with another woman (the feminist teacher), whom one can perceive as a possible variant of oneself. Acknowledging that there may be gradations and complex forms of such identification and allowing that some students can be most critical of the role model with whom they strongly identify, Morgan nevertheless emphasizes that some identification is necessary. Her point is that such identification strengthens the teacher's resulting referent power, and it is viewed as a legitimate process.

However, Morgan says, "By definition, a person who successfully identifies with her teacher will . . . replicate various actions, attitudes, or emotional responses exhibited by her real life or symbolized models." But then she points out, "such replication is, I believe, the replication of the identity of another, not the mark of a unique self-created individual." Thus, she concludes, "feminist autonomy is compromised by the very educative process that is designed to foster it."

I will say straight away that I am not as worried about the function of role models in feminist pedagogy as Kathryn Morgan. I am not persuaded that relying on this form of "identification" does jeopardize autonomy. My skepticism is based upon a number of considerations. First and foremost, it seems to me that we have many actual cases in which this process of identification seems clearly to have been the *catalyst* for autonomy. I propose we examine at least one such case in which the cultivation of a feminist sensibility through identification with a role model may enhance a woman's autonomy. Consider the case of Sara Ruddick (1984b) and her account of how she found autonomy through her identification with a role model. Her account begins, "Virginia Woolf changed my life."

> Before my encounter with Woolf, I was fragmented and anxious, living on the edge of professional life. I depended on the smiles, opinions, and invitations of distinguished thinkers. Along with Hannah Arendt I hoped that the thinking ego was "sexless" and without a "life story." But like many women I secretly be-

lieved that thought belonged to men, women being only its handmaidens and interpreters. Strength too resided in men, and power, for women, in the male connection. Understandably, I resented and feared the men in whose presence I felt inferior and powerless. Yet the idea that my own life might offer a distinctive perspective on shared human concerns did not occur to me. . . .

But Virginia Woolf was the personal, direct agent of change in my life; it was she who forced me from dependence on men's judgment, who made women real for me, who helped me to recover my own mind, eyes and voice. Virginia Woolf taught me to say "we" and to mean women, to say "we" are different, and to value differences. She opened up for me a world of women. . . .

Surrendering to Woolf's influence, I was not left at her mercy, not enthralled by her Greatness. It is true that I had to work through temptations to idealize her and also to suspect and discount her just because she was a woman . . . but she never tempted me to self-loss. . . . Woolf inspired me to find, not lose myself (pp. 137, 138).

Clearly we have here in Sara Ruddick's own words a nice description of the sort of feminist sensibility one hopes to cultivate through identification with a role model. Eloquent one might say, but is this an example of the sort of identification process Morgan has in mind? And how can we be sure Ruddick's autonomy is/was not threatened? Perhaps what we have here is adoring feminist false consciousness. Perhaps we have a case where one intellectual colonization is traded for another.

If what we have here *is* adoring feminist false consciousness or an alternative form of intellectual colonization, then Kathryn Morgan is right—the very processes that we think are catalysts for autonomy really do, paradoxically, jeopardize it. But how can we decide? Obviously, one thing we need to do is clarify more precisely what we mean by our notions of *identification, role models,* and *autonomy.*

A strong initial difficulty lies with the exact characterization of these notions. Identification is a concept whose home is in the theory of psychoanalysis; role model or role-modeling are terms whose origins lie in social learning theories, which dispute much of what psychoanalysis has to say about psychological processes. This means that considerable ambiguity can surround these terms, particularly when they are used in conjunction to describe the phenomenon that interests us. But we can make some attempt at clarity here.

Identification is a technical term referring to a psychoanalytic dynamic that involves, as Schafer (1968) says, "those processes by which the subject transforms . . . real or imagined characteristics of [her] environment into inner regulations and characteristics" (p. 9).

Jerome Kagan (1964) defines identification more simply: "An identification is a belief that some of the attributes of a model . . . belong to the self" (p. 146). The process of identification begins when the individual thinks she has certain characteristics in common with another and comes to think that she must then also have other internal, psychological characteristics that belong to the other person. The inference is an example of the common human tendency to believe that if two objects share some features they probably share others. In the case of identification the assumption is that if one possesses some of the external—and more objective—characteristics of the model (for example, femaleness, femininity), she might also possess her desirable psychological properties (for example, power, competence, ability to succeed). If a child is identified with a model, [she] will behave, to some extent, as if events that occur to the model are occurring to [her] (Kagan 1964, p. 147). And it is when the belief in psychological similarity to the other is associated with the experience of a vicarious emotion that seems appropriate to the model that we say the individual has established an identification. For example, when a daughter who has an intelligent mother feels pride or a daughter of a dishonest mother feels shame. The general point is that the daughter's emotional state is more appropriate to the parent than to the self.

Nancy Chodorow (1978) reminds us: "People may identify with others modifying their self or their activity to resemble someone who has abilities, attributes, or power they want, fear, or admire" (p. 43). She also notes it is an "unnoticeable and unconscious operation" in our psychological experience of others used as a defense "to cope with lack of control, ambivalence, anxiety, loss, feelings of dependence, helplessness, envy" (p. 42). On this description identification seems not a promising process for the birth of autonomy.

There are many definitions of the term 'role model'; a fairly standard one might read as follows: Real or theoretical persons perceived as being ideal standards for emulation in one or a number of selected roles.

It seems to me fair to say that Ruddick's example involves a full-blown case of identification. Ruddick (1984b) speaks of "surrendering to Woolf's influence," "being absorbed in her life." She views criticisms of Woolf as "attacks on the woman I loved." She speaks too of "seeing and hearing the world in Woolfian rhythms" and notes, too, "how oddly, whenever my interest in another woman becomes particularly intense in the way Woolf made possible, somehow Woolf gets mixed up in the relationship too."

Ruddick (1984b) speaks of Woolf as a model of this and it seems to me fair to say that we have here a good example of learning through identification with a role model whose own practice provides a powerful example of the exercise of a feminist sensibility. In short, we have a good example of the sort of psychological processes Morgan thinks is needed in feminist pedagogy. Our next question must be, Has autonomy been realized in this process of identification?

Again, our answer here will depend upon what we mean by autonomy but certainly "acquiring one's own mind, eyes, and voice," and acquiring "the courage of my perceptions," as Ruddick says, has to involve at least some development of autonomy if authenticity has anything to do with autonomy.

Still, doubts may remain. Even if we do grant that Ruddick's is a legitimate example of an individual realizing her autonomy in identification with

Virginia Woolf, how do we explain it as a general possibility? How do we explain that, in general, identification with a role model does not necessarily jeopardize autonomy? It can easily be thought that Ruddick and Woolf are an unusual case. Ruddick was an adult, one with considerable philosophical training before she encountered Woolf. And, perhaps to the point, Woolf is dead. These factors surely ameliorate the process somewhat. The cases that worry Morgan, that ought to worry us, are those involving girls and young women in women's studies classes with role models who are far from dead and who are in positions to wield considerable influence and power over those seeking to emulate them. So the question pressed on us is, How can we show that, in general, identification with a role model need not jeopardize autonomy?

Before proceeding further, we must address one point. Morgan is asserting that the process of identification jeopardizes autonomy, but it is unclear what sort of claim she is making. We might take her to mean that the process of identification necessarily jeopardizes autonomy because it is a process that, as Chodorow (1978) says, is "unnoticeable and unconscious." But Morgan does not say this explicitly and other things indicate that she must be talking about an identification process that can in principle become noticed and available to consciousness. She is, after all, speaking of a process students are alert to and indeed expect to occur; she also assumes that it is one that we can bring to mind sufficiently in order to scrutinize and rationalize it. So I expect she has in mind some process not wholly beyond our control, whether it is the same psychological process psychologists label identification or not. Thus, I take Morgan to be making a contingent claim, that is, that, as a matter of fact, this process of identification with a role model does not lead to autonomy.

To aid our thinking on this matter, it will also be useful to keep in mind certain points about autonomy. The first thing we should notice is that autonomy needs to be contextualized. If we look at the political contexts in which identifications happen, it is clear that, as Elizabeth Young-Bruehl (1987) says, "there is a great deal in our personal and cultural histories suggesting that thinking is not our province, not our privilege, not even our possibility" (p. 207). Men have been the great thinkers and our only models. If we wanted to be good, to be competent thinkers, we have had to be like men. Thinking has been and is forbidden for women, and dangerous—our uterus will fall out, we will be unmarriageable, certainly we will be destroyed or abandoned.

This set of conditions has led women who perceive themselves as thinkers to think they have a male mind. Sara Ruddick (1984b) says, "I had bought the stereotype, minds were male, my mind and my father's" (p. 143). "My well educated head, steeped in conventional definition secretly thought of itself as male and openly declared itself to be genderless" (p. 151). This in turn leads, as Ruddick describes so eloquently, to feelings of self-alienation, to feeling like a fraud, and to waiting for the punishment to happen.

In these circumstances identifying with a woman thinker, countenancing "the idea of a thinking woman," as Ruddick says, "learning to delight in female minds" can be an experience of healing. It is possible to reconcile what the world has said is a contradiction and this can be an experience of great joy.

Alice Walker (1983) reminds us of what it feels like to be rid of the alienation and loneliness in her account of her identification with her role model Zora Neale Hurston: "What I had discovered of course was a model . . . she had provided, as if she knew someday I would come along, wandering in the wilderness" (p. 12). Walker speaks of how this encouraged her to finish her work. Now, she says, she writes as though "with a great many people, ancient spirits, all very happy to see me consulting and acknowledging them, eager to let me know through the joy of their presence, that indeed I am not alone" (p. 13).

Obviously, from self-reports anyway, such identifications with women thinkers and women writers provide a profoundly liberating experience. One becomes autonomous from men's judgments; one no longer experiences oneself as The Other.

My point, in short, is that we cannot know, in the abstract, whether a psychological process will jeopardize autonomy because we cannot determine autonomy in the abstract. Usually discussions of autonomy arise when we suspect undue external influence. Identifying with Virginia Woolf obviously helped Sara Ruddick recognize the undue influence of male thinkers in characterizing her abilities, in determining what sorts of things it was permissible to think about, what questions were interesting to take up, and so forth. It helped at least to free her from this undue influence.

Some might still be skeptical. Certainly Morgan's suspicion is not so easily removed. This could just be exchanging one form of intellectual colonization for another more to our liking. In order to get a real understanding of how autonomy and identification with role models are not necessarily in conflict, we also need to address the presuppositions of the process of identification with role models.

The fear of jeopardizing autonomy in the process of identification with a role model can only arise if we view the psychological process acontextually and ahistorically and if we perceive the student as passive. My main quarrel with the view of role models and identification implied in Morgan's chapter is that there may be a hidden presupposition that the identification is something that *happens* to the student, something unknowingly inflicted upon her by sophisticated feminist pedagogues. This would be, I think, a very misleading view of the matter.

A more accurate picture emerges if we think in terms not just of role models and identification but also, as Fisher (1988) suggests, of "role model making." Taking this perspective of the process we are reminded of certain facts that help to dissolve the paradox of authority Morgan has constructed.

First, we notice that role models and persons are not the same. A role model only comes into existence when we *choose* another as a role model. The point is that the process implies a degree of judgment and consent. We need to notice that we can and do refuse and dissent in this process of identification. Sara Ruddick clearly made Virginia Woolf into a role model but Margaret Laurence did not. In her memoir *Dance on the Earth*, Laurence (1989) says:

> Virginia Woolf is a writer whose perceptions helped shape my view of life, as did her brand of feminism, but by the time I was in my twenties, I began to feel that her writing lacked something I needed, that something was a sense of physical reality. Her characters were beautifully, ironically drawn, but what was lacking was ordinariness, dirt, earth, blood, yelling, a few messy kids. Woolf's novels, so immaculate and fastidious in the use of words, are also immaculate and fastidious in ways that most people's lives are not. She says a great deal, but there is a profound way in which she doesn't speak to my own life (p. 130).

Margaret Laurence rejects Virginia Woolf and adopts as a role model her own mother-in-law, Elsie Laurence, a woman from another generation who could not choose both to have children and to write books, but a woman of talent and courage who enabled Margaret Laurence to choose both. ("Her story became part of mine, she was what is now called a role-model" p. 125.)

A second and more obvious point we need to remind ourselves of is that we not only choose but we *create* a role model. Adopting a role model involves conceptualizing an activity through selecting out certain features of it: We create role models by selecting out those features of someone that best suit our interests from our current points of view. Fundamentally, our desire to follow a role or perform it depends upon our own interest in it. Margaret Laurence chose to create her mother-in-law as a role model because of her love for children as well as her love for writing. Having children and writing were what Margaret Laurence had an interest in.

Finally, we need to notice that the selection of a role model is not something that occurs in a vacuum. Many things affect the making of a model: whether the activity we are trying to have modeled has a clearly recognized tradition; whether the role has been contested or not; whether the prospective individual model fares well or not. Consider two examples that illustrate these points.

Margaret Laurence noticed that for all their similarity in wanting to write she and Virginia Woolf had different circumstances: Virginia Woolf fared well in part because of her class; because she did have money and a room of her own; because she did have a companion devoted to her and her writing; because she did not have children.

Mary Helen Washington (1985) gives a touching account of incidents in her own women's studies classroom that indicates the many factors at work in determining who takes whom as a role model for what. Herself a black woman, a specialist in Afro-American literature, she team taught a women's studies course on images of women with Linda Dittmar, a Jewish woman raised on an Israeli kibbutz. They divided the course into several sections— middle-class women, working-class women, emergent women—each section comparing black women's lives to white women's. Helen Washington taught the black women writers and Linda Dittmar taught the white women writers.

As she reports it, the class went badly. It was immediately polarized with the assumption that the white students would identify with the white teacher and the black students with the black teacher. Students were silent and edgy, afraid of voicing an incorrect racial attitude. Washington recognizes that real communication has been obscured when she asks herself:

> Why did students from predominantly Irish Catholic backgrounds, raised on novenas and confession, the nine first Fridays, and the Threat of sins against the sixth commandment think they had more in common with a woman raised in an Israeli kibbutz than with me, a woman who survived sixteen years of Catholic school upbringing, who can still recite the Act of Contrition and the Memorare by heart? (p. 223)

The point is that one can set up the situation, the course outline, the curriculum along racial lines, the teaching along racial lines, so that the class imitates the syllabus, so that race is primary. But that can prevent other more useful identifications. And as Washington reports, it cannot ensure the conscious obvious identifications one intends. At the end of another course, a happier one on black women writers, one of her students made a comment to Washington that she intended as a compliment: "I could tell the first day you came in here and started talking that you weren't black." The student went on to say that she had since changed her mind and decided Washington was black (Washington 1985, p. 227).

The general point I want to emphasize here is that it is one person's desire that can bring a role model into being. As Bernice Fisher notes, "creating a role model is like love, it's unilateral and involves passion, a passion for what has not been given to oneself, but also for what can be for oneself" (Fisher 1988, p. 220).

Fisher argues that in order to understand the process of identification with role models, we need to contextualize the quest. We need to see what is behind the quest for role models, what is the impulse that drives the process. It is easy to see the point of role models from an educator's point of view, but what is it about for the student?

Bernice Fisher sees the struggle with role models in rather heroic, historical, political, and existential terms. I think her understanding, although somewhat grand, is accurate. Fisher claims that the quest for role models is about trying to solve a problem—the problem of how to make a life that is different from our mothers' and perhaps at odds with our contemporaries'. The tension between tradition and progress, represented by feminism, puts a special burden on women. There is, Fisher says, a rendering of the social fabric of ourselves and so we have a quest for "images of women who have survived and who therefore in some sense negate such contradictions" (p. 217).

The tension, the pain and anguish of this trying to make a life that is different from our mothers' is poignantly captured by Marge Piercy (1982, pp. 278–281). The following excerpts are from her poem about her mother entitled "Crescent Moon Like a Canoe."

> You who had not been allowed to finish
> tenth grade but sent to be a frightened
> chambermaid, carried home every week
> armloads of books from the library
> rummaging them late at night, insomniac.
> riffling the books like boxes of chocolates
> searching for the candied cherries, the nuts.
> hunting for the secrets, the formulae.
> the knowledge those others learned
> that made them shine and never ache.
> You were taught to feel stupid: you
> were made to feel dirty; you were
> forced to feel helpless; you were trained
> to feel lost, uprooted, terrified.
> You could not love yourself or me.
> . . .
> You did not want the daughter you got.
> You wanted a girl to flirt as you did
> and marry as you had and chew the same
> sour coughed up cud, yet you wanted too
> to birth a witch, a revenger, a sword
> of hearts who would do all the things
> you feared. Don't do it, they'll kill
> you, you're bad, you said, slapping me down
> hard but always you whispered, I could have!
> . . .
> You look to men for salvation and every year
> finds you more helpless. Do I battle
> for other women, myself included,
> because I cannot give you anything
> you want? I cannot midwife you free.
> . . .
> My muse, your voice on the phone wavers with tears.
> The life you gave me burns its acetylene

of buried anger, unused talents, rotted wishes,
the compost of discontent, flaring into words
strong for other women under your waning moon.

Bernice Fisher claims that our search for role models is an attempt to find support, validation, and guidance in changing historical circumstances. We search, she says, because no authority figure can provide definite answers or solutions to the questions posed. This means, "We are on a constant moral frontier in which neither our own nor anyone else's knowledge of the world guarantees our transition from the present to the future" (Fisher 1988, p. 217). And this means, she says, that we experience a fundamental existential loneliness. "The loneliness of not knowing where our efforts to change social relationships will take us. And whether, in the end, the struggle will be worth the cost" (pp. 217–218).

For Fisher the core meaning of role models and our identification with them is that they represent "a kind of moral faith that we have, a faith that we can bring into existence, other, better possibilities" (p. 231). Recognition of this as the core meaning of role models has implications for the alleged paradox of authority it is presumed to pose for feminist pedagogy.

The first, most obvious implication that follows is that acting as a role model is not something that is intrinsic to teaching as an activity. Teaching, as Fisher reminds us, is a consensual relationship in which both teachers and students take on responsibilities. When someone agrees to be a teacher, she can be held accountable for doing or not doing certain things for her students. By contrast, as Fisher perceptively notes, role models cannot be held accountable since becoming one does not involve consent.

The second obvious implication is that we must beware of holding teachers responsible for what is essentially the student's responsibility. Given very broad limits, we choose our own political ideals and the responsibility for these remain ours alone. As Fisher (1988) puts it, "The responsibility for choosing and creating role models entails nothing more or less than taking responsibility for ourselves" (p. 229).

Morgan's paradox arises, I think, because she inappropriately employs a social science notion of role models. It is, I think, a notion that is not good enough for feminism. It is too thin a notion. It does not incorporate what girls and women do when they make role models. Fisher's account of role model–making is closer to how it works, and I think her account of the meaning, the purpose, the point of the activity is (more) in keeping with what feminists and feminist students are about. That said, and granting that the choosing and creating of role models entails the student taking responsibility for herself, we still might think that we, as educators, do bear *some* responsibility. Students' role model–making does, after all, occur to some extent within the very broad limits that we educators determine. So, feeling the moral pressure of Morgan's worries, we might ask, What are the conditions in which a student's identification with a role model will not jeopardize her autonomy?

It may help us to think about this question if we reconfigure the problem along the lines I have suggested and see our responsibility as pedagogs to be that of helping students to find a range of alternative models/model-making material all compatible with "the cultivation of feminist sensibility." Sara Ruddick's case is a good example of what one has to make available to students. Virginia Woolf speaks to the problem of trying as a woman to do intellectual work. But obviously we need a wider range of materials available for students, for Margaret Laurence needed someone who was trying to do intellectual work *with children*. We cannot know all the variations needed, but we can make our best guesses and see to it that we try to provide as broad a range of model-making material as possible in our teachers, our texts, and our curriculum. The students will do the rest.

But further, when we do find ourselves *taken* as role models, we need to be honest with our students about the conditions that make success possible, and about the obstacles, difficulties, and realities we have *failed* to overcome. In this way we can repay their faith in us and in the possibility of a better future for themselves. In this way we can preserve and protect the autonomy of the students by keeping the process grounded in realities.

We want the admiration that fuels the creation of role models to grow out of an understanding of the conditions women must face. We want it grounded in an honest recognition of women's difficult situations, for this allows us to open up the process for interpretation and reinterpretation (Fisher 1988).

Although the faith students express through their choice of role models *need* not jeopardize their autonomy, we might well set it to slumber if we let them think that faith is sufficient to smooth their way into the future. The responsibility that at least some feminists recognize is that of keeping the process grounded in realities. The idea is to have the admiration that fuels the creation of role models grow out of an understanding of the conditions we must face so that claiming someone as a role model does not require a denial of realities women face. It should not rest on an ignorance of the high costs of success.

In short, one feminist approach to role models insists on keeping the moral faith that the role-model creation represents grounded in an honest recognition of women's difficult situations. We can best preserve the autonomy of the student by revealing ourselves whole, by being clear about the conditions that make success possible and by honestly acknowledging the realities we have failed to overcome. In this way we open up the process for interpretation and reinterpretation. I suspect it was this sort of honesty that enabled Virginia Woolf to be a catalyst, a role model for autonomy. Woolf did not hide the difficulties. She took responsibility for herself in full recognition of all the difficulties.

PART THREE

Politics

12

An Ethics of

Care Takes On Pluralism

ANN DILLER

In this chapter I sketch an ethics of care approach to pluralism in education. In particular I suggest that using an ethics of care leads us to articulate, and attend to, new forms of pluralism that are (in the spirit of pluralism itself) compatible with each other rather than mutually exclusive. I propose furthermore that these forms of pluralism are appropriate aims for education, but that to pursue them as viable educational practices we must also follow the ethics of care in its insistence on changing our ethical focus from a preoccupation with justification to a concern for better caring relationships.

Four distinctive features structure the ethics of care: (1) a relational ontology; (2) a relational ideal; (3) a methodology of caring attentiveness; and (4) an insistence upon knowledge of the particular. To create, maintain, and enhance caring relationships among ourselves constitutes the central moral task. In order to do so we practice what Nel Noddings (1984) terms *engrossment*, the giving of caring attentiveness to particular persons in particular situations.[1]

What happens when we look at existing pluralisms from an ethics of care perspective? Let us consider two standard forms: (1) pluralisms of coexistence; and (2) pluralisms of cooperation.

Pluralisms of Coexistence and Cooperation

A pluralism of coexistence requires basic noninterference, combined with mutual tolerance. Under ideal circumstances it would also carry a mutual respect for those who differ from us.[2] In a speech near the end of the nineteenth century, William James ([1899] 1958) summed up its features and appeal. "It is negative in one sense, but positive in another. It absolutely forbids us to be forward in pronouncing on the meaninglessness of forms of exis-

161

tence other than our own; and it commands us to tolerate, respect, and indulge those whom we see harmlessly interested and happy in their own ways, however unintelligible these may be to us. Hands off" (p. 169).

Almost a century later, pluralisms of coexistence still have a wide appeal. For example, James's "Hands off" point recurs in a recent statement by a woman of color speaking to white women about the contrast between obligation and friendship; her version of obligation resembles hands off:

> Out of obligation you should stay out of our way, respect us and our distance, and forego the use of whatever power you have over us—for example, the power to use your language in our meetings, the power to overwhelm us with your education, the power to intrude in our communities in order to research us and to record the supposed dying of our cultures, the power to engrain in us a sense that we are members of dying cultures and are doomed to assimilate, the power to keep us in a defensive posture with respect to our own cultures (Lugones and Spelman [1983] 1986, pp. 19–31).

However attractive hands off may be, life in our contemporary world is so interdependent that we can rarely have coexistence without some degree of cooperation. Pluralisms of cooperation do, however, encompass a wide range. At one extreme we may have quite fragile, temporary forms of cooperation such as the one Robert Axelrod (1984, chapter 5) describes in his account of how during World War I along the "Western Front" (a five-hundred-mile line in France and Belgium), enemy soldiers in the trenches managed to cooperate enough to establish their own frontline truces and then to maintain these "Live-and-Let-Live Systems" for extended periods of time. At the other end of the cooperative spectrum, membership in a community may be so extensive that it leads persons to transcend their separate ethnic, racial, class, or gender differences by identifying with the public interest and common good of the larger cooperative.

In any case, most serious efforts at mutual coexistence do enmesh us, to some degree, in pluralisms of cooperation, just as coexistence provides the fall-back position, so to speak, for the closer connections of cooperation.

When we consider pluralisms of coexistence and cooperation from an ethics of care perspective, I believe we must conclude that they are necessary and valuable but also insufficient. Although each helps us to regulate, to negotiate, and to benefit from our human differences, they are not sufficient for the relational tasks of human communities. For example, pluralisms of coexistence can provide necessary conditions, basic ground rules, to enable other more demanding forms of pluralism to flourish. But for the rearing of children, the care of the sick and the elderly, the enhancement of personal relations, the endeavors of friendship and affection, a pluralism of coexistence is simply not enough.

Similarly most pluralisms of cooperation, although crucial for facilitating constructive forms of interdependency, are also insufficient to meet the concerns of an ethics of care. For one thing, the relations among persons need not be taken as ends-in-themselves but can be merely instrumental. There is no intrinsic reason to care for each other. This does not mean caring cannot arise or is not often part of a cooperative endeavor; it simply means caring is not essential or constitutive and thus may be absent or avoided.

Thus, neither pluralisms of coexistence nor of cooperation are sufficient for an ethics of care even though both may provide important and necessary conditions. At least two additional forms of pluralism seem to me to be in keeping with an ethics of care and are also at work in recent feminist dialogues: (1) a pluralism of co-exploring, and (2) a pluralism of co-enjoyment.

Pluralism of Co-Exploring

The concept of co-exploring as I am using it here exemplifies and also extends the basic engrossment methodology of an ethics of care. An insistence on the practice of receptive attention not only recurs among advocates of an ethics of care, it appears in recent feminist writings as well.

While Noddings (1984) favors the term engrossment and talks also of receptivity, Sara Ruddick (1989) calls it *attentive love*. Marilyn Frye (1983) uses the image of the *loving eye* and contrasts it to the *arrogant eye*. Lisa Delpit (1988) describes a "special kind of listening" that entails "really hearing." And Sarah Hoagland (1988) simply advocates *attending*.

Although these authors diverge in other ways, their views on attentiveness show a remarkable convergence. They all agree that when we attend to each other in this special way we must temporarily suspend our own projects, set aside our own agendas, and bracket our a priori expectations; we do this in order to apprehend another's reality on their own terms.

In addition to distinguishing receptive attending from other ways of attending such as projection, these authors as well as Carol Gilligan (1982) and other proponents of an ethics of care agree with Iris Murdoch (1970) when she says that to undertake such attentiveness constitutes a distinctively moral act. "I have used the word 'attention', which I borrow from Simone Weil, to express the idea of a just and loving gaze directed upon an individual reality. I believe this to be the characteristic and proper mark of the active moral agent" (p. 34).

Once we begin practicing engrossment, transformations occur. Nel Noddings (1984) describes the transformation in her own personal experience that occurred with a colleague for whom she had "never had much regard" and "little professional respect." She writes that it was "as though his eyes and mine have combined to look at the scene he describes. I know that I would have behaved differently in the situation, but this is in itself a matter of indifference. I feel what he says he felt. . . . I shall never again be completely without regard for him" (pp. 30–31).

Noddings's account is apropos in that it makes explicit both the changed perception and also the fact of continuing differences. The recognition of plurality has not been diminished; indeed it may be heightened by additional specificity, but the relationship between the persons has changed. A new understanding alters the landscape; it lessens the power of differences to build barriers and to maintain fences of disregard.

But what Noddings recounts is only a one-way, unidirectional understanding. She gives no indication that there has been mutual understanding, or even a reciprocal effort at engrossment. In order to do *co*-exploring all the parties must engage in engrossment practices.

For an unmistakable example of co-explorers, I want to turn to an often-cited dialogue between Maria Lugones, Hispana, and Vicky Spelman, Anglo woman. Sometimes each of the coauthors speaks singly in her own voice and at other times they speak jointly. This published Lugones-Spelman dialogue ([1983] 1986) gives us an in-print example of the co-exploring process. It addresses both the procedures and the substantive issues for pluralistic exploration. The following quotation is found near the end of the dialogue, spoken "Problematically in the voice of a woman of color": "To attain the appropriate reciprocity of care for your and our well-being as whole beings, you will have a stake in us and in our world, you will be moved to satisfy the need for reciprocity of understanding that will enable you to follow us in our experiences as we are able to follow you in yours" (p. 30). It is this emphasis on a "reciprocity of understanding," a mutual attentiveness, that marks a pluralism of *co*-exploring.

In addition to its clear call, both by precept and example, for a reciprocity of understanding, the Lugones-Spelman dialogue brings out some further aspects for serious co-explorers to consider. For one thing we have to confront the personal discomfort that arises when we try to follow another person into their own culture and life experiences. Maria Lugones describes the problem when she observes that "the task at hand for you is one of extraordinary difficulty. . . . [it] calls for circumspection, for questioning of yourselves and your roles in your own culture" (Lugones and Spelman [1983] 1986, p. 30).

To follow another person into their reality can be uncomfortable and threatening. Lisa Delpit (1988) describes the problem when she talks about how difficult it is to get white educators to listen to what parents and teachers of color say about their own children, how hard it is to hear each other across cultural, racial, ethnic, and economic barriers:

> To do so takes a very special kind of listening, listening that requires not only open eyes and ears, but open hearts and minds. We do not really see through our eyes or hear through our ears, but through our beliefs. To put our beliefs on hold is to cease to exist as ourselves for a moment—and that is not easy. It is painful as well, because it means turning yourself inside out, giving up your sense of who you are, and being willing to see yourself in the unflattering light of

another's angry gaze. It is not easy, but it is the only way to learn what it might feel like to be someone else and the only way to start the dialogue (p. 297).

This feeling of discomfort helps to explain the strong resistance most of us experience when faced with honest, and often angry, cross-cultural encounters.

In addition to the fact that none of us likes to be criticized, there is also, I believe, another deeper fear that blocks us from full engagement in listening and hearing another culture on its own terms. This is the fear that the "rightness" of our own position may be undermined, that our grip of certainty on our own beliefs may be loosened. So long as we are preoccupied with justifying and defending the superiority of our own beliefs we are caught in this fear.

Changing the Problem

If co-exploring among members of different "cultures," or even between persons who have "real differences," is to have a chance of success, we may need to follow the ethics of care in its insistence on changing our focus from a preoccupation with moral justification to a concern with how we can create and maintain better relationships for all of us. Noddings (1984), for example, contrasts the pursuit of justification with the practices of an ethics of care. "As one-caring, I am not seeking justification for my action: I am not standing alone before some tribunal. What I seek is completion in the other—the sense of being cared-for and, I hope, the renewed commitment of the cared-for to turn about and act as one-caring" (p. 95). Thus an ethics of care changes what we take to be the moral problem.

In his fascinating book on creativity, D. N. Perkins (1981) tells the following story of a changed problem.

> Early on in the space race, NASA spent much time and effort seeking a metal robust enough to withstand the heat of reentry and protect the astronauts. The endeavor failed. At some point, a clever person changed the problem. The *real* problem was to protect the astronauts, and perhaps this could be done without a material that could withstand reentry. The solution, the ablative heat shield, had characteristics just opposite to those originally sought. Rather than withstanding the heat, it slowly burnt away and carried the heat away from the vehicle (p. 217).

From an ethics of care perspective, to persist in trying to determine who is "right," and by implication who is "wrong," resembles the NASA search for a metal to withstand the heat of reentry. We need instead to solve the real problem, which is how to improve our relationships with each other. And, as with the NASA heat shield, the characteristics most appropriate for this task may be just the opposite of those that lead us to insist on and defend our rightness.

On this interpretation the framework for co-exploring can shift to a pluralistic search for better relationships. As co-explorers we can then work together to achieve reciprocal understanding, we can pursue complex truths via shared inquiry, we can be attentive to each person's account of the terrain as each of us travels it. If we make serious efforts to attain reciprocal understanding of each other's worlds, differences and misunderstandings will not cease to exist. Quite the contrary. We shall take differences for granted as the nature of the terrain and accept misunderstandings as one of the inevitable hardships of the expedition. But to continue as co-explorers does mean that we face these hardships together and that we stay with the expedition.

At this point one might well observe that given the admitted discomforts and inevitable hardships of such co-exploring expeditions, we are still faced with strong reasons for resistance and perhaps for desertion as well. Why would anyone undertake this? When Maria Lugones (Lugones and Spelman [1983] 1986) raises this question she answers: "out of friendship" or "from within friendship you may be moved by friendship" (pp. 23, 30).

When she identifies friendship as the appropriate moving force, Lugones (Lugones and Spelman [1983] 1986) points us toward the recursive effects of reciprocal understanding. Such encounters can cultivate the grounds for transformative friendships.[3] But for this recursive effect to occur the process must get going in the first place. How does it start? Here is where I believe we need another new pluralism: a pluralism of co-enjoyment.

Pluralism of Co-Enjoyment

How can we give friendship a chance to develop, to get started? To answer this question we need to return to the issue of particularity, to the insistence that moral knowledge consists of specific knowledge about particular persons. But which specific knowledge do we need to attend to? When we ask Simone Weil's (1951) question, "What are you going through?" we tend to hear about suffering, sorrows, grief, or pain. All of which do constitute an integral part of our lives. But only a part.

In his essay "On a Certain Blindness in Human Beings" William James ([1899] 1958) calls upon an extended quotation from Robert Louis Stevenson's "The Lantern-Bearers" to make the point that "to miss the joy is to miss all. In the joy of the actors lies the sense of any action. That is the explanation, that the excuse" (pp. 154–155). Here we have, as James, the Pluralist, well knew, the clue for a crucial refinement on our claims about knowledge of the particular: which particulars it is that give us the most essential knowledge of someone? "To miss the joy is to miss all."

Can anyone really know us who knows nothing of our personal joys? In this connection, Spelman (1988, pp. 124–125) reminds us of Nikki Giovanni's lines from her poem "Nikki Rosa":

> *and I really hope no white person ever has cause*
> *to write about me*
> > *because they never understand Black love is*
> *Black wealth and they'll*
> > *probably talk about my hard childhood*
> *and never understand that*
> > *all the while I was quite happy.*

It is not enough, then, to have moved from the general to the particular—to concrete specific knowledge of persons-in-situations—unless we have also begun to understand what "really matters" to this particular person. And here is where "to miss the joy" is at least to miss a great deal, if not all.

In advocating a pluralism of co-enjoyment, I believe that experiences of co-enjoyment can work as moving forces to encourage and sustain efforts at mutual attentiveness. I also believe that as educators we ourselves would do well to practice and teach the pluralisms of both co-enjoyment and co-exploring. Indeed I suggest that in education we need to give serious conscious attention to all four forms of pluralism. Let us look more closely at what this might mean.

Teaching Pluralism

In contrast to large political configurations, such as nation-states, educational institutions (schools, colleges, universities) are small community-sized units with relatively stable groups of people, many of whom meet face-to-face on a regular basis. Educational institutions are, therefore, already in a favorable position to practice the four forms of pluralism that we have been discussing.

In the first place, educational institutions are in a position to enforce and implement a pluralism of coexistence. One can expect and insist that members of an educational institution will refrain from harming one another and shall exhibit outward tolerance as well as being respectful, or at least polite, regardless of inward feelings or attitudes.

In the second place, the pluralism of cooperation gives us effective and appropriate educational practices; effective in part because of their indirectness. A cooperative effort often elicits mutual understanding, camaraderie, and bonding. John Dewey's influence has, of course, made cooperative practices widespread in education; and at present, methods of "cooperative learning" seem to be in the ascendancy. Whether or not these methods successfully incorporate pluralism is a further question.

Third, appearing under other names, such as *the dialectic*, certain forms of co-exploring have a long, respectable history in educational inquiry. But to practice a true pluralism of co-exploring, one that entails reciprocal understanding across cultural and racial differences, requires conditions that are not easily met. Although the details are beyond the scope of this short chapter, I believe that, in brief, we need to create educational spaces that are both safe and expansive: (1) safe psychologically as well as physically and linguistically, so that exchanges of particular, and personally revealing, knowledge become possible, so that students can take risks both in speaking and in hearing; and (2) expansive enough that new, and sometimes discomforting, possibilities can be seriously entertained.

In the fourth place, I think we should, as educators, aim straight for the pluralism of co-enjoyment not only as a long-term, distant possibility but also as an everyday "happening" consciously structured into our teachingand-learning lives.

And finally, if our educational efforts are successful, all four forms of pluralism—coexistence, cooperation, co-exploration, and co-enjoyment—will become possibilities for us and for our students. We can then set out together on expeditions into new, unexplored territories. Adrienne Rich (1978, p. 31) gives us a poet's account of the possibilities:

> *The rules break like a thermometer,*
> *quicksilver spills across the charted systems,*
> *we're out in a country that has no language*
> *no laws, we're chasing the raven and the wren*
> *through gorges unexplored since dawn*
> *whatever we do together is pure invention*
> *the maps they gave us were out of date*
> *by years.*

Notes

1. I am using Nel Noddings, *Caring* (Berkeley: University of California Press, 1984), as the primary source for this discussion of an ethics of care. Two other widely discussed sources are Carol Gilligan, *In a Different Voice* (Cambridge, MA: Harvard University Press, 1982), and Sara Ruddick, *Maternal Thinking* (Boston: Beacon Press, 1989).

2. The role of respect in pluralism is complex. In his presidential address to PES, Walter Feinberg distinguished three forms of respect; Feinberg's first two, "Laissez-Faire" and "Respect as Constraint," would come under pluralisms of coexistence, but his third form, "Respect as Cultural Encounter," is closer to what I term *co-exploring*, as is much of Feinberg's own account of his encounters with Japanese culture. See W. Feinberg, "A Role for Philosophy of Education in Intercultural Research: A

Reexamination of the Relativism-Absolutism Debate," in *Philosophy of Education 1989* (Normal, IL: Philosophy of Education Society, 1989) pp. 2–19.

3. Audrey Thompson gives a relational account of the transformative effects of friendship in "Friendship and Moral Character: Feminist Implications for Moral Education" in *Philosophy of Education 1989* (Normal, IL: Philosophy of Education Society, 1989) pp. 61–75.

I wish to thank Debra Shogan, Susan Franzosa, Barbara Houston, Jane Martin, Beatrice Nelson, Jennifer Radden, and Janet Farrell Smith for helpful comments on earlier versions of this chapter.

13

The Moral Politics

of Sex Education

KATHRYN PAULY MORGAN

Many contemporary advocates of sex education ground their position in liberal theory. In the area of sexuality, liberalism maintains a strong commitment to equality, sexual subjectivity, unrestricted individual choice, and individual responsibility limited only by the Harm Principle. Sex education is seen as a necessary means to responsible sexual self-determination and is accorded high instrumental value. In this chapter, I argue that educational materials commonly recommended to children and adolescents do not, in fact, promote central liberal values. This leads to the central paradox of the shaping of illiberal sexual subjectivity in the name of sexual liberalism.

Individual sexual subjectivity is founded on choice and responsibility. The development of such a model of subjectivity should be at the heart of sex education materials directed at children and adolescents. In order to determine whether or not this moral and political focus is at work, I will explore four questions in the process of examining two ostensibly liberal sex education sources: (1) the very popular book (and video) *Where Do I Come From?* (Mayle [1973] 1980) and (2) "Discovering Yourself," the free pamphlet distributed to adolescent girls by Kimberly-Clark (no date) (the manufacturer of feminine hygiene products, hereafter referred to as KC). In the course of my analysis, I will situate these two textual analyses in a larger cultural/discursive setting of contemporary North American culture.

The Question of Sexual Subjectivity: Who Initiates?

In North American culture full social approval goes to men who are (and are expected to be) sexual initiators in an overt, public sense. If women do initiate, women are instructed that such initiation should be more covert, more ambiguous. In a private setting, if a woman tries to initiate overtly, she may be warned of the devastating consequences of male impotence as the price she must pay or, in a public setting, she could possibly be arrested for soliciting. From the perspective of individual psychosexual histories, women have been expected to be virgins or to simulate being virgins upon marriage. Under such arrangements, it is clear that the husband functions not only as sexual initiator but as sexual tutor as well. Obviously such practices legitimize male initiation and relative female passivity (and put enormous pressures on men to be initiators and risk-takers).

Contemporary discursive practices display the same emphasis on male sexual subjectivity. As Robert Baker (1975) points out (and many speakers of the language confirm), there are several categories of terms used almost exclusively by men to refer to women. Such categories may refer to various kinds or parts of animals (e.g., *chick, bird, fox, tail*), to playthings (*babe, doll*), and to fetishized body parts (*cunt, pussy, piece of ass, piece*). None of these items is noted for its capacity to initiate human action, the prime emphasis of virtually all liberal accounts of sexual subjectivity. The model of sexual interaction we arrive at is that of a human man initiating sexual activity with a sub- or nonhuman entity.

The expectation of male initiation is manifest in widely available sex education materials that can be found in liberal households and schools. In the popular book *Where Do I Come From?* we find the following passage:

> Let's say the man and the woman are lying in bed together. The man loves the woman. So he gives her a kiss. And she gives him a kiss. And they hug each other very tight. After a while, the man's penis becomes stiff and hard, and much bigger than it usually is. It gets bigger because it has lots of work to do. By this time the man wants to get as close to the woman as he can, because he's feeling very loving to her. And to get really close the best thing he can do is lie on top of her and put his penis into her vagina.

Notice the implications of the description involved. The man initiates the entire series. It is his penis that is described as having "work to do." It is then suggested that the most loving position for them to be in is for him to be on top of her in the male superior position, a position that leaves the woman minimally mobile (and, which is, incidentally, not the optimal position for conception to occur). So far, in all this activity, all the woman has done is return the initial kiss.

Moving ahead to consideration of the early years of puberty, it is instructive to examine the Kimberly-Clark (KC, no date) pamphlet already referred to. Proudly announcing that it is reviewed and approved by a committee of medical and educational authorities, this pamphlet is widely distributed to young girls entering puberty. In a section (non-ironically) entitled "Straight Talk About the Sex Urge," the authors say,

Without discipline, dependability, sound values, inner strength and self-respect, no sexual relationship can be good or gratifying. Without mutual, profound and ongoing emotional commitment, sexual intercourse cruelly violates the "I" of you. . . . It is important to acknowledge that you, as a young woman, have a very special responsibility to the young men in your life. Male sexual feelings are aroused, in general, much more quickly and easily than your own. A sweater that seems merely fashionable to you may appear sexually provocative to your date. The necking that you consider as little more than friendly communication may stimulate him to physical passion. Obviously the best way to cope with this unwanted state of affairs is to avoid setting the stage for it or irresponsibly provoking it. Turn off the heat long, long before your date reaches the boiling point (pp. 13–14).

This passage resonates with a fear of sexuality and promotes an erotic double standard. It maintains that although sexual desire in boys and men is aroused quickly and passionately, normal good girls are expected either to feel no sexual arousal in what one would think of as a paradigmatically sexual context or to be unconsciously "sexy." As the man's cerebral superiority becomes clouded by dangerous sexual passion, it becomes incumbent upon the (always sober?) girl or woman to act as the restraining brake in a situation in which the initiating action and sexual acceleration is assigned to the man. Although it appears as if the woman is in a position of power, it is essentially regulative power of a negative sort. Merely being in a position of saying "no" to a sexually aroused man is not a position of optimal or even equal power. It would be farcical to regard it as a choice.

Moreover, this asymmetrical assignment of responsibility often requires a young woman either to feel abnormal if she is becoming aroused as quickly as her partner or to deny her own sexual feelings. Thus, the situation can easily compound feelings of sexual alienation and hypocrisy.

Situating these texts again in a larger discursive setting, we can find this illiberal Tarzan/Jane model of male sexuality at work in a more sophisticated setting for sex education—gynecology and obstetrics textbooks. One of the standardly used gynecology books states: "The frequency of intercourse depends entirely upon the male sex drive. . . . The bride should be advised to allow her husband's sex drive to set their pace and she should attempt to gear hers satisfactorily to his" (Novak, Jones, and Jones 1970, pp. 662–663). And yet another notes: "An important feature of sex desire in the man is the urge to dominate the woman and subjugate her to his will; in the woman acquiescence to the masterful takes a high place" (Jeffcoate, 1967, p. 726).

In general, then, the message that comes through is that men should be the sexual initiators and women the sexual receivers whose behavior and sexual sensibility should display passivity. The upshot of this is only men are seen and evaluated as fully active sexual objects, a message in direct violation of the liberal principle of according full human subjectivity to men and women.

The Question of Sexual Egalitarianism: Is This an Equal Opportunity Setting?

Contemporary linguistic practices in North America do not support an egalitarian erotic norm. For example, the phrase "going all the way" is usually taken to refer to penis/vagina intercourse with ejaculation by the man serving as both necessary and sufficient conditions. In the law, marital "consummation" and adultery are defined in these terms.[1] And many definitions of rape have required the emission of semen into the vagina as a necessary condition. Looking at a potentially more promising set of texts, liberation-orientation sex manuals, a critical sexual sensibility should note precisely which behaviors are placed in the categories of *foreplay* and *afterplay*, behaviors that bracket **THE ACT** (Rotkin 1976).[2] More often than not, female clitoral orgasm is put into one of the subordinate categories—into the category of foreplay if it is seen as a useful prelude to and stimulus to further male arousal or into the category of afterplay when "equal time" principles seem to require it. It is seen as the friendly sort of need to attend to once the main fireworks are over with. **THE ACT,** in this context, invariably refers to the male orgasm.

The centrality of men's orgasm and male sexuality is underscored in two further ways: (1) by attending to what the sex education materials tell us about the clitoris, and (2) by examining the growing narrative material surrounding the problems of male sexual impotency (David and Brammer 1976; Farrel 1975; Fasteau 1975; Julty 1979; Lewis 1981; Pleck and Sawyer 1981; Snodgrass 1977). I will examine only the first of these here.

Let us look at the book *Where Do I Come From?* (Mayle [1973] 1980), since this is a book that promises to "name all the labels (vagina, penis, etc.) and show all the important parts of the body."[3] In the text, a modest anatomy lesson is offered to the reader. A woman's breasts and hips are carefully explained. Moving to the genital region, there is a brief discussion of pubic hair followed by the question, "But what does the woman have between her legs?" The answer that is given is that she has a little opening called a vagina. That's it! There is nothing else of significance in the location in question. Although emphasis is placed on mutual orgasm (which is described as a "tickly" feeling that ends in a "tremendous big lovely shiver for both of them"), what activates this feeling for both the woman and the man is ejaculation taking place in the woman's vagina. Thus we find that a prima facie sexual egalitarianism, signified by mutual orgasm, is seriously undermined by silence with respect to the primary locus of women's sexual pleasure. And the clinical literature on women's alleged and consequent frigidity documents the loss of sexual subjectivity on women's part as a result of this silence. This is a culpable silence.

Where the role of the clitoris in women's sexuality is discussed, the clitoris is described in relation to the penis, which is assumed to be the paradigm erotic organ. Consequently, the clitoris is described, alternately, as "an immature penis," a "little penis," a "miniature penis," or a "tiny" penis. (It requires no imagination to see how descriptions of the penis might go were we to take the clitoris as the normative organ.) Often the function of the clitoris remains quite mysterious. For example, in the Kimberly-Clark pamphlet, the clitoris is described as "a small organ which is especially sensitive" and that is sheltered by soft folds of flesh (KC, p. 6). This is all that is said about the clitoris. Reading this, a young girl might be apt to think that it was something like an eyeball, requiring a protective clitoral "lid." That it might be remotely associated with sexual pleasure would involve a wild extrapolation. This obscurity is followed by a profoundly misleading definition of mutual orgasm. "The effect of the sexual embrace is profoundly emotional. It also has physical manifestations of the most dramatic kind. . . . At the climax of the sexual act, the penis ejaculates its semen. *Although no similar ejaculation occurs in women, this climax is called orgasm in both the male and the female*" (KC, p. 14, emphasis added). Given this definition of female orgasm, it is not surprising that there is nothing more said about the role of the clitoris in female sexuality.

Here again, under the guise of liberal sex education materials, we find evidence of a phallocentric interpretation of human sexuality. Male sexual arousal patterns and a man's sexual pleasure are seen as central to the most fulfilling sexual acts. A woman's sexual pleasure is put into a subordinate category (although not neglected altogether). And the physiologically most focused site of female eroticism is either devalued, demeaned, or dismissed altogether. Although mutuality of sexual desire and pleasure is called for in the liberal model, education designed to further erotic development is more likely to render actual mutuality of pleasure and erotic recognition impossible for girls and women. Thus the very educational means designed to foster liberal erotic egalitarian goals in fact undermine them and lead to asymmetry and inequality.

Defining the Range of "Normal" Sexual Behavior: Where Should "Normal Sex" Take Place?

In this culture, it is clear that penis/vagina intercourse functions as the paradigm case of normal sex. If the sex of the participants is unspecified, the phrase "to have sex with" is taken to be synonymous with penis/vagina intercourse. In normative contexts, such as philosophical and psychological discussions of perversion and sexual deviance, penis/vagina intercourse is taken to be the benchmark against which other sexual acts are measured even when reproductive concerns are explicitly disavowed. Philosophers argue that no theory of sexual normalcy would be an adequate theory that led to the conclusion that penis/vagina intercourse is perverted (although one can easily imagine contexts in which one might find it immoral, e.g., adultery, incest, prostitution, rape, etc.). And it may appear to the reader, as well, that this position is the only obvious one to hold. Nevertheless, there is considerable literature to support the hypothesis that heterosexual men are more likely to see this as a synthetic a priori truth than are heterosexual women, gay men, lesbians, and bisexuals. It is clear that for most heterosexual men, vaginal placement of the penis is a circumstance that produces considerable stimulation, pleasure, and orgasmic release. It is not so for women. That the vagina is a preferred site of sexual pleasure is a view that, apparently, many women have to be socialized into with considerable effort. And the sex education materials are there to perform precisely that role.

Recall the passage from *Where Do I Come From?* (Mayle [1973] 1980): "By this time, the man wants to get as close to the woman as he can, because he's feeling very loving to her. And to get really close the best thing he can do is lie on top of her and put his penis inside her, into her vagina." This may well be the most loving thing for *him*, but it is not at all clear that it is the most loving thing for *her*. Nevertheless, the book continues, "This is the closest two people can get." It may well be the closest, physically speaking, but it is not the most erotically satisfying for a woman, although it may well be for a heterosexual man. A woman's sexual satisfaction is unlikely to be achieved by this sexual act. Often, she will be labeled *unresponsive* or *cold* or given some more pathological label as a consequence so that no critical attention is directed to the act itself (Barker-Benfield 1976; Ehrenreich and English 1973, 1978; Irvine 1990; Scully 1980).

To reinforce the devaluing of clitorally based sexual pleasure, sex education materials warn girls about masturbation. In the Kimberly-Clark pamphlet, in the section entitled "'Social' Ills You Should Know About," the authors first say that masturbation is not, technically, a physical or social problem for a young girl, although it can arouse someone who masturbates to feel guilty or withdrawn from society. With this warning, they continue: "As one approaches maturity, intense self-preoccupation should pass. New interests and activities capture the imagination. The satisfaction with self grows as these outgoing preoccupations are pursued with zest and enthusiasm. *The urge to masturbate diminishes and eventually disappears*" (KC, p. 24, emphasis added). As a result of messages like this, any woman who continues to find sexual pleasure through clitoral stimulation either with a partner or by herself cannot help but label her sexual feelings as deviant and experience feelings ranging from embarrassment to fear and shame. She has been socialized into a sexual belief set that defines penis/vagina intercourse as the preferred normal site of sexual pleasure. Should she not experience any sexual pleasure in this context—in likely contrast to heterosexual males—she cannot help but regard her other sexual experiences as strange and potentially pathological.

Phallocentric concerns are not only primary; they can involve the appropriation of women's vaginas. They are involved when, after giving birth, a woman's episiotomy is remedied and she is given the extra stitches commonly referred to as "husband stitches." They are at work when approximately 74 million women in the Middle East and Africa undergo devastatingly painful clitoridectomies so that their clitoris cannot serve as an alternate source of pleasure (Hosken 1979). They are involved where there is an emphasis on penis/vagina intercourse as the only legitimate or mature form of heterosexuality. They are at work when men refuse to wear condoms and to practice safe sex because condoms interfere with their own pleasure. Risks of transmitting disease and potentially lethal transmission of bodily fluids to women pale in significance when placed in the balance with male sexual pleasure. Such phallocentric concerns are inconsistent with liberal commitment to equality.

A commitment to liberal sexual values would lead, if orgasm is seen as the goal, to some sort of equality.[4] To advocate as normal sexuality only those processes that led to maximum sexual pleasure for one partner seems unfair and in violation of liberal commitments to equality and equality of erotic opportunity. Moreover, the intense singular focus on penis/vagina intercourse is consistent with the principled pluralism of the original liberal position.

Setting Limits on Legitimate Sexual Choice: Who Is Permitted to Have Sex with Whom?

Throughout this chapter, my focus has been largely heterosexual. This is not surprising. In many cultures, heterosexual sex is the only approved form of sexual experience even when a culture is striving to reduce its population. Such a focus is buttressed by the ideology of heterosexism and the psychopolitical dynamic of homophobia, which institutionally prohibit sexual activity between gay men, lesbians, and bisexuals in a variety of ways ranging from mild disapproval or awkwardness to the death penalty as it was practiced in Nazi Germany and is at present law, for example, in Iran (Rich 1980).[5]

The Kimberly-Clark pamphlet addresses, somewhat obliquely, the question of homosexuality. Suggesting that attraction of girls to other girls is natural in early adolescence, it is described as involving "a perfectly natural stage of life during which she prefers to share her pursuits and her ideas with members of her own sex." At this point, there has been no mention of anything remotely sexual. The manual continues, "If sexual interest in the same sex does continue into adulthood, progressing to the exclusion of interest in the opposite sex, it is a symptom of maladjustment. This is called homosexuality and indicates that the normal response to persons of the opposite sex has been somehow damaged" (p. 24). Note again the heterosexist assumptions at work here. The claim is made that all human beings, normally, are heterosexual but that this form of attraction can be "damaged" by being sexually attracted to and loving members of one's own sex. For the young adolescent girl reading this, who might be hesitant or confused about understanding her own desires and who might be intensely attracted to other women, or to both women and men, the outcome can only be one of a sense of shame and of sexual crippling. Similar messages are directed at boys and men. In both cases, heterosexist "expert" opinion can lead to serious psychological and moral erosion of a sense of erotic legitimacy. As such, the sexual subject of the liberal position is threatened.

Heterosexist assumptions can also function in conceptually a priori ways to restrict, control, and skew human sexual behavior. Gay men and lesbians are expected to role-play heterosexual stereotypes. In a male supremacist culture, gay men are often labeled *effeminate* and are seen as playing a female role in a sexual encounter, that of "one who is penetrated." He is thereby devalued for his sexual choices and his sexual behavior. Similarly, lesbians' erotic interactions can only be understood, according to heterosexist stereotypes, as necessarily involving one *butch* and one *femme* role. The phallocentric modulation of heterosexism becomes most explicit when someone is puzzled about what lesbians "do" if there is no penis present. One "solution" is to fashion erotic devices exclusively in penile form to remind women of what is "missing" in masturbatory or lesbian sexual settings.

Heterosexism and heterosexist sex educational materials contradict the fundamental tenets of political liberalism. Liberal sexual values cannot, in principle, specify or restrict the gender of the sexual participants or the range of legitimate sexual behaviors (although it, obviously, can invoke the Harm Principle). An exclusive emphasis on heterosexual penis/vagina intercourse in the context of social institutions that cultivate and orchestrate high levels of homophobia is inconsistent with this liberal set of values.

Conclusion

The moral politics of sex education is a profoundly confused domain. Liberal moral values are cited both by opponents and advocates of sex education. The same values are used in recommending particular curriculum materials. However, those very materials can be seen to contradict the values of individual sexual self-determination, subjectivity, and equality. At the very heart of materials that purport to further liberal goals, we find an emphasis on male initiation and male sexual satisfaction in a site that maximizes male sexual pleasure, all within an exclusively heterosexual context. This asymmetric model of power relations, of compulsory heterosexual socialization patterns designed to produce dominant men and subordinate women, is inconsistent with any reading of the principles of liberal equality.

Can we move to a genuine understanding and practice of sexuality that implements those liberal values? Not in a vacuum. Sexual behavior is powerfully integrated within a larger social structure (however intimate and private it might feel). Sexuality serves as a supportive microcosm of larger social dynamics that involve the systematic use of the power of men over women. Ironically, it is the conservative critics of sex education in the public schools who correctly perceive that if the schools genuinely promoted liberal sex education, that education would be revolutionary indeed.

Notes

This chapter was presented to the Philosophy of Education Society (1995) under the title "Sex, Sex Education, and the Paradoxes of Liberalism."

1. Note how "dangerous" it might be to require female orgasm as a necessary condition for adultery: This could entail the possibility of numerous nonorgasmic sexual encounters involving sexual intercourse that would not count as adultery.

2. In this analysis, I am indebted to Karen Rotkin's (1976) illuminating article.

3. In all fairness, it should be noted that the book omits any identification and discussion of the scrotum and testicles although they are clearly pictured.

4. It is interesting to see how different operationalizations of the notion of equality could lead to very different outcomes. One definition of equality might suggest a "one orgasm each" model, since that is most likely what a man is going to be capable of experiencing. A second definition of equality might advocate that each should experience that of which they are capable, a kind of "orgasm commensurability" model, which would, in many cases, require (?) multiple orgasms for women. An "equality of orgasmic opportunity" model might generate yet a third sort of outcome.

5. For a devastating account of the use of violence in societies supporting compulsory heterosexuality, see Adrienne Rich, Compulsory Heterosexuality and Lesbian Existence, in *Signs*, vol. 5, no. 4 (1980), 641–660.

14

Women's Physical Education: A Gender-Sensitive Perspective

ANN DILLER AND BARBARA HOUSTON

Active exercise was my delight. . . . No boy could be my friend till I had beaten him in a race, and no girl if she refused to climb a tree, leap fences, and be a tomboy (Louisa May Alcott, quoted in Lerner 1977, p. 7).

Why should one talk about *women's* physical education? Why not talk about physical education for both women and men, for children, for adolescents, for adults, for persons? Some would argue that to raise the separate question of women's physical education is to already affirm and perpetuate a detrimental distinction based on biological sex where such a distinction is neither required nor desirable.

There is no question that physical education has been differentiated for the sexes for reasons having to do with both perceived biological and social differences between them.[1] Women have played an active role in the development of their own formal physical education since its modern beginnings in the mid-nineteenth century, and it has differed in character from men's physical education in the following ways (Kennard 1977, pp. 835–843):

1. The philosophy of physical education for women has emphasized the importance of securing "the greatest good to the greatest number" (Spears 1978, p. 11) and has all along placed a greater emphasis on amateur as opposed to professional sport, on cooperation rather than competition, and on the basic benefits to be gained by everyone rather than pursuit of the scarce benefits affordable to the few.
2. Women and men have differed in their conceptions and administration of competitive athletics. In women's programs extramural sport has been developed within the educational context, with goals and staff allocations the same for general education, professional prepara-

179

tion, and intramural and extramural programs. Men's physical education has been characterized by a severance between physical education
and extramural competitive sport.

3. There have been different explicit curricula for women and men.
   Although sport has been a major ingredient of both programs, the selection of sports has been different; and when the sports were the
   same, women developed them differently "by way of such affectations
   as shortened matches, divided basketball courts and special rules and
   techniques" (Kennard 1977, p. 836).

4. Curriculum development has borne a different emphasis in the two
   programs with dance and movement education developed primarily by
   women and given more attention within women's programs and colleges.[2]

A more significant observation to make, however, is that in contemporary
North American society it is obvious that equality has not been realized
through gender-differentiated physical education programs. Women's physical education has received less money for programs and personnel, and
women have had unequal access to facilities. In general, women's sports have
been underfunded and less well coached and equipped, and players have not
had equal fringe benefits such as medical benefits, housing, and food and
travel allowances. Women have not had equivalent opportunities for athletic
scholarships. In schools and in society, women's sports have been accorded
much less status and attention than men's.[3]

In short, it is fair to say that the gender-differentiated programs have suffered from sexism; they have been different and unequal. This has made
many educators properly skeptical of proposals that we continue to take sex
and gender differences into account when designing physical education programs.[4] But there is still fierce debate about the best way to realize sex equality.

On a general level the disagreement about sex equality has a dual focus. In
part it concerns our interpretation of the concept of sex equality.[5] Does sex
equality entail the elimination of activities in which there might be significant sex differentiation by virtue of natural and ineradicable sex advantages?
Or does it allow for significant sex differentiations and merely require the
elimination of sexist attitudes and values now associated with these differences?[6] Additional disagreement arises over the best means to realizing the
ideal of sex equality, however it is interpreted. Should we, need we, take account of gender in the methods we propose for the realization of our ideal?[7]
In physical education this controversy takes the form of a debate over the extent to which physical education programs should be sex integrated or sex
segregated.

In this chapter we assume the viewpoint of an educator who is already
strongly committed to sex equality and to equal educational opportunity but

recognizes that this still leaves a number of practical questions and policy problems undetermined. First, we examine the physical education debate over sex integration in an effort to identify central legitimate concerns on each side. Second, we introduce the concept of a gender-sensitive perspective as one way of doing justice to the concerns of both sides. We then take this gender-sensitive perspective as our viewpoint on women's physical education for the rest of the chapter. Third, we apply the gender-sensitive perspective to our definition of physical education and discover the importance of the hidden curriculum. Fourth, we sketch some prominent features of the hidden physical education curriculum for girls and women. Fifth, we address the question of the educator's responsibility for dealing with undesirable hidden curricula and suggest a number of alternative approaches. Finally, we provide a brief summary of our conclusions on what it means to take a gender-sensitive perspective toward women's physical education.

Sex-Integrated Physical Education

In this section we will examine some of the major arguments for and against sex-integrated physical education. We shall start with those that favor integration.

In addition to the prima facie case against sex segregation in physical education[8] there are strong considerations that favor sex integration. Integrationists urge that we will never come to have an accurate knowledge of the abilities of girls and women until we have sex-integrated classes and similar expectations for the two sexes. Many constraints have been unfairly imposed on girls and women because of erroneous beliefs about physiological differences between the sexes. Specialized rules for girls have circumscribed their play and women are still kept from competing in certain events.[9] These sorts of constraints have led to serious confusion about the causes of the differential in female and male sports performance. Differences arising from unequal experience have been mistakenly attributed to natural or physical differences.

A well-known example of this mistake is captured in the phrase "throwing like a girl." The implication is that girls throw badly by nature. Dr. Jack Wilmore (1969) of Arizona University devised an ingenious experiment that is easy to replicate: "When he asked boys and girls to throw the ball, the boys did much better than girls. Then he asked each of them to throw with their non-dominant arm (i.e., right-handers throw with their left hand and vice versa). On this occasion both boys and girls threw the same distances."[10] The point this simple experiment makes is that physiological differences alone obviously do not account for performance differences. We cannot know what accounts for performance differences until we give equal training to girls and boys. The same point might also be made with respect to attitudinal differences. For example, women's attitudes toward competition may have been so thwarted or distorted by our continually being forced to compete in unfair circumstances that these attitudes may be more a testament to our imposed disadvantages than to our moral superiority.

The general failure to differentiate between performance discrepancies attributable to physiological differences and those resulting from training has also given us inaccurate estimates of the gap between the athletic potential of the two sexes. Very few women have ever had training equivalent to that of many men. Consequently, women are nowhere near exploring the limits of their potential. As more women become involved in sports, we see amazing improvements in their world records. For example, when Don Schollander won his Olympic medals for men's swimming in 1964, no one would have predicted that ten years later his times would not be good enough to win the women's gold medal.[11]

The integrationist concludes that since we do not and cannot know for some time what a realistic estimate of the sex distinction in athletic potential might be, it is premature to think of having anything other than coeducational physical education.

A second argument posed by those favoring integration is that the differences in athletic potential, once we do know more about them, will deserve relatively little attention in physical education. As with research on sex differences in general, more attention has been paid to the differences than to the relevant similarities. Even if we were to rely on our presently available estimates of sex differences, we should beware of exaggerating their significance for physical education.

Granted that some physiological differences between the sexes are relevant for the sports performance of equally well trained world class competitors, there are several points more salient for physical education. Whatever their differences, "neither sex has a structure that is unsuitable for sports" (Cochrane, Hoffman, and Kincaid 1977, p. 80), and both sexes have physiological advantages dependent upon the choice of sport. A physical education program designed to include only or mostly activities favoring one of the sexes would be a poor program. There are other activities one should want to include for a variety of reasons, such as their appeal to student interest, their contribution to physical fitness, their lifetime playability, the facilities they require, and their expense.

Further, females and males are similar physiologically in such areas as coordination and the ability to learn particular skills. These similarities, along with other considerations, are more relevant to the design of physical education programs than are the sex differences in the performances of world class competitors. It is not the point of physical education classes to train top level sports competitors.

Another argument in favor of sex integration is that it offers girls a better opportunity to realize their potential. This view is expressed rather clearly by two 15-year-old girls who explain why they prefer coeducational physical education:

> I feel I have to set higher goals when playing with the boys. . . . I do better, too, when I compete with them.
>
> When I was in an all girls class I knew I was the best and it was easy to slack off. Now I really have to work to stay near the top. It's better that way (Mikkelson 1979, p. 63).[12]

It might be argued that integration provides a better opportunity only for the very best girls and not for the others. But this argument relies on assumptions about the overall ability of girls as a group in comparison with boys and this is the very point at issue. The expectations of performance for girls have generally been lower than for boys and this itself may account for most of the differences at a physical education class level.[13] Sex-integrated classes and ability groupings within these classes should reduce the chances that sex, rather than individual abilities and interests, will determine the performance expectations.

Those who favor sex-segregated classes or a gender-differentiated physical education curriculum acknowledge many of the points raised by integrationists, but still remain unconvinced of the desirability of coeducational programs. They are concerned not only with the advantages any physiological differences might give boys and men but also with the social power advantages that males hold in our sexist culture. They call attention to the fact that males dominate coeducational interactions in ways that limit female participation, undermine women's values, and discount their concerns.[14] They argue that integration will, contrary to what has been claimed, bring about a *greater* loss of opportunity for girls.

Empirical research reported by Patricia Scott Griffin (1980) legitimates the concern that sex-integrated physical education classes will not necessarily eliminate sex bias. For example, observations of game interactions among fifth grade integrated classes showed that

> girls tended to be left out of game interactions by the boys. This was true even when the girls had a higher skill level than the boys did. Additionally, both girls and boys regarded boys as better players even when the girls were more highly skilled. Boys preferred to pass the ball to an unskilled boy rather than to a skilled girl. Girls tended to give away scoring opportunities to boys. Unskilled girls were almost completely left out of game action. However, both skilled and unskilled girls received fewer passes than boys did. (In Griffin, p. 10.)

A second argument against sex integration is a straightforward political argument about male dominance. There are more men than women involved in physical education and athletics; they are better established in the hierarchy; and men are and will continue to be regarded more favorably by the general educational administration, which is also male dominated. Therefore, whatever we think of it in principle, in *practice* integration in physical education is a bad political strategy if we are concerned about furthering women's interests and increasing their autonomy in this field.

Among women physical educators a further worry is that women's distinctive interests and values will be submerged in integration so that coeducational programs will be shaped in a masculine mold. A frequently cited example is the way in which cooperative participation may be devalued in the face of a male preoccupation with competitive excellence.[15]

Another argument arising from concern about male dominance is somewhat more complex. In its most sophisticated versions the argument is a plea for diversity and pluralism. It rests on the contention that women and men have distinctive cultures that need to be preserved. The strong segregationists argue that we can better realize equality by opting for an organizational arrangement that recognizes genuine differences and provides protection for them.[16]

A Gender-Sensitive Perspective

In philosophy of education this same tension, between the case for sex integration and the apparent need for some gender differentiation, finds its expression in the search for a just and unbiased conception of the educated person. In her Presidential Address to the Philosophy of Education Society, Jane Roland Martin (1981b) speaks to this issue. She talks about the evolution of her own views on the "ideal of the educated person." Martin concludes that at this time we need what she calls a *gender-sensitive ideal*. She summarizes her position as follows:

> For some time I assumed that the sole alternative to a biased conception of the educated person was a gender-free ideal, that is to say an ideal which did not take sex or gender into account. I now realize that gender may have to be taken into account if an ideal of the educated person is not to be biased according to sex. Plato was wrong when, in Book V of the *Republic*, he said that sex is a difference which makes no difference. I do not mean by this that there are inborn differences which suit males and females for separate and unequal roles in society. Rather I mean that identical educational treatment may not yield identical results so long as that treatment contains a male bias. And supposing it were to yield identical results, so long as those results themselves involve the imposition of a masculine mold, sex bias will not be overcome. To opt at this time for a gender-free ideal is to beg the question. There are sex differences in the way people are perceived and evaluated. There may be sex differences in the way people think and learn and view the world. A conception of the educated person must take these into account. What is needed is a gender-sensitive ideal, one which takes sex or gender into account when it makes a difference and ignores it when it does not. Such an ideal would truly be gender-just.

Martin raises two separate questions: (1) should our ideals of the educated person be different for the sexes? and (2) should our way of going about the realization of even a common ideal be different for each sex? In this chapter we shall concern ourselves with the second question and argue in favor of a *gender-sensitive perspective*. We use the term *perspective* to indicate a particular point of view, or standpoint, which is taken in order to give proportional importance to the component parts, in this case those having to do with gender.

We shall use the term *gender-sensitive* in the spirit outlined by Martin—as an alternative both to a gender-free perspective, which completely ignores gender, and to a sex-differentiated approach, which chooses to perpetuate sex differences. Thus, one should take gender into account when doing so makes a difference by furthering sex equality or by preventing sexist bias.

What would a gender-sensitive perspective mean for physical education, especially for women's physical education? The rest of our chapter will be an extended answer to this question.

The Domain of Physical Education

Up to this point we have talked of "physical education" in an ordinary language sense without defining it precisely. It is time now to look more closely at our concept of physical education. How would a gender-sensitive perspective view the domain of physical education? What is included? What ought to be included? This is an important question because the issue of which gender differences need to be taken into account will be determined, in part, by what one includes within the domain of physical education.

Deliberate Physical Education or What Is Taught

What is *physical education?* What are we talking about when we talk of anyone's physical education, whether woman or man, girl or boy? A first, perhaps obvious, clear-cut answer is to say that physical education consists of the formal instruction given in "physical education classes."

Since physical education classes are usually required of all high school students, these classes are the one instance of deliberate instructional efforts to attend to physical learning for all young persons. But there are numerous other instances of deliberate physical education. Within formal schooling itself, the extracurricular sports often include effective teaching. Physical education in nonschool settings is done in classes at summer camps and playgrounds, fitness classes, Y programs, Little League baseball, private and group lessons in tennis, swimming, and so on.

What all of these instances share is a deliberate, intentional effort to do physical education; almost everything else about these classes varies. The expectations, the participation levels, the facilities, and staffing all range from high-quality levels to the barest minimum.

What is of more philosophical interest is the wide variety of educational aims and curricular emphases. Physical fitness and physical health have been a more or less constant theme and concern of all physical educators. But the form these have taken and the additional emphases have varied considerably.[17] As noted previously, some women's programs have developed movement education and have included dance, neither of which has been emphasized in male programs.

The role of sports has been varied and controversial. In some cases sports and physical education have been entirely separate, recognizing that physical education need not entail sports. In other cases, many physical education programs consist almost entirely of a combination of intramural and extramural sports. But even where sports are dominant, different ideals are reflected in the emphases that vary from competitive sports to lifetime sports to noncompetitive "new games."

Anyone addressing educational questions from a gender-sensitive perspective would want to consider how these different educational aims have affected each sex. This then requires us to ask a further question: What does each sex actually learn from their physical education?

What Is Learned

So far we have defined physical education from the point of view of the educator—that is, in terms of what is taught. If we consider the student's point of view as well, then we must broaden our definition to include what is actually learned by students.

For many students, especially those with able teachers or high motivation, their education includes a large amount of what is deliberately taught—the physical skills, the knowledge, and information as well as attendant values and attitudes. But this is not the sum total of any student's physical education. A more inclusive view must also ask what else students have learned about their physical selves, their physical abilities and capacities. What physical propensities have they acquired? What have they learned about their physical being-in-the-world? A gender-sensitive perspective needs to know whether these learning outcomes are different for girls and boys.

If we want to know what girls and women learn about themselves as physical beings in a physical world, especially from informal settings and situations, we must turn to the hidden curriculum.

The Hidden Curriculum

In *Memoirs of an Ex-Prom Queen*, Alix Kates Shulman (1972) describes, with wit, humor, and incisive accuracy, much of the hidden and not-so-hidden

curriculum for girls' physical learning. Shulman's account of minimally su-
pervised school playground activities and their cumulative effect for girls and
boys provides us with an instructive microcosm of the informal, incidental,
and exceedingly powerful lessons girls learn about their physical being-in-
the-world. If we read Shulman's description from an educational point of
view, we can see that it captures the major features of many girls' informal
physical education.

> Once I started school I learned I would have to choose between hair ribbons and
> trees, and that if I chose trees I'd have to fight for them. The trees, like the hills,
> belonged to the boys.
>
> Before and after school, the boys would fan out over the school grounds and
> take over the ball fields . . . we played girls' games under the teachers' protective
> eyes. We could jump rope, throw rubber balls for a-meemy-a-claspy, practice
> tricks on the bars nestled in the ell of the building, play jacks or blow soap bub-
> bles—all safe, dependable and sometimes joyous games which the boys dis-
> dained because we did them. . . . Though in my summers and on my street I had
> wandered freely, taking to the woods and the very tips of the trees, in my first
> weeks of first grade I learned to stay uncomplainingly in my place on the steps or
> in the shadow of the school. I learned masculine and feminine.
>
> "Go to the Mountain, girls, it's a gorgeous day," Mrs. Hess would urge us as
> we stood on the steps at recess trading cards. Or, "Why don't you play some
> freeze tag? You need the exercise." But we knew better. We knew that going near
> the ball fields or behind the backstop or near the basket hoop or in among the
> fruit trees or around the Mountain or near the skating pond were extremely dan-
> gerous expeditions, even if we went in a pack—for that was all boys' territory, ac-
> knowledged by everyone. Despite Mrs. Hess' prods and assurances, we knew
> that at any moment out there a pair or trio or more of boys might grow bored
> with their own game and descend on us with their bag of tricks. If a girl was
> spotted on their territory the boys felt perfectly free to: give her a pink belly, or
> lock her in the shed or not let her down from a tree, or tie her to the flagpole
> or . . .
>
> We knew better than to tell Mrs. Hess. The one time I ran crying to her with
> my dress ripped after Bobby Barr had pulled me out of an apple tree, she hugged
> and comforted me with a double message: "I know, dear, those boys are rough
> boys. Why don't you play with the girls?" . . . from the moment we got kicked
> out of the trees and sent into the walk-in doll house back in kindergarten, our
> movements and efforts had been so steadily circumscribed, our permissible
> yearnings so confined, that the only imprint left for us to make was on ourselves.
> By the third grade, with every other girl in Baybury Heights, I came to realize
> that there was only one thing worth bothering about: becoming beautiful (pp.
> 18–21).

One thing to notice in Shulman's account is the extent to which these informal sex-segregated playground activities mirror the standard forms of sex
discrimination and the undesirable outcomes we have already discussed as
part of our historically sex-segregated formal physical education programs;
the unequal distribution of resources, facilities, and "territory"; the reifica-

tion of gender differences; the stratification with male dominance; and finally the attendant loss of opportunities for girls. Shulman's passage illustrates how the hidden curriculum for girls includes, indeed demands, their acquiescence to these inequalities.

The girls learn to accept gender-differentiated constraints on their physical movements, whereas male-imposed limits on their rights to physical space are established and maintained by physical intimidation. The girls' physical being-in-the-world is circumscribed and confined in direct contrast to the physical freedom of the boys. And the girls soon learn that their games are devalued and the one and only physical priority for their own sex is physical beauty.

What is of further interest to us here is the way in which the school setting both allows for and contributes to a hidden curriculum that runs counter to the explicit values and directives for physical education. So Mrs. Hess urges the girls to go to the mountain, to play freeze tag because they "need the exercise." Thus we have a deliberate physical education directive for girls—*exercise*. But the situation, the setting, and the girls' own experiences, as well as Mrs. Hess's unguarded comments about "rough boys," teach the girls that for them to engage in any interesting or strenuous physical activity will be difficult, dangerous, and costly.

In most contemporary schools the hidden curriculum is presumably less blatant and the deliberate physical education program is better organized. We nevertheless have reason to suspect not only that it still exists but also that the essential content of the hidden curriculum for many, if not most, girls remains substantially the same, whether from school or nonschool settings.[18] If we take a gender-sensitive perspective we must address this problem: What should the educator do about sexist hidden curricula?

Before we attempt to answer this question, there are several remarks that need to be made about our use of the term *hidden curriculum*.[19] We use the term in a broad, but nontrivial, sense to refer to learning that is not openly intended. Our usage allows us to speak not just of the hidden curriculum of the school but also of the hidden curriculum in other settings, whether overtly educational or not. But more importantly our usage allows us to focus on the hidden curriculum there may be for an identifiable group of learners. We are specifically interested in what women learn from a variety of settings that can interfere with the success of physical education programs designed for them.

One might well object to our use of the term hidden curriculum to cover this informal learning. In particular, in the case of the hidden curriculum of sexism, it could be argued that it is no longer hidden, it has been found and articulated rather clearly. Thus, if we mean to discuss unintended educational outcomes perhaps the term *informal curriculum* might seem preferable. But we shall purposely keep the term *hidden* for two reasons: First, the exercise of a sexist curriculum may be clear to some but there are many who are quite unaware of it still; second, and more importantly, the term hidden indicates a concern for recognizing that we have not agreed upon or chosen to teach this curriculum and students have neither been asked nor told about these learning outcomes.

Confronting the Hidden Curriculum

Hidden curricula are, of course, not confined to physical education; and we can ask, in general, what educators should do when the content of their students' hidden curricula runs counter to the aims and values of the deliberate formal curriculum that they are trying to teach. Let us consider, for a moment, the general problem of hidden curricula and the possible alternatives open to the educator. We will then return to the particular problem of the hidden curricula for women's physical education.

1. Faced with an undesirable hidden curriculum, an educator or educational institution can make one or more of the following moves:

   a. *Give up.* The educator can simply give up and change the deliberate curriculum to bring it in line with the hidden curriculum so as to eliminate any inconsistency.[20]

   b. *Do nothing.* In this case one merely goes about one's business as usual, teaching the deliberate curriculum and ignoring what is not a direct part of it, assuming either that these other influences already get too much time and attention, or that they are not serious impediments.

   c. *Create a more desirable alternative.* A more positive move is to alter the emphasis of the deliberate curriculum or create a new deliberate curriculum to counterbalance the undesirable effects of the hidden curriculum.

   d. *Reform the organizational structures.* A more drastic move is to intervene directly in the educational setting, altering structures and organizations so as to eliminate, as much as possible, those practices and situations that contribute to or perpetuate the undesirable learning that arises from or occurs under the jurisdiction of the educational institution itself. This might involve changes in classroom formal instruction, teacher-student interactions, and administrative organization, or changes within the institutional environment affecting rules, procedures, or informal relationships.

   e. *Study the hidden curriculum.* In this case one addresses the hidden curriculum directly by making articulation and scrutiny of it an integral part of the deliberate curriculum. In short, make the hidden curriculum part of the subject matter to study.

   f. *Take the offensive.* Perhaps the most far-reaching move is to teach students self-defense skills "against the onslaught of unasked for learning

states" (Martin 1976, p. 149), that is to say, teach students how to identify hidden curricula, how to discover the sources, and how to avoid the
learning outcomes one does not wish to acquire.

2. These six alternatives sketch what the educator *can* do in response to undesirable hidden curricula. But we have yet to answer the question of what an
educator *should do*. In particular, what is the educational responsibility toward
hidden curricula as seen from a gender-sensitive perspective? In order to answer this question we shall distinguish three types of cases. Our criterion is
the extent to which the locus of control for an undesirable hidden curriculum
lies within the educational institution:

    I. The hidden curriculum is a direct outcome of educational practices or
       in-school procedures.
    II. The hidden curriculum comes from the larger society but manifests it-
       self within the school in ways that are amenable to direct educational
       intervention and control.
    III. Both the source and the control of the hidden curriculum lie outside
       the school, but the learning outcomes constitute a serious impediment
       to the achievement of educational goals.

3. Let us start with the first case. Whether one finds sexism hidden in the
explicit curriculum or in the institutional practices, the educator's responsibility for direct intervention is clear. This responsibility is generally acknowledged; and a number of appropriate reforms, which exemplify our fourth alternative, have been proposed and undertaken; for example, efforts to
arrange a fairer allocation of resources and attempts to redress the blatant inequalities in physical education expenditures for women. Reallocation of resources is also necessary to prevent perpetuation of the assumption that
men's programs are more important and valuable than women's.

Equalizing the numbers of women and men who teach physical education,
coach, and carry administrative responsibilities is another example of organizational reform. But we still need to change the pattern in which males frequently coach females although females rarely coach males if we are to avoid
the implicit message that sports is a male domain in which males have the expertise.

The proposal to integrate sport activities using ability groupings is often
seen as an important way to counter the belief that biological sex is relevant
to athletic participation. Heide (1978) makes the point that "girls and boys,
women and men must participate together in sports with decisions about
participation of individuals and groups to be based on current skill, agility,
experience, strength, size, weight, interest, speed and/or other relevant criteria, not the irrelevant factor of biological sex" (p. 197).

Our discussion so far indicates that the most obvious way of countering
undesirable learning outcomes from in-school hidden curricula is to reform

the organizational structures. But the third approach of curriculum change in order to create a more desirable alternative may also be necessary and useful. Suggestions that we introduce new sports for which women are naturally advantaged would be another way to counter beliefs that male biological sex determines general athletic prowess (English 1978, pp. 269–277).

The efforts of many women physical educators to preserve a sex-differentiated curriculum in order to avoid what they believe to be immoral or unhealthy attitudes toward competition and violence hidden in men's programs might plausibly be seen as examples either of the Do Nothing or of the Create a More Desirable Alternative approach.

4. Let us now turn to case II, in which the manifestations of the society's hidden curriculum are amenable to educational intervention. Patricia Griffin's examples (1980) of teacher-student interactions illustrate ways in which teachers can intervene to offset standard sexist stereotypes and to discourage sexist comments:

> (Male student to another male student who is crying): John, if you're going to act like a girl, get off the field.
> Teacher: Tom, anyone, boy or girl, who gets hit and knocked down that hard might cry.
> Student: Why do the girls have to play?
> Teacher: John, the girls want to play as much as you do. Everyone will have a fair turn to play.
> Student: Mark throws like a girl.
> Teacher: No, Jane, Mark throws like he needs practice throwing. Lots of girls throw well and lots of boys don't (pp. 137–138).

Thus a gender-sensitive perspective would emphasize the important difference between saying that "Mark throws like he needs practice" and "Mark throws like a girl," even though both comments are criticisms of Mark's throwing.

Another pertinent example of behavior that manifests standard sexist presumptions is male students poaching from female students' territory in games, also cited by Griffin. Notice the difference between a teacher who encourages poaching: "Susan, if you can't catch it, back off and let Steve get it" and a gender-sensitive approach: "John, that was Susan's ball" or "Don't crowd her out, Dan" (p. 136).

These are examples of a gender-sensitive perspective because they illustrate ways in which a teacher takes gender into account in order to further sex equality or to prevent sexist bias. But how does a teacher come to notice these numerous incidental cases of gender bias in the first place, especially when they are part of the prevailing culture? It seems likely that many teachers will neither notice nor intervene unless they themselves have studied the hidden curriculum.

Thus one might argue that the first students to study the hidden curriculum, and take the offensive, ought to be teachers themselves. If curricular and organizational changes are to succeed, teachers must know what the hidden curricula are, how to identify sources, and how to make the necessary interventions. Courses and workshops on sexism in education and on sex roles are needed for teacher education and in-service teacher training.[21]

Once teachers are prepared to notice and intervene in sexist interactions, the case for sex integration becomes stronger. Since the interactions in sex-integrated programs are more likely to reveal sexist hidden curricula, an attentive teacher can then address this explicitly. Furthermore, one of the findings on coeducational teaching in university physical education is that both teachers and students are challenging and correcting one another's biases (Blair 1979, p. 77). Griffin (1980) shows that similar corrections could also occur with younger students:

> Student: I'm the third base person, not the third base man.
> Teacher: You're right, Sue. Thanks for correcting me (p. 139).

5. We believe there is also a strong educational case to be made for extending previous alternatives e and f, that is, the study of the hidden curriculum and teaching students to defend against it, whenever we suspect that the hidden curriculum for a group of students is a direct impediment to these students' learning. This brings us to case III, our final case for examination in this chapter. Here the issue of responsibility is much less clear than in cases I and II; and our discussion must be somewhat speculative. Indeed it is important to emphasize at the outset that study of the hidden curriculum cannot and should not take the place of able teaching, sound training, regular practice, and equal opportunities for participation, all of which have been historically unavailable to most girls and women.

But what if we do have good pedagogy and relatively equal opportunities for women? Can we then discount the hidden curriculum? Not if we believe the literature on female physicality. In her book *Body Politics*, Nancy Henley (1977) quotes and then verifies Marge Piercy's description of the different ways women and men move and occupy space. Piercy (1973) describes Wanda teaching a theater group about movement:

> Wanda made them aware how they moved, how they rested, how they occupied space. She demonstrated how men sat and how women sat on the subway, on benches. Men expanded into available space. They sprawled, or they sat with spread legs. They put their arms on the arms of chairs. They crossed their legs by putting a foot on the other knee. They dominated space expansively.
>
> Women condensed. Women crossed their legs by putting one leg over the other and alongside. Women kept their elbows to their sides, taking up as little space as possible. ... Women sat protectively using elbows not to dominate space, not to mark territory, but to protect their soft tissues (p. 438).

But what does this have to do with impediments to women's physical education? Let us compare Piercy's description with Iris Young's (1980) phenomenological description of the difference between the movements of untrained males and untrained females when they engage in athletic activity.

> Now most men are by no means superior athletes, and their sporting efforts more often display bravado than genuine skill and coordination. The relatively untrained man nevertheless engages in sport generally with more free motion and open reach than does his female counterpart. Not only is there a typical style of throwing like a girl, but there is a more or less typical style of running like a girl, climbing like a girl, swinging like a girl, hitting like a girl. They have in common, first, that the whole body is not put into fluid and directed motion, but rather, in swinging and hitting, for example, the motion is concentrated in one body part; and second, that the women's motion tends not to reach, extend, lean, stretch, and follow through in the direction of her intention.
>
> For many women as they move in sport a space surrounds them in imagination which we are not free to move beyond; the space available to our movement is a constricted space. Thus, for example, in softball or volleyball women tend to remain in one place more often than men, neither jumping to reach nor running to approach the ball (p. 143).

The point here is that the restrictions women have learned to accept or to impose on their physical being in the world may explain why many so-called *unathletic* women seem unable to move freely in athletic activity. If this is true, then it is hard to imagine how such deep-rooted physical inhibitions can be altered without direct attention to both their sources and their behavioral manifestations. In other words, one would need to study the society's gender-differentiated physical norms and help students identify the ways in which these norms can interfere with physical self-determination on a basic level.

But the question of educational efficacy as well as educational responsibility remains problematic in these III cases, where both the source and the control of the hidden curriculum lie outside the scope of formal education. We can urge the importance of studying the impact of society's physical norms on women's physicality; and we can attend to the ways in which our norms may even prescribe physical vulnerability for women. But we must also recognize that educational efforts alone are bound to be limited when women's ability to protect themselves depends in large part upon social and political conditions. The prevalence of rape and physical violence against women is a case in point. Although it is difficult to determine the precise impact of such conditions, it is also unrealistic to ignore the complex connections between physical freedom and educational equality.[22]

6. Our discussion of educational responsibility for hidden curricula leads us to conclude that alternatives c, d, e, and f are still necessary for women's physical education. But different approaches need to be taken at different times.

In elementary school less reification of gender differences has occurred and the creation of a concrete alternative model of coeducational physical activities should be relatively successful. Children's conceptions about what is and is not sex-role appropriate are still comparatively loose. However, because of their limited experience and less-developed reasoning abilities, children are more dependent upon the examples in their immediate environment than are older students who have better abilities to imagine alternatives and to avoid overgeneralizing from single cases. We also have a greater degree of control over the young child's environment.

Thus the emphasis in elementary school should perhaps rest on the energetic and thorough construction of a better alternative. We can, to a great extent, more systematically control the sexism in elementary school through this method than we can later on. But a gender-sensitive perspective for elementary schools would also require us to notice that between the ages of four and twelve, boys usually have a number of outside school advantages, including additional athletic practice, coaching, advice, information about sports, many male role models, and general encouragement for their physical feats. We would recommend, therefore, that in addition to integrated physical education classes and sports, there be opportunities for extra activities for girls, such as additional coaching and teaching. This is especially important in elementary school because most sports and physical activities that one engages in as an adolescent or an adult require early development of physical motor skills and build on these.

In the present situation, at the older ages this structural intervention is probably not adequate to deal with the sexism that has become entrenched. At this level one must both create an alternative and address the hidden curricula from other settings. At adolescence whatever sex differences there are emerge most obviously; and much social attention is given to accentuating them. The socialization literature on girls consistently reports that although there is some tolerance for *tomboys* and a greater latitude in expectations of gender role conformity given to prepubescent girls, with adolescence there is increasing pressure for girls to come to terms with their physical femininity and to develop the "properly feminine" beliefs, attitudes, and behaviors.[23]

Gender roles are, however, interdependent; and as Money and Ehrhardt (1972) noticed early on, one only learns what girls are supposed to do and be like by simultaneously learning what boys are supposed to be like and vice versa (p. 19). This symbiotic interplay of norms defining femininity and masculinity means that we cannot hope to alter one without having the other come under critical scrutiny as well. Although there may be a greater need for girls to examine the hidden curriculum for themselves because of a greater incongruity between the socialization message and the developmental objectives of the physical education programs, we know that in general sex roles can be limiting to educational achievement for both females and males (Maccoby 1966, pp. 25–55).

Beyond Sexism in Physical Education

We have tried to address the transitional problems of moving from a sexist education in a sexist culture to a nonsexist education that will nevertheless continue for some time to be influenced by a wider sexist culture.

We have argued that inasmuch as it will affect the success of educational practices, one cannot separate the sexism in the larger context of society from the educational setting. Hence, educators must, if they are to be responsible, adopt a gender-sensitive perspective. A gender-sensitive perspective on physical education requires that we be sensitive to what the larger society is teaching that is relevant to its subject matter, what girls and women are learning about their physical selves. It requires that we attend to this learning, recognize its influence upon our goals and find ways of dealing with it that are appropriate to each level of education.

A gender-sensitive perspective is not a blueprint for physical education that will answer all our questions about particular practices. Rather, it is a perspective that reminds us of conditions that must be met before we are entitled to hold our physical education theories up for admiration or even for adoption. We have contrasted a gender-sensitive perspective with a gender-differentiated ideal, suggesting that the latter is often negligent with respect to sex equality. We are now in a position to indicate what the concept of gender sensitivity might require of any women's physical education:

1. Theories or proposals for women's physical education should be formed in the knowledge of the sexism that has been associated with the history of women's physical education.
2. Theories or program proposals should be able to demonstrate that they are nonsexist.
3. Theories or program proposals should acknowledge some responsibility for foreseeable educational outcomes even when these are partially attributable to hidden sexist curricula from other settings.

Our gender-sensitive perspective is like the Pushmi-Pullyu in the Dr. Dolittle story. It has two heads that look in different directions, one ahead to our ideal of sex equality, one backward to the social realities from which our ideal has emerged. It is useful to have two heads, for the ideal of equality has been with us a long time, but there is an equally long history of its failure in practice. It is only by constantly exploring the tension between the views from both heads that physical education can help women achieve physical freedom as well as physical well-being.

Notes

1. The historical documentation of attitudes toward women's physical education and, in particular, women's own views about what their physical education should be can be found in several articles. See Park (1974, 1978) and Vertinsky (1979).

2. For a more elaborate discussion of the history of these developments within physical education see Daryl Siedentop (1972), especially chapter 6.

3. Documentation of the inequality of opportunity in physical education and sports may be found in: Fishel and Pottker (1977), Saario, Jacklin, and Tittle (1973), and Eitzen (1979), chapter 11.

4. One of the common distinctions employed in the literature on sex roles is that between sex and gender. When the distinction is drawn, *sex* refers to the biological differences between females and males and *gender* refers to the social differences between the sexes. However, the matter is far from simple; usage of the terms is often inconsistent and some have argued that the distinction itself is unsuccessful because of the complex linkage between biological and social aspects of sex. Granted there are difficulties. We will, nevertheless, employ the distinction in this chapter. We use the term gender-sensitive perspective precisely because we believe that not just biological differences between the sexes are relevant to the development of physical education programs. We do not wish to beg any questions about the nature or causal explanation of gender differences. We are interested in the implications we think they should have for educational practice. Hence, we invoke the concept of gender, but we use it solely as a descriptive term. For an insightful discussion of the difficulties with the distinction between sex and gender see Eichler (1980), pp. 10–19.

5. A good general introduction to the problem of the interpretation of the ideal of sex equality may be found in English (1977), section II. For a discussion of whether this ideal requires the abolition of sex roles see Alison Jaggar (1979), "On Sexual Equality."

6. An interesting discussion of this controversy and its implications for sports activities is set out in two papers: Wasserstrom (February 1977), pp. 581–615; and Boxill (Fall 1980), pp. 281–299.

7. The philosophical discussion of this point occurs in the context of debate about the morality of affirmative action programs. See Bishop and Weinzweig (1979), chapter 7, Gould and Wartofsky (1976), section IV, and Gross (1977).

8. The prima facie case against sex-segregated sports is summed up by Mary Anne Warren (1983), chapter 1. The same case holds against sex-segregated physical education classes.

9. For a chronicle of the limited participation permitted women in the Olympic games see Gerber, Felshin, Berlin, and Wyrick (1974), chapter 4.

10. This experiment is reported in Cochrane, Hoffman, and Kincaid (1977), p. 81. See also Wilmore (1969). It is doubtful that one can overestimate the powerful impact early sex-role socialization has on a child's sense of her own physical abilities. One study, for example, reports that as early as twenty-four hours after birth parents have different expectations for infants based on sex alone. Among infants who did not differ on any physical or health measures, fathers judged sons as "firmer, larger featured, *better coordinated, more alert, stronger* and hardier"; daughters were judged as "softer, finer featured, *more awkward, more inattentive, weaker,* and more delicate" (emphasis ours). See also Rubin, Provenzano, and Luria (1976), p. 183.

11. See Jackie Hudson (in Oglesby 1978, p. 52) for scientific refutation of many myths about women's natural inferiority in sports. In addition to the tremendous increase in women's performances in conventional Olympic events, Hudson reports on women's world records in endurance events such as long-distance running and swimming.

12. Something akin to this sentiment was expressed long ago by Elizabeth Cady Stanton. She recalled her own experience in an all girls school: "The thought of a school without boys, who had been to me such a stimulus both in study and play, seemed to my imagination dreary and profitless." Quoted in Park (1978), p. 39.

13. For a discussion of the literature on sex bias in teacher expectations in physical education see Griffin (1980).

14. "The Classroom Climate: A Chilly One for Women," issued by the Project on the Status and Education of Women, Association of American Colleges, 1982, documents this sort of male domination in coeducational settings. For a recent review of the literature on the role of social power in coeducation and on the differential effects of single-sex education and coeducational settings on the educational attainments of girls and boys see Finn, Reis, and Dulberg (June 1980), pp. 33–52.

15. For a concise exploration of the ambivalence some women coaches have about women adopting so-called male attitudes toward competition see Rohrbaugh (1979), chapter 17.

16. This argument is put forth by both women and men physical educators and it appears in its sophisticated form in Boxill (1980). Interestingly, those male and female physical educators who argue against coeducation do so on the same grounds, but their interpretation of the reasons differ. Both contend that it will mean a loss of opportunity and a change in the valuation of the activities. However, women contend it will mean a loss of opportunity for all but the very best girls; men contend that it will mean a loss of opportunity for the better male athletes. Women worry that girls will pick up what they consider to be morally questionable male attitudes toward competition; men worry that the girls' participation will trivialize or devalue the activities or increase the risk of male humiliation in defeat. It should, of course, be noted that the sex differences in those attitudes are not clear cut. There are many men who defend coeducation in this area and deplore the dominant combative model for sports. There are also women who argue that girls should not infringe on male sports territory. A good discussion of these general attitudes can be found in Jan Felshin's chapter, "The Social View," in Ellen Gerber et al. (1974), *The American Woman in Sport*.

17. For an extended discussion of the different conceptions of physical education that have influence in contemporary education, see Siedentop (1972). For a less systematic but fairly representative sampling of contemporary influences, see Cobb and Lepley (1973).

18. The sexist hidden curriculum of schools is fully documented in Frazier and Sadker (1973), Stacey, Bercaud, and Daniels (1974), and Freeman (1978), pp. 207–242. See also a two-part special issue, on Women and Education, *Harvard Educational Review*, 49(4) (November 1979) and 50(1) (February 1980). A good general introduction to what we call the sexist hidden curricula for women in nonschool settingsw is Gornick and Moran (1971). The best general introduction to a systematic explication of sexism in society can be found in the chapter "Theory of Sexual Politics," Kate Millett (1970).

19. Our usage of the term hidden curriculum follows closely that employed by Martin (1976) in her paper "What Should We Do with a Hidden Curriculum When We Find One?" pp. 135–151. To our knowledge Martin is the first to draw a distinction between the hidden curriculum of a setting and the hidden curriculum for a learner. For a further discussion of the hidden curriculum see Vallance (1973–1974).

20. For example, the 1981 proposal for a "Family Protection Act" made a pointed effort to force the deliberate curriculum into even greater alignment with sexist conventions in the larger society. The act was designed to prohibit the use of federal funds for educational materials that "do not reflect a balance between the status role of men and women, do not reflect different ways in which women and men live, and do not contribute to the American way of life as it has been historically understood" (Pelham 1981, p. 1916).

21. Projects funded by the Women's Equal Equity Act Program (WEEAP) have developed materials to aid teachers in addressing sexism in education. A complete listing of these can be found in the catalog of materials published by WEEAP.

22. Adrienne Rich eloquently reminds us: "Women and men do not receive an equal education because outside the classroom women are perceived not as sovereign beings but as prey. The growing incidence of rape on and off campus . . . is certainly occurring in a context of widespread images of sexual violence against women, on billboards and in so-called high art. More subtle, more daily than rape is the verbal abuse experienced by the woman student on many campuses. . . . The undermining of self, of a woman's sense of her right to occupy space and walk freely in the world, is deeply relevant to education. The capacity to think independently, to take intellectual risks, to assert ourselves mentally, is inseparable from our physical way of being in the world, our feelings of personal integrity" (Rich 1979a, pp. 241–242).

23. There is an enormous literature on sex-role socialization. Some frequently cited books include Weitz (1979), Weitzman (1979), Kaplan and Bean (1976), and Frieze et al. (1978). A short summary of the literature may be found in Weitzman (1979), pp. 153–216. Much research and writing on sex differences and sex-role socialization is fraught with bias. A good explication of some of the difficulties plaguing the literature can be found in Eichler (1980).

15

Political Correctness:

The Debate Continues

MARYANN AYIM

The debate surrounding political correctness is hampered by misunderstandings so fundamental that one must consider whether it is fueled by a passion to achieve understanding and truth or a desire to make mischief. *Mischief,* however, like *political correctness,* is a mischievous term, for it makes light of serious concerns in ways that are inappropriate. The debate itself promotes this making light, for one of its deepest misunderstandings is the reduction of serious moral considerations to matters of mere etiquette. One can dismiss demands for political correctness, unlike moral or ethical improvement, as interfering, irrational, or hysterical.

In this milieu, the imposition of labels and categories will be more highly fraught with difficulty than usual; nonetheless, it is necessary to introduce some labels to render the discussion intelligible. Hence, with some misgivings, I identify the two major positions on political correctness as the liberal position and the reform position. One of my misgivings is that *liberal*[1] usually connotes reform, suggesting a system both desirous and capable of eliminating deficiencies within, and hence capable of self-correction. The opposition of liberal, to reform, thus seems antithetical to part of the established meaning of liberal. Nonetheless, the position that I identify as the liberal position on political correctness is strongly distinguished from the position I have called *reform* in terms of whether or not universities should comply with reform measures for more inclusive, more positive, and less stereotypic language and curriculum.

The term liberal appears to be a misnomer for another reason as well; a position that urges that any form of expression, no matter how sexist or racist, ought to be protected within the university in order to promote academic freedom and higher academic standards, appears to smack more of conservatism than liberalism. Ironically, this is also true of the reform posi-

tion. In urging the outlawing of certain forms of expression, the reform position necessarily advocates repression, or even censorship of certain kinds of
communication, and hence adopts a stance more usually associated with conservatism than reform. I shall argue, nevertheless, that in certain contexts, repression or even censorship of certain forms of expression is not only consistent with reform but may be genuinely necessary to it. In spite of these
shortcomings, I shall use both terms throughout the remainder of this chapter as a means of distinguishing the two prominent positions on this issue.

Advocates of the liberal position reduce genuinely ethical considerations to
merely political ones. Dinesh D'souza (1991), for example, refers to universities' attempts to outlaw racist, sexist, and stereotypic language as "racial etiquette" (p. 140), "social etiquette" (p. 156), and as "a kind of liberal or political etiquette" (D'souza and MacNeil 1992, p. 36). Racist, sexist, homophobic
speech is reduced to "insensitive speech" (D'souza 1991, p. 141), "unpopular
forms of expression" (p. 142), or "offences against the sensitivities of blacks,
feminists, and homosexuals" (p. 146). In a similar vein to D'souza, Nat
Hentoff (1992) equates hurt to "hurt feelings" (p. 17), as though all those
who oppose racist and sexist slurs, for example, are prima donnas who feel irrational hurt in the presence of such language, and that minority students
who feel hurt when confronted with stereotyped expectations or outright
racism would be well advised to grow thicker skins so that they can live in the
real world. "Increasingly, at colleges and universities, students are being
taught to see themselves as fragile," Hentoff (1992, p. 17) laments. What
D'souza and Hentoff are claiming, essentially, is that racist language may be
rude, but even rude language must be protected by a right to freedom of expression. On the other side of this issue is John R. Van de Wetering (1991),
who states that it is not simple etiquette that forbids us to use racist slurs,
"but a long and dreadful history of rock-pelting, derision, and segregation.
. . . Nomenclature, in short, is not devoid of significant history and education" (p. 100).

In this chapter, I shall argue for Van de Wetering's perspective on this issue. In other words, I shall argue that racist and sexist language descend to
lower depths than mere rudeness and that they may involve severe harm far
in excess of the hurt feelings of the emotionally fragile (although hurt feelings should not be dismissed as trivial either). No attempt will be made to develop any particular inclusive or fair language policy in this chapter; my task
is the more formal one of exploring the assumptions made by several contemporary thinkers who would a priori outlaw such policies. I shall argue that
the trivializing of sexist and racist language as mere bad manners is rooted in
three erroneous assumptions: First, all speech is lumped together in terms of
its right to protection; hence, speech that interferes with other people's freedom of expression, such as sexist or racist speech, receives no special analysis
or censure. Second, all harms (and hence avenues to overcome such harm)
are perceived as specific and individual, with no cognizance of their historical

and contextual grounding, resulting in the inability to understand the impact of systemic harms and the necessity of systemic solutions to some sorts of harm. Third, whereas reform measures and policies, such as guidelines for nonracist language and affirmative action in hiring, are perceived as highly political and hence suspect in an academic institution, the status quo is perceived as apolitical and hence suited to institutions of "higher learning." If my responses to these assumptions appear simplistic, I urge that this is a consequence of the simplicity of the assumptions themselves.

Following a discussion of these three mistaken assumptions, I shall examine the links made by several of the participants in this debate between the tradition of a liberal education and their rejection of political correctness. I shall argue in this regard that these writers ignore at least two major philosophical justifications of the educational curriculum, focusing on one specific theory of curriculum justification, and that their rendition of even this theory involves oversimplification and misrepresentation.

Three Mistaken Assumptions of the Liberal Position

The first mistaken assumption is that all speech is to be lumped together in terms of its right to protection; hence, speech that interferes with other people's freedom of expression, such as sexist or racist speech, is to receive no special analysis or censure. In other words, all forms of expression, whether racist slur, scientific formula, or radical social criticism, are treated alike as being equally deserving of protection; hence, attempts to eradicate any of these forms of expression also score equally on a villainy scale, with feminist attempts to institute inclusive language guidelines being perceived as McCarthyism. There is no apparent cognizance of the fact that some forms of expression, in and of themselves, erode freedom of expression. As Van de Wetering (1991) points out:

> Political correctness has, today, become confused with issues of censorship and totalitarianism. . . . PC, starting first as a satire of the excesses of the language of affirmative action and multiculturalism, became later, in the hands of frightened scholars and laymen, a convenient label for curricular changes which seemed threatening to the traditional and established structure of the white, masculine-dominated educational system.
>
> Simple humane rules of decent conduct thus become targets for tests of free speech, under the mocking aegis of politically correct (p. 101).

Dinesh D'souza, for example, laments the suffering that he perceives as imposed on professors and students who "trespass on prevailing orthodoxies" (D'souza and MacNeil 1992, p. 45), making no mention of the suffering imposed on professors and students who trespass on prevailing racist and sexist norms. "Perhaps the most important lesson universities can teach their students is to think and search for truth in freedom" (D'souza and MacNeil 1992, p. 46), says D'souza, but without elucidating further on freedom for whom. "Offensive, erroneous, and obnoxious speech is the price of freedom" (p. 47), he continues, again avoiding the question of freedom for whom. Consider the following example of offensive speech between two tenth-grade students, a female and a male, which was documented in a Canadian study on sexual harassment in the high school. "I was talking to this guy who sits beside me in class. He ended up calling me a bonehead and I said you're the one that's a boner and he said, you'd better not say that or I'll stick my dick up your ass so far you won't even be able to breathe, and then he started laughing" (O'Connor, 1992, p. 16). Whose freedom is assured, and whose freedom is curtailed, by protecting this speech? Unfortunately, the liberal theorists never provide an answer to this question; although there is deep concern with the suffering of those who "trespass on prevailing orthodoxies" (D'souza and MacNeil 1992, p. 45), and for "whites [who] are the real victims now" (D'souza 1991, p. 132), there is no evidence of concern for the suffering of those who struggle to eradicate social inequities. Not only are whites victimized by restraints on their speaking in sexist and racist ways, according to D'souza (1991), but they are also falsely accused, for it is the restraints themselves that produce such speech. "Campus browbeating and balkanization come to public attention by way of the public outcomes they produce—the racial joke and the racial incident. Both represent white exasperation with perceived unfairness, double standards, and suppression of independent thought on the American campus" (p. 239). Why this represents white exasperation rather than white bigotry is not made clear. According to D'souza (1991), these harsh "censorship codes" do not lead to greater sensitivity, only to a tighter regulation of "outward expression" (p. 241). This remark only makes sense if racism is being looked at *solely* from the perspective of those not victimized by it—for there is no doubt that the victim of racism is better off if the bigot ceases to utter racist slurs in public, even if still thinking them in private.

Although I focus on sexism and racism in this chapter, similar arguments about harm could be made regarding language widely used in the past and still to some extent today in referring to people with disabilities. Terms such as *retard, moron, cripple, mute,* and *deaf and dumb* are cruel words that impart false and unnecessary connotations to their referents. People who are unable to vocalize are no more likely to be dumb, in the everyday sense of that term, than anyone else in the population. It is so clear that those who are limited in their ability to vocalize are better off if they are not labeled as dumb, and that people should therefore not refer to them in such a way, that I find it hard to imagine any sensible objection to a fair language policy prohibiting the use of such terms. Attitudes of the hearing community toward the language of the deaf also leaves much to be desired.

Allan Bloom (1987) laments that when people hold back from making claims for which they fear being branded sexist or racist this creates an atmosphere that makes "detached, dispassionate study impossible" (p. 355). D'souza (1991) worries that charges of racism and sexism are directed toward white males, whereas black women are immune to being branded by such charges (p. 130). No concern is expressed for an atmosphere so poisoned against women or people of color, for example, that they are denied access to "detached, dispassionate study."

It is worth reiterating an observation made earlier—advocates of the liberal position reduce genuinely ethical considerations to merely political ones. Occasionally reform measures are likened, not to political etiquette, but to religious fervor. This confusion is abetted by the use of terms that equate the social reformer to the religious zealot, such as "prevailing orthodoxies" rather than "reform measures to achieve egalitarianism."

A similar move is made by Christina Sommers (1991) in her critique of radical socialist feminism and her defense of liberal feminism, in which she likens the claims of non-liberal feminists to the religious convictions of Zoroaster (pp. 141–158). Allan Bloom (1987) takes this move one step further when he speaks of "the radical orthodoxy" (p. 355) of reformers who seek to remove racist and sexist bias from the classroom, where scholars who trespass against this orthodoxy are treated as "the equivalents of atheist or communist in other days with other prevailing prejudices" (p. 355). The attempt to alleviate racist and sexist bias, not the bias itself, has been cast in the role of prejudice.

D'souza (1991) appeals to Mill for justification of the view that there should be no constraints on expression; D'souza speaks of "John Stuart Mill's argument, in *On Liberty*, that even offensive speech served the purpose of illustrating error" (p. 153). D'souza neglects to mention that according to Mill's analysis in *On Liberty*, any behavior that injures other people is appropriately subject to "moral reprobation, and, in grave cases" (Mill 1972, p. 135), to "moral retribution and punishment" (p. 135). Mill includes among those actions injurious to other people "unfair or ungenerous use of advantages over them" (p. 135). It is important to notice that he deems as immoral and "*fit* subjects of disapprobation" (p. 135), not only direct actions that injure others, but also "the dispositions which lead to them" (p. 135). Among these dispositions, he includes "the love of domineering over others; the desire to engross more than one's share of advantages . . . ; the pride which derives gratification from the abasement of others; the egotism which thinks self and its concerns more important than everything else, and decides all doubtful questions in its own favour" (Mill 1972, p. 135). Mill's (1972) discussion raises a host of fascinating questions: What is to distinguish the imposition of a Eurocentric curriculum on all students from an "unfair or un-generous use of advantages over them"? (p. 135) Does resistance to any affir-mative action based on race or gender reflect a "desire to engross more than one's share of advantages"? (p. 135) Is this insistence on the centrality of the "classics," as traditionally perceived, an instance of "the love of domineering over others"? (p. 135) Are the liberal theorists' constant references to the un-derachievement of black students an indication of "the pride that derives gratification from the abasement of others"? (p. 135) Does Bloom's (1987) and D'souza's (1991) persistent use of male language which excludes females illustrate an "egotism which thinks self and its concerns more important than everything else, and decides all doubtful questions in its own favour"? (Mill 1972, p. 135).

Having raised these questions, which any serious appeal to Mill suggests, it is interesting to ask what presuppositions bolster the liberal theorists' mini-malization of the seriousness of such language. I believe there are two possi-ble answers to this question, both of which receive support from the liberal position. The first presupposition is that the university milieu represents a true meritocracy (or at least it did until affirmative action came along), a mer-itocracy done up in a Rushton color scheme where white and yellow repre-sent achievement and worth, but black doesn't quite cut it. In other words, to speak poorly of black people, quite the opposite of racist discrimination, is simply to tell it like it is. Furthermore, since the pursuit of truth is the raison d'être of the university, language choices that appear to trivialize black people could be seen as positively desirable. There is evidence that the liberal theo-rists uphold this first presupposition. For today's students, "considerations of sex, color, religion, family, money, nationality, play no role in their reactions" (Bloom 1987, p. 88), Bloom assures us.

We are told that white students harbor no racist attitudes toward black stu-dents (Bloom 1987, p. 92). Not surprisingly Bloom also believes that sex is no longer a significant factor in the university setting (p. 107). For Bloom, then, students—at least white students—are both gender-blind and color-blind. There is a not-so-subtle suggestion that black students fail to share the typical white student's indifference to skin color, however. We are told that black students maintain a kind of separatism from the rest of the university population via black studies courses (Bloom 1987, pp. 92–93). Not only is black studies a form of separatism, it is also, according to Bloom, an academic cop-out, a desperate attempt to placate black students who are not achieving up to par in the regular curriculum (pp. 94–96). The same point is made by D'souza (1991, p. 247). D'souza (1991) quotes with approval a Michigan un-dergraduate who says that "Black Power says you don't need to do well in university. . . . You don't need to improve your SAT scores. You are special as you are" (p. 129). D'souza argues that pressure for a "minority-oriented" (p. 247) curriculum emanated from the failure of minority students to succeed in "the core curriculum of Western classics" (p. 247). Neither white nor Asian students require any watering down of the regular curriculum, presumably because they are sufficiently competent to manage it in its pure form (Bloom 1987, pp. 96–97).

The glue holding all these color claims together is the assumption of the intellectual purity of the university. Bloom assures us that "the real community of man [*sic*] . . . is the community of those who seek the truth" (p. 381). In the same vein, Schmidt (1991) insists that "the most important lesson universities can teach their students is to think and search for truth in freedom" (p. 46). According to D'souza (1991), the "fundamental purpose . . . [of the university is] the disinterested pursuit of truth" (p. 120) and the university is defined by "liberty of mind" (p. 142). The questions of "Which community?" and "Freedom for whom?" and "Disinterested according to whom?" are not raised by Bloom, Schmidt, or D'souza.

I have discussed what I regard as the first presupposition of this minimalization of the seriousness of such language—the university campus is a meritocracy, and any belittlement of black students that exists is a function of the absence of black merit, not a function of the presence of white bias. I believe there is a second presupposition at work here—existence of a strong distinction between speech and behavior, with the result that behavior, but not speech, is seen as reasonably subject to restrictions. This assumption makes it easy to slide into the "sticks and stones can break my bones, but words will never hurt me" position, which sees only restrictions on speech or expression as harmful, never the speech or expression itself, which can at worst be mere bad taste capable of hurting feelings perhaps, but not of doing any real harm. If speech is totally unlike other forms of behavior, it is possible to make a special argument for absolute freedom of expression; without this assumption, it is difficult to make sense of the liberal position on this issue.

The second mistaken assumption of the liberal position is that harm is strictly an individual matter; there is no understanding of systemic harms, with the result that relevance of context is consistently ignored. In particular, the context of social/political power is ignored in any analysis that perceives the social system as a pure meritocracy to which all individuals have equal access and from which each individual has an equal chance of gain. As June Jordan (1992) points out, "there is difference and there is power. And who holds the power shall decide the meaning of difference" (p. 18).

Although much of the discussion on political correctness from the liberal perspective assumes that the situation is somehow context-free, in fact the context must be taken into account. There can be no a priori assumptions about the amount of harm done by racist speech, for example, because the harm will be in part determined by one's race, class, and gender membership. This mistaken ignoring of the context has led to other related errors in the liberal position, for example, a rejection of affirmative action as unfair and a favoring of gender-blind and color-blind approaches to social policy. I shall address each of these points in turn. D'souza, for example, states that affirmative action in faculty hiring and student admission policies represents a denial rather than an affirmation of equality of opportunity (D'souza and MacNeil 1992, p. 30). Such a position on affirmative action only makes sense if one assumes that the world is a true meritocracy, and that social goods are already being dispensed to individuals strictly on the basis of their individual qualities, with no race or gender bias, for example, interfering with people's access to these goods.

As Scott (1992) points out, however, in a less than utopian "society where individuals are not equals to begin with, a policy of neutrality can only protect the already privileged group(s)" (p. 7). So long as we live in a world in which social, political, and economic structures bar certain groups of people from attaining full equality, it is reasonable to endorse affirmative action measures to counter such systemic bias. Seen in this way, affirmative action, far from undermining equality of opportunity, is rather a necessary condition for achieving it.

The notions of truth and freedom are given pride of place in much of the liberal discussion of political correctness with the understanding that they will naturally emerge from an open debate among the many differing parties. This claim will receive a more detailed discussion later in this chapter when I turn specifically to curriculum considerations, but I must point out at this time its assumption that each individual "discussant" has an equal opportunity to participate in the discussion, to be heard, and to influence the outcome of the discussion; the reality, unfortunately, is quite different. Systemic race, sex, and sexual preference biases preclude equal participation of all in the debate, without even raising the question as to whether debate is the best mechanism for generating truth and freedom. So long as racist, sexist, and homophobic slurs, for example, are not merely tolerated, but zealously protected in the name of freedom of expression, people of color, women of all colors, and gay and lesbian people will continue to be gagged in the very forum that prides itself on fostering freedom of expression.

I claimed earlier that the mistaken ignoring of the context has led to two related errors in the liberal position, namely, a rejection of affirmative action as unfair and a favoring of gender-blind and color-blind approaches to social policy. Having addressed the liberal rejection of affirmative action, I turn now to a discussion of gender and color-blindness. D'souza specifically promotes color-blindness as a mechanism for generating racial equality (D'souza and MacNeil 1992, p. 38). Like the liberal position on affirmative action, the policy to ignore race (or gender) in the allocation of social goods only makes sense on the assumption that it has already been ignored in the broader system. It is inconsistent to both acknowledge that race has indeed been paid attention to (via racism) in our social organization and to urge that it should be ignored in our dealings with people within that organization. If race, for example, had been irrelevant to the formation of social structures, then refusing to give it any credence in making social policy decisions could be a sensible decision. It is hard to argue, living on a continent that participated in the slave trade, among other atrocities, that race has been irrelevant to the formation of our social structures.

It does not follow, however, that such an argument has not been made. Bloom (1987), for example, states with what I consider unbelievable naïveté that

> contrary to fashionable opinion, universities are melting pots, no matter what may be true of the rest of society. Ethnicity is no more important a fact than tall or short, black-haired or blond. What these young people have in common infinitely outweighs what separates them. The quest for traditions and rituals proves my point and may teach something about the price paid for this homogenization. The lack of prejudice is a result of students' failing to see differences and of the gradual eradication of differences. When students talk about one another, one almost never hears them saying things that divide others into groups or kinds. They always speak about the individual. The sensitivity to national character, sometimes known as stereotyping, has disappeared (pp. 90–91).

Hand-in-hand with the view discussed earlier that students harbor no ethnic or racial prejudice against other students and that stereotyping has disappeared from the university campus goes the view that the university is a meritocracy in which black students are not as good as white students.

The basis for Bloom's belief that the university is a meritocracy can perhaps be traced to his claim that "reason cannot accommodate the claims of any kind of power whatever, and democratic society cannot accept any principle of achievement other than merit" (1987, p. 96). If we presume that reason and democracy reign supreme on the university campus, then perhaps we can at least understand Bloom's belief. It is not surprising that Bloom also rules sex out as a factor of any importance in the university. The numerous studies that attest to the importance of sex in classroom dynamics notwithstanding (French and French 1984; Spender 1981, 1982, 1984; Cline and Spender 1987), Bloom (1987) confidently states that "academically, students are comfortably unisexual; they revert to dual sexuality only for the sex act. Sex no longer has any political agenda in universities except among homosexuals, who are not yet quite satisfied with their situation" (p. 107). Bloom fails utterly to see the political parameters of noninclusive language, sexual harassment, date rape, and heterosexual privilege. Bloom notwithstanding, where people's opportunities, aspirations, self-concepts, even their language, have been shaped according to race, it makes no sense to drop cognizance of race out of the formula governing allocation of social goods. In other words, at this juncture of our racist history, it is too late to ignore race. Of course, if the case can be made for specific contexts that have evolved free of any considerations of race, then an argument can be made for policies of color-blindness within that context, on the grounds that where color really does not make a difference, ignoring it is a sensible option.

If we close our eyes to color, we also close our eyes to the systemic structures of racism; a color-sensitive rather than a color-blind approach is required to allow us to take account of racism as a structural impediment to equality. (See Wasserstrom 1979; Martin 1981a; and Houston Chapter 4, this volume for a detailed development of these concepts.) In other words, it is important to remember that in rejecting skin color as a possible basis for dealing with people, we also ignore what a history of racist imperialism has meant for people of color.

The third mistaken assumption of the liberal position is that although reform measures and policies, such as guidelines for nonracist language and affirmative action in hiring, are highly political and hence suspect in an academic institution, the status quo is apolitical and hence suited to institutions of "higher learning." Schmidt (1991) captures this assumption when he states that society is denouncing those who "use their academic positions to indoctrinate students in bizarre ideologies" (p. 45). But we need to ask who gets to decide what is bizarre. If a feminist view is perceived as bizarre, how should we perceive a male chauvinist view? It seems self-evident that if feminism, for example, represents a political stance, so too does patriarchy. Conservatism is as deeply based in ideology as any of the more radical stances are. It is true that supporting hiring quotas involves taking a side on a much politicized issue, but not supporting hiring quotas is as deeply political as supporting them.

D'souza maintains that special interest courses endorse separatism and segregation rather than integration, on which liberal education should be focused (D'souza and MacNeil 1992, p. 30). Again, however, we must ask why courses that offer, for example, a feminist interpretation of events are any more conducive to separatism and segregation than more traditional courses that offer a patriarchal interpretation of events. Furthermore, what makes a feminist course a special interest course, whereas a traditionally male-oriented course is considered generally applicable to all students? And why should black studies entail separatism and segregation? Why shouldn't black studies, rather, be included in everyone's curriculum so that all students attain a broader, deeper, and more critical understanding of their history? As Van de Wetering (1991) states, "Multiculturalism is . . . an acknowledgement, not an invention, of who we are" (p. 102).

As we have seen in our earlier discussion, proponents of the liberal position claim that merit ought to be the only factor taken into consideration in student admissions and faculty hirings, with no apparent realization that people's concepts of merit vary widely, and the particular concept of merit selected as a student admissions criterion, for example, will be consistent with the political views of its proponents. Two years ago my faculty made a decision to consider work experience, in addition to academic records, in selecting student applicants for admission. This was not a decision to move away from merit as the sole criterion of admission, but a decision to broaden the concept of merit so as to include both academic grades and work experience.

Not everyone agreed with this particular expansion of the concept of merit, of course, and not everyone who supported it did so on academic grounds. Some argued, for example, that we needed to include experience in our admissions policy because there was intense pressure from the school boards to do so, and to ignore this pressure would be to risk these boards' refusal to hire our students. It is also important to point out that not all supporters of the grades-only admissions policy based their support in academic considerations. An efficiency argument for this policy was voiced by some faculty members, who claimed that decisions based strictly on grades could be made quickly and easily, with significant saving of faculty and staff time; some voiced a legalistic addendum to this efficiency argument—justification of student rejections based simply on grades would be a straightforward matter, unlike justification of student rejections based on their work experience, which could be very messy and involve the faculty in appeals and law suits that they might well lose.

There is significant overlap between this third assumption of the liberal position and issues surrounding the multicultural curriculum; I turn now to a discussion of the multicultural curriculum.

Curriculum Justification, Liberal Education, and Political Correctness—Some Misunderstandings

Of the three standard theories of curriculum justification—the transmission of knowledge theory, the student-centered theory, and the social reform theory (see Milburn 1977, pp. 192–198, for a succinct discussion of these three theories)—it is strictly the transmission of knowledge theory that is presupposed by what I have characterized as the liberal approach to political correctness. The liberal theorists assume, without discussion, that transmission of knowledge is what our schools—at least our universities—ought to be about. Although one might argue that the second of these three theories, the student-centered theory, which focuses on the self-actualization and development, both affective and intellectual, of the students themselves, is more suited to a justification of a primary rather than a tertiary curriculum, the liberal theorists have not advanced any such argument. The most D'souza offers is a snide dismissal of a student-centered curriculum. In a chapter section entitled "Profiles in Cowardice," D'souza (1991) quotes disparagingly a critic of Bloom who claimed that "the purpose of liberal education was to 'address the need for students to develop both a private self and a public self, and to find a way to have those selves converse with each other'" (p. 246). Nor have the liberal theorists put forward any argument against the third theory, that of social reform, which is far less easily dismissed as an underlying rationale for the university curriculum. The liberal theorists simply *assume* that the function of the university curriculum is the transmission of knowledge to its students. (See, for example, Bloom 1987, p. 341.) These theorists are so single (narrow?) minded about the overall purpose of education that their position gives the impression of backlash against alternative accounts. John A. Howard (1991) makes a somewhat similar point when he refers to these theorists as "altogether intolerant of a different view of educational purpose" (p. 757).

Equally worrisome are the liberal theorists who assume without question that the traditional male Eurocentric curriculum constitutes precisely the knowledge that the universities should transmit to their students. Throughout the entirety of their books, for example, both Bloom (1987) and D'souza (1991) use language that excludes females. Undoubtedly, these authors would view any admonition to use neutral (i.e., *they*) or specifically inclusive (i.e., *she or he*) pronouns as an infringement upon their freedom of expression. They probably also believe, in spite of overwhelming empirical evidence to the contrary (Eberhart 1976; Graham 1973; Hamilton 1985, 1988a, 1988b; Harrison 1975; Harrison and Passero 1975; Henley 1989, Hyde 1984; MacKay 1980a, 1980b, 1983; MacKay and Fulkerson 1979; Martyna 1978, 1983; Moulton, Robinson, and Elias 1978; Schneider and Hacker 1973; Shepelak, Ogden, and Tobin-Bennett 1984; Sniezek and Jazwinski 1986; Switzer 1990; Tittle, McCarthy, and Steckler 1974; Wilson 1978; Wilson and Ng 1988) that females are in fact fully included in their pseudo-generic terms *he* and *man*.

Bloom (1987) also speaks of "the moral unity of learning" and "the goodness of science" (p. 356), adding that "our way of life is utterly dependent on the natural scientists, and they have more than fulfilled their every promise" (p. 356). Challenges occur only at the margin according to Bloom, in the raising of such issues as the application of science to the production of nuclear weapons, but these are merely peripheral, for in science "in general . . . all is well" (p. 356). Even though the professional schools are lacking insofar as they fail to emphasize a liberal education, according to Bloom (p. 370).

The liberal theorists never address the social and political implications of the whole process of defining knowledge. They ignore totally June Jordan's (1992) questions: "And who shall decide what these many peoples of America shall know or not know? And what does that question underscore besides the political nature of knowledge?" (p. 23) According to Bloom (1987):

> The real community of man . . . is the community of those who seek the truth. . . . But in fact this includes only a few, the true friends, as Plato was to Aristotle at the very moment they were disagreeing about the nature of the good. Their common concern for the good linked them; their disagreement about it proved they needed one another to understand it . . . this, according to Plato, is the only real friendship, the only real common good. It is here that the contact people so desperately seek is to be found. The other kinds of relatedness are only imper-

fect reflections of this one trying to be self-subsisting, gaining their only justification from their ultimate relation to this one (p. 381).

Bloom (1987) neglects to point out that one possible reason why this "real community of man . . . includes only a few" (p. 381) is that the many were performing the forms of supportive labor required for even a few to indulge in careers devoted to "disagreeing about the nature of the good" (p. 381). Although a host of well-known, little-known, and totally unknown intellectuals have spent their lives enmeshed in such disagreement, countless others, whether through choice or not, have spent their lives raising children, growing crops, preparing food, tending the sick, and disposing of garbage. It is these other lives that have made it possible for a privileged few to attain the leisure to seek and disagree about the nature of the truth.

The oddness of identifying as "the common good" (Bloom 1987, p. 381) something that "includes only a few" (p. 381) apparently does not occur to Bloom; nor does he anywhere indicate that the identification of the common good with the search for and disagreement about truth rather than, for example, good health or adequate food for all is a value judgment, and a contentious one at that.

Equally worrisome is Bloom's (1987) failure to challenge the primacy of the impersonal relationship among truth-seekers, which he attributes to Plato. Why does this relationship have primacy over the parent-child relationship. Who is it exactly "who so desperately seek" (p. 381) this contact rather than other forms of relationships? Would it be unfair to answer, "Perhaps those incapable of what is more usually perceived as an intimate or a caring relationship"? (For an extended discussion of this perspective, see Roe 1952, 1956; Ayim 1992, pp. 9–11; Shakeshaft 1987.) It is interesting to speculate on whether scientific, philosophic, and educational traditions would have been radically different had the relevant scholars chosen their areas of research because of a "liking for and interest in people" (Shakeshaft 1987, p. 173) rather than the politically headier passion for seeking "the truth . . . [and] the nature of the good" (Bloom 1987, p. 381).

At any rate, the liberal theorists have assumed without question the rightful place of the traditional male Eurocentric perspective in the center of the university curriculum. It is therefore not surprising that alternative perspectives, such as those found in a multicultural curriculum, receive little sympathy. Roger Draper (1992), for example, claims that "for a generation now, we have been living in this country with a conservative ascendancy. Multiculturalism, despite its radical pretensions, has strongly promoted that ascendancy. It is a part of the problem, not a part of the solution" (p. 17).

D'souza correctly urges that the multicultural curriculum should be, and often is not, studied critically (D'souza and MacNeil 1992, p. 31). The same point is made by Konstantin Kolenda (1991, p. 40). I am in agreement with this important point—if multiculturalism is to be part of the university (or secondary school, or even elementary school, for that matter) curriculum, then it must be studied within a critical context. However, the same admonition applies to the traditional mainstream curriculum, from which any form of critical analysis has often been abysmally absent. For example, the sexist and racist outrages of Canadian history were never made apparent to me and never discussed in my formal schooling, which stretched from elementary school through to university.

Critics are eager to point out that young girls standardly undergo genital mutilation in certain African countries—D'souza (1991), for example, generalizing to all of Africa, advises us that "authentic African virtues such as spiritual depth and freedom from materialism must be balanced against human sacrifice, tribal warfare, executions, female circumcision, infanticide, and primitive medicine" (p. 121). Such critics seldom mention that clitorectomies are commonly performed on females in Canadian psychiatric institutions, as a "corrective" measure for masturbation, that the tribal warfare in Ireland is as long-lasting as any in Africa, and that political executions in Bosnia have become "run-of-the-mill" occurrences.

Two of the arguments employed by the liberal theorists against "censorship regulations outlawing racially and sexually offensive speech" (D'souza 1992, p. 30) are that regulations will erode not only free speech but academic standards as well. D'souza (1991), for example, refers to "a recent Michigan gag rule prohibiting racially stigmatizing speech against minorities" (p. 129). Those who are inclined to use racially stigmatizing speech are described as being gagged by antiracist speech legislation; there is no sense in D'souza's discussion of how black or native people, for example, are gagged by racist language. As discussed previously, it is imperative that we ask whose freedom of speech is being considered. As for the preservation of academic standards, it is far from apparent that sexually and racially offensive language stand as paradigms of academic rigor. In fact, although the liberal theorists appeal to a historical notion of liberal education as a justification for many of their educational ideas, their justification of racist and sexist language violates one of the most prominent contemporary accounts of liberal education—that of R. S. Peters.

In his spelling out of the criteria for the educational ideal, Peters (1965) stipulates that "something of value should be passed on" (p. 92). For education to have occurred, "some change for the better" (p. 91) must have occurred in the student's state of mind. Although Peters does not raise this point, I suggest that the transmission of racist and sexist ideologies violates this requirement, hence providing a strong *educational* reason for justifying a curriculum that promotes an egalitarian ideology.

In addition, Peters maintains that the educational ideal rules out any procedures of transmission in which the students' engagement in the educational enterprise lacks voluntariness or wittingness (p. 96). Although Peters was concerned to rule out conditioning and indoctrination as true forms of education, I believe this requirement also eliminates from the educational realm classrooms where the students unwittingly participate in, for example, a white supremacist ideology. Of course, the unwitting participation of students in a black supremacist ideology would equally be disqualified as education, but in our present historical context, the likelihood of unwitting participation in a black supremacist ideology seems far more remote.

The same point can be made about sex. Classrooms where students unwittingly participate in a male or female supremacist ideology would fail one of R. S. Peters's educational requirements. At the present moment in time, it is hard to imagine the unwitting participation of students in a female supremacist ideology—empirical research makes it clear that when females, who constitute one-half the student number, receive even one-third of a teacher's attention, male students are perceived as being cheated of their fair share of the teacher's attention (Cline and Spender 1987; French and French 1984; Spender 1982).

Conclusion

I have argued in this chapter that the debate surrounding political correctness is hampered by some fundamental misunderstandings; I have attempted to elucidate three of the issues contributing to the misunderstanding: first, the absence of any distinction between levels of speech, which would have both permitted a general endorsement of free speech and discouraged or even prohibited speech and other behavior harmful to others; second, the limitation of all harms to the specific and individual, with no attention to historical and contextual grounding, resulting in the inability to understand the impact of systemic harms and the necessity of systemic solutions to some sorts of harm; third, a politicizing of reform measures and policies, such as guidelines for nonracist language and affirmative action in hiring, together with an overall neglect of the political nature of the status quo. I have attempted as well to show that the liberal theorists' views on the multicultural curriculum admit only one of several justifications of the curriculum, and that they have interpreted even this justification too narrowly.

One of the deepest misunderstandings to emerge from the debate on political correctness is the reduction of serious moral considerations to matters of mere etiquette. D'souza (1991) and Hentoff (1992) claim, as we have seen, that racist and sexist language may be rude, but even rude language must be protected by a right to freedom of expression. I have argued against the equation of racist, sexist language with rudeness, urging instead, as Van de Wetering (1991) does, that racism can be neither understood nor corrected in a vacuum, but must be seen in its full (and dreadful) historical context. Against such a context, racist and sexist language is not simply rude, but is morally and educationally problematic. Were racist and sexist language as trivial as the liberal theorists would have us believe, it would be difficult to understand their resistance to reform and the thousands of pages of print that they have produced to shield those who engage in such language.

Issues of racism and sexism in language are not simply matters of *political correctness;* they are, however, deeply political and, like the concepts of intelligence and knowledge, will go a long way toward determining the allocation of privilege, dignity, and even human worth. Those who have traditionally defined such concepts have wielded an enormous power, for we all have a stake in which particular definitions gain acceptance as correct. If we want, like Charles Sanders Peirce (1931–1958), to insist that scholarship "not block the way of inquiry" (p. 56, vol. 1, paragraph 1.135) on such important issues, we must begin by not reducing them to matters of etiquette, but by acknowledging their profound impact on all of us.

Notes

1. I use the term "liberal" because of the emphasis these writers place on the traditional liberal ideal of freedom of expression and academic freedom, as well as their attempt to use the work of John Stuart Mill as justification for their position. In retrospect, I think that "pseudo-liberal" would have been a better term and "neo-conservative" better yet.

References

Acker, S. (1993). Women and other academics. *Women's Studies International Forum,*
   6(2), 191–201.
Agonito, R. (Ed.). (1977). *History of ideas on woman: A source book.* New York: G. P.
   Putnam's Sons.
Ahmad, F. (1994). How do you identify? *Canadian Women's Studies: les cahiers de la*
   femme, 14(2), 29–30.
Aisenberg, N., and M. Harrington. (1988). *Women of academe: Outsiders in the sacred*
   grove. Amherst, MA: University of Massachusetts Press.
Alcoff, L. (1988). Cultural feminism versus post-structuralism: The identity crisis in
   feminist theory. In E. Minnich, J. Barr, and R. Rosenfeld (Eds.), *Reconstructing the*
   academy. Chicago: University of Chicago Press.
Allen, J. (1986). *Lesbian philosophy: Explorations.* Palo Alto, CA: Institute of Lesbian
   Studies.
American Association of University Women. (1992). *How schools shortchange girls.*
   Washington, DC: American Association of University Women Educational
   Foundation: National Education Association.
Anzaldua, G. (1987). La conciencia de la mestiza: Towards a new consciousness.
   Borderlands: La Frontera. San Francisco: Aunt Lute Books.
Anzaldua, G. (Ed.). (1990). *Making face: Making soul—Haciendo caras: Creative and crit-*
   ical perspectives by women of color. San Francisco: Aunt Lute Books.
Aquinas, T. ([1266–1272] 1973). On the first man. From *Summa Theologica.* Question
   92, Reply to Objection 2. From *Basic Writings of Saint Thomas Aquinas,* Ed., A.
   Pegis. New York: Random House. Included in Mahowald (1983).
Aristotle. *Politics,* Book I. Trans. Benjamin Jowett. (1885). Oxford: Clarendon Press.
   Cited in Mahowald (1983).
Ascher, C., L. DeSalvo, and S. Ruddick. (Eds.). (1984). *Between women.* Boston:
   Beacon Press.
Association of American Colleges. (1982). *The classroom climate: A chilly one for women?*
   Washington, DC: Association of American Colleges.
Atwood, M. (1982). *Second words.* Boston: Beacon Press.
Auel, J. M. (1980). *The clan of the cave bear.* New York: Crown.
Auerbach, J., L. Blum, V. Smith, and C. Williams. (1985). Commentary on Gilligan's
   "In a Different Voice." *Feminist Studies, 11*(1).
Axelrod, R. (1984). *The evolution of cooperation.* New York: Basic Books.
Ayim, M. (1982). Wet sponges and bandaids: A gender analysis of speech patterns.
   Semiotics 1982, Proceedings of the Seventh Annual Meeting of the Semiotics
   Society of America. Bloomington, IN: Semiotics Society of America.
———. (1986). Wet sponges and band-aids: A gender analysis of speech patterns. In
   G. Nemiroff (Ed.), *Women and men: Interdisciplinary readings on gender* (pp.
   418–430). Toronto, ON: Fitzhenry and Whiteside.

215

———. (1988). Violence and domination as metaphors in academic discourse. In T. Govier (Ed.), *Selected issues in logic and communication.* Belmont, CA: Wadsorth.

———. (1992). Dominance and violence in scientific discourse: A portrait of the scientist as a young man. In C. Peden and J. K. Roth (Eds.), *Rights, justice, and community* (pp. 9–23). Lewiston/Queenston/Lampeter: The Edwin Mellen Press.

Ayim, M., and B. Houston. (1982). A conceptual analysis of sexism and sexist education. In D. Cochrane and M. Schiralli (Eds.), *Philosophy of education: Canadian perspectives* (pp. 145–170). Don Mills, ON: Collier Macmillan.

Ayim, M., and B. Houston. (1985). The epistemology of gender identity: Implications for social policy. *Social Theory and Practice, 11*(1), 25–59.

Backhouse, C., R. Harris, G. Michell, and A. Wylie. (1989). The chilly climate for faculty women at the University of Western Ontario: Postscript to the Backhouse Report. London, ON: University of Western Ontario.

Baier, A. (1985). What do women want in a moral theory? *Nous, 19*(1), 53–63.

———. (1986). Trust and antitrust. *Ethics, 96*(2), 231–260.

Baker, R. (1975). "Pricks" and "chicks": A plea for "persons." In R. Baker and F. Elliston (Eds.), *Philosophy and sex* (pp. 45–64). Buffalo, NY: Prometheus Books.

Bandura, A., and R. H. Walters. (1963). *Social learning and personality development.* New York: Holt, Rinehart, and Winston.

Banks, J. (1991). A curriculum for empowerment, action and change. In C. E. Sleeter (Ed.), *Empowerment through multicultural education* (pp. 125–142). Albany, NY: State University of New York Press.

Banks, J. A., and C. A. M. Banks. (1989). *Multicultural education: Issues and perspectives,* Boston: Allyn and Bacon.

Bannerji, H., L. Carty, K. Dehli, S. Heald, and K. McKenna. (1991). *Unsettling relations: The university as a site of feminist struggle.* Toronto, ON: The Women's Press.

Bardwick, J. M., and E. Douvan. (1971). Ambivalence: The socialization of women. In V. Gornick and B. K. Moran (Eds.), *Women in sexist society: Studies in power and powerlessness* (pp. 225–241). New York: Basic Books.

Barker-Benfield, G. J. (1976). *The horrors of the half-known life: Male attitudes towards women and sexuality in 19th century America.* New York: Harper and Row.

Bartky, S. (1990). *Femininity and domination.* New York: Routledge.

Barton, L., R. Meighan, and S. Walker (Eds.). (1980). *Schooling, ideology and the curriculum.* Sussex, Eng.: The Falmer Press.

Bazin, N. T., and A. Freeman. (1974). The androgynous vision. *Women's Studies, 2*(2), 186.

Beardsley, E. (1967). Referential genderization. In C. C. Gould and M. Wartofsky (Eds.), *Women in philosophy* (pp. 285–293). New York: G. P. Putnam Sons.

Beauvoir, S. d. (1952). *The second sex.* Trans. H. M. Parshley. New York: Alfred A. Knopf.

Belenky, M. F., B. M. Clinchy, N. R. Goldberger, and J. Tarule. (1986). *Women's ways of knowing.* New York: Basic Books.

Bem, S. L. (1976). Probing the promise of androgyny. In A. G. Kaplan and J. Bean (Eds.), *Beyond sex role stereotypes: Readings toward a psychology of androgyny* (pp. 47–62). Boston: Little, Brown and Co.

Benhabib, S. (1992). *Situating the self.* New York: Routledge.

Benhabib, S., and D. Cornell (Eds.). (1987). *Feminism as critique.* Minneapolis: University of Minnesota Press.

Bennett, W. (1988). *Our children and our country.* New York: Simon and Schuster.

Bernstein, B. (1971). *Class, codes, and control.* vol. 1. London, Eng.: Routledge and Kegan Paul.

———. (1977). *Class, codes, and control.* vol. 3. London, Eng.: Routledge and Kegan Paul.

Bishop, S., and M. Weinzweig (Eds.). (1979). *Philosophy and women.* Belmont, CA: Wadsworth.

Black, N. (1989). Man is the measure. In C. Filteau (Ed.), *Proceedings of a Conference on Women in Graduate Studies in Ontario.* Toronto, ON: Ontario Council on Graduate Studies.

Blair, L. L. (1979, November/December). Implementing Title IX: Concerns of undergraduate physical education majors. *Journal of Physical Education and Recreation,* 438.

Block, J. H. (1976). Conceptions of sex role: Some cross-cultural and longitudinal perspectives. In A. G. Kaplan and J. Bean (Eds.), *Beyond sex role stereotypes: Readings toward a psychology of androgyny.* Boston: Little, Brown and Co.

Bloom, A. (1987). *The closing of the American mind: How higher education has failed democracy and impoverished the souls of today's students.* New York: Simon and Schuster.

Blum, L., M. Homiak, J. Housman, and N. Scheman. (1976). Altruism and women's oppression. In C. C. Gould and M. W. Wartofsky (Eds.), *Women and philosophy: Toward a theory of liberation.* New York: G. P. Putnam's Sons.

Bourdieu, P. (1971). Systems of education and systems of thought. In M. F. D. Young (Ed.), *Knowledge and control.* New York: Collier-Macmillan.

———. (1973). Cultural reproduction and social reproduction. In R. Brown (Ed.), *Knowledge, education, and cultural change.* London, Eng.: Tavistock.

———. (1977). *Outline of a theory of practice.* London, Eng.: Cambridge University Press.

Bourdieu, P., and J. Passeron. (1990). *Reproduction: In education, society, and culture.* London, Eng.: Sage.

Bowles, S., and H. Gintis. (1976). *Schooling in capitalist America.* New York: Basic Books.

Boxill, B. (1980). Sexual blindness and sexual equality. *Social Theory and Practice, 6,* 281–299.

Brant, B. (1993). The good red road: Journeys of homecoming in Native women's writing. *And still we rise: Feminist political mobilizing in contemporary Canada.* Toronto, ON: The Women's Press.

Brewer, R. M. (1993). Theorizing race, class and gender: The new scholarship of black feminist intellectuals and black women's labor. In S. M. James and P. A. Busia (Eds.), *Theorizing black feminisms: The visionary pragmatism of black women* (pp. 13–30). New York: Routledge.

Briskin, L. (1990). *Feminist pedagogy: Teaching and learning liberation.* Ottawa, ON: Canadian Research Institute for the Advancement of Women.

Bronowski, J. (1968). Science in the new humanism. *The Science Teacher,* p. 14. Reprinted in Easlea (1985).

———. (1973). *The ascent of man.* Boston: Little, Brown and Co.

Broughton, J. (1983). Women's rationality and men's virtues. *Social Research, 50*(3), 597–642.

Broverman, I. K., D. M. Broverman, F. E. Clarkson, P. S. Rosencrantz, and S. R. Vogel. (1970). Sex role stereotypes and clinical judgments of mental health. *Journal of Consulting and Clinical Psychology, 34*(1), 1–7.

Buber, M. (1947) *Between man and man.* Trans. R. G. Smith. London, Eng.: Collins, The Fontana Library.

Burbules, N. (1986). A theory of power in education. *Educational Theory, 36*(2), 95–114.

Butler, J. (1985). Toward a pedagogy of Everywoman's Studies. In M. Culley and C. Portuges. *Gendered subjects: The dynamics of feminist teaching.* New York: Routledge and Kegan Paul.

———. (1987). Variations on sex and gender: Beauvoir, Witting and Foucault. In S. Benhabib and D. Cornell (Eds.), *Feminism as critique.* Minneapolis: University of Minnesota Press.

———. (1989). Transforming the curriculum: Teaching about women of color. In J. A. Banks and C. A. M. Banks. *Multicultural education: Issues and perspectives* (pp. 145–164). Boston: Allyn and Bacon.

———. (1990). *Gender trouble.* New York: Routledge.

———. (1994). *Bodies that matter: On the discursive limits of "sex."* New York: Routledge.

Byrne, E. M. (1978). *Women and education.* London, Eng.: Tavistock.

Cammaert, L. (1985). How widespread is sexual harassment on campus? *International Journal of Women's Studies 8*(4), 388–397.

Camper, C. (Ed.). (1994). *Miscegenation blues: Voices of mixed race women.* Toronto, ON: Sister Vision Press.

Canadian Women's Studies, 12(3). (1992). Special Title: *Gender equity and institutional change.* Educational equity, submitted by the Ontario Confederation of University Faculty Associations, 99–102.

Cannon, L. W. (1990). Fostering positive race, class, and gender dynamics in the classroom. *Women's Studies Quarterly.* Topic: Curricular and Institutional Change, vols. 1 and 2, 126.

Caplan, P. (1992). *Lifting a ton of feathers: A woman's guide to surviving in the academic world.* Toronto, ON: University of Toronto Press.

Card, C. (1985). Virtues and moral luck. Unpublished manuscript. Working Papers Series I, No. 4, Institute for Legal Studies, University of Wisconsin Law School.

———. (1991). *Feminist ethics.* Lawrence, KS: University of Kansas Press.

Carmichael, C. (1977). *Non-sexist childraising.* Boston: Beacon Press.

Carty, L. (1991). Black women in academe: A statement from the periphery. In H. Bannerji, L. Carty, K. Delhi, S. Heald, and K. McKenna. *Unsettling relations: The university as a site of feminist struggles.* Toronto, ON: Women's Press.

Chesler, P. (1972). *Women and madness.* New York: Doubleday.

Chodorow, N. (1978). *The reproduction of mothering: Psychoanalysis and the sociology of gender.* Berkeley: University of California Press.

Clark, J. et al. (1989). *Summary of women's needs assessment survey: Women's views of their experiences as students at Princeton University.* Princeton: Princeton University.

Clark, M. (1989). *The great divide.* Canberra, Australia: Curriculum Development Centre.

Clarke, C. (1993). Living the texts *out*: Lesbians and the uses of black women's traditions. In S. M. James and P. A. Busia (Eds.), *Theorizing black feminisms: The visionary pragmatism of black women* (pp. 214–227). New York: Routledge.

Clausen, J. (Ed.). (1968). Perspectives on childhood socialization. *Socialization and society*. Boston: Little, Brown and Co.

Cleverdon, C. (1974). *The woman suffrage movement in Canada*. Toronto, ON: University of Ontario Press.

Cline, S., and D. Spender. (1987). *Reflecting men at twice their natural size*. London, Eng.: Andre Deutch Ltd.

Cobb, R., and P. Lepley (Eds.). (1973). *Contemporary philosophies of physical education and athletics*. Columbus, OH: Merrill.

Cochrane, J., A. Hoffman, and P. Kincaid. (1977). *Women in Canadian sports*. Toronto, ON: Fitzhenry and Whiteside.

Cole, S. G. (1995). Jane Rule: Rule's realm. *NOW Magazine*. Toronto, ON: NOW Communications.

Collins, P. H. (1990). *Black feminist thought: Knowledge, consciousness, and the politics of empowerment*. New York: Routledge.

Connell, R. W., R. W. Ashenden, D. J. Kessler, and G. W. Dowsett. (1982). *Making the difference*. Boston: George Allen and Unwin.

Constantinople, A. (1976). Masculinity-femininity: An exception to a famous dictum. In A. G. Kaplan and J. Bean (Eds.), *Beyond sex role stereotypes: Readings toward a psychology of androgyny* (pp. 48–62). Boston: Little, Brown and Co.

Cook, R., and C. Brown. (1976). *Canada: A nation transformed*. Toronto, ON: McClelland and Stewart.

Cornell, D., and A. Thurschwell. (1987). Feminism, negativity, and intersubjectivity. In S. Benhabib and D. Cornell (Eds.), *Feminism as critique*. Minneapolis: University of Minnesota Press.

Courtenay-Hall, P. (1992). From justified discrimination to responsive hiring: The role model argument and female equity hiring in philosophy. In W. Cragg (Ed.), *Contemporary moral issues* (3rd edition). Toronto, ON: McGraw-Hill Rynerson. Revised and reprinted in D. Shogan (Ed.), *A reader in feminist ethics*. Toronto, ON: Canadian Scholars Press.

Culley, M. (1985). Anger and authority in the introductory Women's Studies classroom. In M. Culley and C. Portuges, *Gendered subjects: The dynamics of feminist teaching*.

Culley, M., A. Diamond, L. Edwards, S. Lennow, and C. Portuges. (1985). The politics of nurturance. In M. Culley and C. Portuges (Eds.), *Gendered subjects: The dynamics of feminist teaching*. New York: Routledge and Kegan Paul.

Culley, M., and C. Portuges (Eds.). (1985). *Gendered subjects: The dynamics of feminist teaching*. Boston: Routledge.

Dagg, A. I., and P. Thompson. (1988). *MisEducation: Women and Canadian universities*. Toronto, ON: Institute for Studies in Education Press.

Daly, M. (1973). *Beyond God the father: Toward a philosophy of women's liberation*. Boston: Beacon Press.

Danziger, K. (1971). *Socialization*. Harmondsworth, Eng.: Penguin Books.

Darwin, C. (1874). *The descent of man* (2nd edition), revised. Part 3, Ch. 19. London, Eng.: John Murray. Included in Agonito (1977).

David, D., and R. Brammer. (1976). *The forty-nine percent majority.* Lexington, MA: Addison Wesley.

Davies, B. (1989). Education and sexism: A theoretical analysis of the sex/gender bias in education. *Educational Philosophy and Theory, 21*(1), 1–19.

Davis, D. L. (1972). The woman in the moon: Prolegomenas for women's studies. In R. L. Siporin (Ed.), *Female Studies V: Proceedings of the Conference—Women and Education: A Feminist Perspective.* Pittsburgh: Know.

Day, D. (1990). *Survey of 1600 adolescent girls in Nova Scotia.* Halifax, NS: Nova Scotia Advisory Council on the Status of Women.

Delamont, S. (1980). *Sex roles and the school.* London, Eng.: Methuen.

Delpit, L. C. (1988). The silenced dialogue: Power and pedagogy in educating other people's children. *Harvard Educational Review, 58*(3), 280–298.

Diller, A. (1984). The virtues of *Philia* and justice: Who learns these in our society? *Philosophy of Education 1984: Proceedings of the Philosophy of Education Society.* Normal, IL: Philosophy of Education Society.

———. (1992). Pluralisms for education: An ethics of care perspective. In H. Alexander (Ed.), *Philosophy of Education 1992: Proceedings of the Philosophy of Education Society.* Normal, IL: Philosophy of Education Society.

Diller, A., and B. Houston. (1983). Women's physical education: A gender-sensitive perspective. In B. C. Postow (Ed.), *Women, philosophy, and sport: A collection of new essays.* Metuchen, NJ: Scarecrow Press. Revised for Chapter 14, this volume.

Dinnerstein, D. (1978). *The mermaid and the minotaur.* New York: Harper and Row.

Draper, R. (1992). Writers and writing: P. C. pipe dreams. *The New Leader, 75*(5), 16–17.

D'souza, D. (1991). *Illiberal education: The politics of race and sex on campus.* New York: The Free Press.

D'souza, D., and R. MacNeil. (1992). The big chill? Interview with Dinesh D'souza. In P. Berman (Ed.), *Debating P. C.: The controversy over political correctness on college campuses* (pp. 29–39). New York: Laurel, Dell Publishing.

Dziech, B. W., and L. Weiner. (1984, 1990). *The lecherous professor.* Urbana and Chicago, IL: University of Illinois Press.

Easlea, B. (1981). *Science and sexual oppression: confrontation with women and nature.* London, Eng.: Writers and Readers Publishing Coop.

———. (1985). *Fathering the unthinkable: Masculinity, scientists, and the nuclear arms race.* London, Eng.: Weidenfield and Nicholson.

Eberhart, O. M. Y. (1976). Elementary students' understanding of certain masculine and neutral generic nouns. *Dissertation Abstracts International, 37,* 4113A–4114A.

Ehrenreich, B., and D. English. (1973). *Complaints and disorders: The sexual politics of sickness.* Old Westbury, NY: Feminist Press.

———. (1978). *For her own good: 150 years of experts' advice to women.* Garden City, NJ: Doubleday Anchor Press.

Eichler, M. (1980). *The double standard: A feminist critique of feminist social sciences.* London, Eng.: Croom Helm.

———. (1988a). The elusive ideal—Defining equality. *Canadian Human Rights Yearbook, 5,* 167–188.

———. (1988b). *Non-sexist research models.* London, Eng.: Winchester and Unwin, reprinted by Routledge.

Eitzen, S. D. (Ed.). (1979). *Sport in contemporary society: An anthology*. New York: St. Martin's Press.

Elgin, S. H. (1989). Damned if we do . . . *The Women's Review of Books*, 6(8), 15–16.

Eliade, M. (1967). *Myths, dreams and mysteries*. New York: Harper and Row.

Ellsworth, E. (1989). Why doesn't this feel empowering? Working through the repressive myths of critical pedagogy? *Harvard Educational Review*, 59(3), 297–324. Reprinted in Luke and Gore (1992).

English, J. (1977). *Sex equality*. Englewood Cliffs, NJ: Prentice-Hall.

———. (1978). Sex equality in sports. *Philosophy and Public Affairs*, 7(3), 269–277.

Esland, G. M. (1971). Teaching and learning as the organization of knowledge. In M. F. D. Young (Ed.), *Knowledge and control*. New York: Collier-Macmillan.

Falk, W. D. (1970). Morality, self and others. In K. Patel and M. Schiller (Eds.), *Readings in contemporary ethical theory*. Englewood Cliffs, NJ: Prentice-Hall.

Farrel, W. (1975). *The liberated man*. New York: Bantam.

Fasteau, M. (1975). *The male machine*. New York: McGraw Hill.

Feinberg, W. (1989). A role for philosophy of education in intercultural research: A reexamination of the relativism-absolutism debate. *Philosophy of Education 1989*. Normal, IL: Philosophy of Education Society.

Filteau, C. (Ed.). (1989). *Proceedings of a conference on women in graduate studies in Ontario*. Toronto, ON: Ontario Council on Graduate Studies.

Finn, G. (1982). On the oppression of women in philosophy—Or, whatever happened to objectivity? In A. Miles and G. Finn (Eds.), *Feminism in Canada—From pressure to politics*. Montreal, PQ: Black Rose Books.

Finn, J., J. Reis, and L. Dulberg. (1980). Sex differences in educational attainment: The process. *Comparative Educational Review*, 24(2), Part 2, 333–352.

Fiol-Matta, L., and M. Chamberlain. (Eds.). (1994). *Women of color and the multicultural curriculum*. New York: Feminist Press.

Fischel, A., and S. J. Pottker. (Eds.). (1977). *Sex bias in the schools*. New Brunswick, NJ: Rutgers University Press.

Fisher, B. (1988). Wandering in the wilderness: The search for women role models. *Signs: Journal of Women in Culture and Society*, 13(2), 211–233.

Fishman, P. (1977, May). Interactional shitwork. *Heresies: A Feminist Publication on Art and Politics*, 99–101.

Fitzgerald, L. F., L. M. Weitzman, Y. Gold, and M. Ormerod. (1988). Academic harassment: Sex and denial in scholarly garb. *Psychology of Women Quarterly*, 12(3), 329–340.

Foucault, M. (1977). *Discipline and punish: The birth of the prison*. New York: Vintage Books.

———. (1980). *Power/knowledge: Selected interviews and other writings, 1972–1977*. New York: Pantheon.

Fowlkes, D., and C. McClure. (1984). *Feminist visions: Toward a transformation of the liberal arts curriculum*. Tuscaloosa, AL: University of Alabama Press.

Fox, E. K. (1983). Gender and science. In S. Harding and M. B. Hintikka (Eds.), *Discovering reality: Feminist perspectives on epistemology, metaphysics, methodology, and philosophy of science* (pp. 187–205). Dordrecht, Holland: D. Reidel Publishing Company.

Frankenberg, R. (1993). *White woman, race matters: The social construction of whiteness.* Minneapolis: University of Minnesota Press.

Frazier, N., and M. Sadker. (1973). *Sexism in school and society.* New York: Harper and Row.

Freeman, B. C. (1978). Female education in patriarchal power systems. In P. Altbach and J. Kelly. *Education and colonialism* (pp. 207–242). New York: Longman.

Freire, P. (1968). *Pedagogy of the oppressed.* Trans. M. Bergman Ramos. New York: Seabury Press.

———. (1973). *Education for critical consciousness.* New York: Herter and Herter.

French, J., and P. French. (1984). Sociolinguistics and gender divisions. In S. Acker, J. Megarry, S. Nisbet, and E. Hoyle (Eds.), *World yearbook of education 1984: Women and education* (pp. 52–63). New York: Kogan Page/London, Eng.: Nichols Publishing Company.

Frieze, I. et al. (1978). *Women and sex roles.* New York: Norton.

Frye, M. (1975). Male chauvinism: A conceptual analysis. In R. Baker and F. Elliston (Eds.), *Philosophy and sex* (pp. 65–79). Buffalo, NY: Prometheus Books.

———. (1983). *The politics of reality: Essays in feminist theory.* Trumansburg, NY: The Crossing Press.

Galloway, P. (1980). *What's wrong with high school English? It's sexism—un-Canadian—outdated.* Toronto, ON: Ontario Institute for Studies in Education.

Garry, A., and M. Pearsall (Eds.). (1989). *Women, knowledge and reality: Explorations in feminist philosophy.* Boston: Unwin Hyman.

Gaskell, J., and A. McLaren (Eds.). (1987). *Women and education: A Canadian perspective.* Calgary, AB: Detselig Enterprises Ltd.

Gaskell, J., A. McLaren, and M. Novogrodsky. (1989). *Claiming an education: Feminism and Canadian schools.* Toronto, ON: Garamond Press.

Gerber, E., J. Felshin, P. Berlin, and W. Wyrick. (1974). *The American woman in sport.* Reading, MA: Addison-Wesley.

Gilligan, C. (1982). *In a different voice: Psychological theories about women's development.* Cambridge, MA: Harvard University Press.

Gilligan, C., N. P. Lyons, and T. J. Hanmer (Eds.). (1990). *Making connections: The relational worlds of adolescent girls at Emma Willard School.* Cambridge, MA: Harvard University Press.

Gilligan, C., J. V. Ward, and J. M. Taylor, with B. Bardige. (1988). *Mapping the moral domain: A contribution of women's thinking to psychology and education.* Cambridge, MA: Harvard University Press.

Gilman, C. P. ([1915] 1979). *Herland.* New York: Harper.

Giroux, H. A. (1989). Schooling as a form of cultural politics: Toward a pedagogy of and for difference. In H. A. Giroux and P. McLaren (Eds.), *Critical pedagogy, the state, and cultural struggle.* Albany, NY: State University of New York.

Glasser, W. (1984). *Control theory.* New York: Harper and Row.

Goldberg, S. (1977). The inevitability of patriarchy. In M. Levin. *Sex equality* (pp. 203–204). Englewood Cliffs, NJ: Prentice-Hall.

Goldstein, E. (1979). Effect of same-sex and cross-sex role models on the subsequent academic productivity of scholars. *American Psychologist, 34,* 407–410.

Gore, J. (1990). What can we do for you! What *can* we do for you? Struggling over empowerment in critical and feminist pedagogy. *Educational Foundations, 4*(3), 5–26. Reprinted in Luke and Gore (1992).

Gornick, V., and B. Moran (Eds.). (1971). *Women in sexist society*. New York: New American Library.

Gould, C., and M. Wartofsky (Eds.). (1976). *Women and philosophy: Toward a theory of liberation*. New York: Capricorn Books.

Gould, L. (1974). *X: A fabulous child's story*. In M. Trip (Ed.), *Woman in the year 2000* (chapter 20). New York: Arbor House.

Graham, A. (1973). The making of a nonsexist dictionary. *Ms. 2*, 12–16.

Greene, M. (1988). *The dialectic of freedom*. New York: Teachers College Press.

Griffin, P. S. (1980). Developing a systematic observation instrument to identify sex role dependent and sex role independent behavior among physical education teachers. Doctoral dissertation, University of Massachusetts. *University Microfilms International*. No. 8101326.

Grimshaw, J. (1986). *Philosophy and feminist thinking*. Minneapolis: University of Minnesota Press.

Gross, B. (Ed.). (1977). *Reverse discrimination*. Buffalo, NY: Prometheus Books.

Gutmann, A. (1987). *Democratic education*. Princeton: Princeton University Press.

Hall, M. A. (1981). Sport, sex roles and sex identity, *The CRIAW Papers*. Ottawa, ON: CRIAW.

Hall, R. M., and B. R. Sandler. (1982). *The classroom climate: A chilly one for women?* Washington, DC: Project on the Status and Education of Women, Association of American Colleges.

———. (1983). *Academic mentoring for women students and faculty: A new look at an old way to get ahead*. Washington, DC: Project on the Status of Education of Women, Association of American Colleges.

———. (1986). The chilly climate revisited: Chilly for women faculty, administrators, and graduate students. Washington, DC: Project on the Status and Education of Women, Association of American Colleges.

Hamilton, M. C. (1985). Linguistic relativity and sex bias in language: Effects of the masculine "generic" on the imagery of the writer and the perceptual discrimination of the reader. *Dissertation Abstracts International, 46*, 1381B.

———. (1988a). Masculine generic terms and misperception of AIDS risk. *Journal of Applied Social Psychology, 18*(14), 1222–1240.

———. (1988b). Using masculine generics: Does generic he increase male bias in the user's imagery? *Sex Roles, 19*(11–12), 785–799.

Hanmer, J., and M Maynard (Eds.). (1987). *Women, violence, and social control*. Atlantic Highland, NJ: Humanities Press International.

Harrison, L. (1975). Cro-Magnon woman—In eclipse. *Science Teacher, 42*(4), 8–11.

Harrison, L., and R. N. Passero. (1975). Sexism in the language of elementary school textbooks. *Science and Children, 12*(4), 22–25.

Hartman, J., and E. Messer-Davidow (Eds.). (1991). *(En)Gendering knowledge: Feminists in academe*. Knoxville, TN: University of Tennessee Press.

Harvard Educational Review, *49*(4) (November 1979), and *50*(1) (February 1980).

Hegel, G. (1896). *The philosophy of right*. Trans. S. W. Dyde. Part 3, section 161–173. London, Eng.: George Bell and Sons.

Heide, W. S. (1978). Feminism for a sporting future. In C. A. Oglesby (Ed.), *Women and sport: From myth to reality* (p. 22). Philadelphia: Lea and Febiger.

Heilbrun, C. G. (1973). *Toward a recognition of androgyny*. New York: Harper and Row.

———. (1974). Recognizing the androgynous human. In R. Francoeur and A. Francoeur. *The future of sexual relations*. Englewood Cliffs, NJ: Prentice-Hall.

Held, V. (1984). *Rights and goods: Justifying social action*. New York: The Free Press.

———. (1986). Non-contractual society. Paper presented at the University of Cincinnati Twenty-third Annual Philosophy Colloquium on *Feminist Moral, Social and Legal Theory*. Cincinnati.

———. (1993). *Feminist morality: Transforming culture, society, and politics*. Chicago: University of Chicago Press.

Henley, N. M. (1977). *Body politics*. Englewood Cliffs, NJ: Prentice-Hall.

———. (1989). Molehill or mountain? What we know and don't know about sex bias in language. In M. Crawford and M. Gentry (Eds.), *Gender and thought: Psychological perspectives* (pp. 59–78). New York: Springer-Verlag.

Hentoff, N. (1992). Who's on first? Hurt feelings and free speech. *The Progressive, 56*(2), 16–17.

Hill, S. (1975). Self-determination and autonomy. In R. Wasserstrom (Ed.), *Today's moral problems* (pp. 171–186). New York: Macmillan.

Hoagland, S. L. (1986). Moral agency under oppression. *Trivia, 9*.

———. (1988). *Lesbian ethics*. Palo Alto, CA: Institute of Lesbian Studies.

Holland, D. C., and M. A. Eisenhart. (1990). *Educated in romance: Women, achievement, and college culture*. Chicago: University of Chicago Press.

hooks, bell. (1989). *Talking back: Thinking feminist, thinking black*. Boston: South End Press.

———. (1992). Theory as liberatory practice. *Yale Journal of Law and Feminism 4*(1), 1–2. Excerpted under the title Out of the academy and into the streets, *Ms. 3*(1), (July/August), 80–82.

Hosken, F. (1979). *The Hosken report: Genital and sexual mutilation on females*. Lexington, MA: WIN News.

Houston, B. (1985). Gender freedom and the subtleties of sexist education. *Educational Theory, 35*(4), 359–369.

———. (1987). Rescuing womanly virtues: Some dangers of moral reclamation. In K. Nielsen and M. Hanen (Eds.), *Science, morality and feminist theory*. Calgary, AB: University of Calgary Press. *Canadian Journal of Philosophy*, Supplementary vol. 13, 237–262.

———. (1988a). Gilligan and the politics of a distinctive women's morality. In L. Code, S. Mullett, and C. Overall (Eds.), *Feminist perspectives: Philosophical essays on methods and morals*. Toronto, ON: University of Toronto Press.

———. (1988b). Sex, gender, and identity. *Atlantis: Canadian Journal of Women's Studies 13*, 2.

———. (1989). Prolegomena to future caring. In M. Brabeck (Ed.), *Who cares? Theory, research and educational implications* (pp. 150–183). New York: Praeger Press.

Houston, B., and A. Diller. (1987). Trusting ourselves to care. *Resources for feminist research, 16*(3), 371–381. Reprinted in Shogan (1992). *Feminist ethics* (pp. 109–129).

Howard, J. A. (1991). Lifting education's iron curtain: To rebuild the civic and moral capitol. *Vital Speeches of the Day, 57*(24), 756–761.

Hrdy, S. B. (1986). Empathy, polyandry, and the myth of the coy female. In R. Bleier (Ed.), *Feminist approaches to science* (pp. 119–146). New York: Pergamon Press.

Hudson, J. (1978). Physical parameters used for female exclusion from law enforcement and athletics. In C. A. Oglesby (Ed.), *Women and sport: From myth to reality*. Philadelphia: Lea and Febiger.

Hull, G. T., P. B. Scott, and B. Smith (Eds.). (1982). *All the women are white, all the blacks are men, but some of us are brave*. Old Westbury, NY: Feminist Press.

Hyde, J. S. (1984). Children's understanding of sexist language. *Developmental Psychology, 20*(4), 697–706.

Irvine, J. (1990). *Disorders of desire: Sex and gender in modern American sexology*. Philadelphia: Temple University Press.

Jackson, P. (1968). *Life in classrooms*. New York: Holt, Rinehart, and Winston.

Jaggar, A. (1979). On sexual equality. In S. Bishop and M. Weinzweig (Eds.), *Philosophy and women* (pp. 77–87). Belmont, CA: Wadsworth.

Jaggar, A., and P. R. Struhl. (Eds.). (1978). *Feminist frameworks: Alternative theoretical accounts of the relations between women and men*. New York: McGraw Hill.

James, S. M. (1993). Mothering: A possible black feminist link to social transformation? In S. M. James and P. A. Busia (Eds.), *Theorizing black feminisms: The visionary pragmatism of black women*. New York: Routledge.

James, W. ([1899] 1958). *Talks to teachers on psychology and to students on some of life's ideals*. New York: Norton.

Jeffcoate, T. (1967). *Principles of gynecology*. London, Eng.: Butterworth.

Johnson, P. (1978). Women and interpersonal power. In I. Frieze, J. Parsons, P. Johnson, D. Ruble, and G. Zellman. *Women and sex roles: A social psychological perspective*. New York: W. W. Norton.

Jordan, J. (1980). *Passion: New Poems 1977–1980*. Boston: Beacon Press.

———. (1992). Just inside the door: Toward a manifest new destiny. *The Progressive, 56*(2), 18–23.

Julty, S. (1979). *Men's bodies, men's selves*. New York: Dell Publishing.

Kagan, J. (1964). Acquisition and significance of sex typing and role identity. In Hoffman and Hoffman (Eds.), *Review of child development research*. New York: Russell Sage Foundation.

Kant, I. (1764). *Observations on the feelings of the beautiful and the sublime*, Section 3. Trans. J. T. Goldthwait. Berkeley, CA: University of California Press (1960).

Kaplan, A. G. (1976). Androgyny as a model of mental health for women: From theory to therapy. In A. G. Kaplan and J. Bean (Eds.), *Beyond sex role stereotypes: Readings toward a psychology of androgyny*. Boston: Little, Brown and Co.

Kaplan, A. G., and J. Bean (Eds.), (1976). *Beyond sex role stereotypes: Readings toward a psychology of androgyny*. Boston: Little, Brown and Co.

Keller, E. F. (1984). *Reflections on gender and science*. New Haven: Yale University Press.

Kelly, L. (1987). The continuum of sexual violence. In J. Hanmer and M. Maynard (Eds.), *Women, violence, and social control*. Atlantic Highland, NJ: Humanities Press International.

Kennard, J. A. (1977). The history of physical education. Review Essay in *Signs: Journal of Women in Culture and Society, 2*(4), 835–842.

Kenway, J., and H. Modra. (1989). Feminist pedagogy and emancipatory possibilities. *Critical Pedagogy Networker, 2*(2 and 3). Reprinted in Luke and Gore (1992).

Ketchum, S. A. (1979). Liberalism and marriage law. In S. Bishop and M. Weinzweig (Eds.), *Philosophy and women* (pp. 184–189). Belmont, CA: Wadsworth.

Key, M. R. (1975). *Male/female language: With a comprehensive bibliography*. Metuchen, NJ: Scarecrow Press.

Kimberly-Clark Ltd. (no date). Discovering yourself. *Life Cycle Library*. Toronto, ON: Kotex Products.

Kittay, E., and D. Meyers (Eds.). (1987). *Women and moral theory*. Totowa, NJ: Rowman and Littlefield.

Klein, S. S. (1988, Spring). Using sex equity research to improve education policies. *Theory into Practice*, 152–160.

Klein, S. S. (Ed.). (1985). *Handbook for achieving sex equity through education*. Baltimore: Johns Hopkins University Press.

Kohlberg, L., C. Levine, and A. Hewar. (1983). *Moral stages: A current formulation and response to critics*. New York: Karger.

Kolenda, K. (1991). Philosopher's column: E pluribus unum. *The Humanist, 51*(5), 40–44.

Koveski, J. (1967). *Moral notions*. London, Eng.: Routledge and Kegan Paul.

Kramarae, C., and D. Spender. (1992). *The knowledge exposition: Generations of feminist scholarship*. New York: Teachers College Press.

Kramarae, C., and P. Treichler. (1992). *Amazons, bluestockings and crones, a feminist dictionary*. London, Eng.: Pandora Press.

Kramer, H., and J. Sprenger. (1971). *The Malleus Maleficarum*. Trans. with introductions, bibliography, and notes by Rev. Montague Summers. New York: Dover.

Kristeva, J. (1981). Women's time. *Signs: Journal of Women in Culture and Society, 7*(1), 13–35. Trans. A. Jardine. Reprinted in T. Moi (Ed.), *The Kristeva reader*. Oxford, Eng.: Basil Blackwell.

———. (1981). *The Kristeva reader*. Ed. T. Moi. New York: Columbia University Press.

Larkin, J. (1994). *Sexual harassment: High school girls speak out*. Toronto, ON: Second Story Press.

Lather, P. (1991). *Getting smart: Feminist research and pedagogy with/in the postmodern*. New York: Routledge.

Laurence, M. K. (1989). *Dance on Earth: A memoir*. Toronto, ON: McClelland and Stewart, Inc.

———. (1989). Role models—Importance and availability. In C. Filteau (Ed.), *Proceedings of a Conference on Women in Graduate Studies in Ontario*. Toronto, ON: Ontario Council on Graduate Studies.

Laviqueur, J. (1980). Co-education and the tradition of separate needs. In D. Spender and E. Sarah (Eds.), *Learning to lose: Sexism in education* (pp. 180–190). London, Eng.: Women's Press.

Leach, M. (1989). Reviewing the "subject(s)." *Educational Philosophy and Theory, 21*(1), 21–32.

Leach, M., and B. Davies. (1990). Crossing the boundaries: Educational thought and gender equity. *Educational Theory, 40*(3), 321–332.

Lerner, G. (1976a). New approaches to the study of women in American history. In B. A. Carroll (Ed.), *Liberating women's history: Theoretical and critical essays*. Chicago: University of Chicago Press.

———. (1976b). Placing women in history: A 1975 perspective. In B. A. Carroll (Ed.), *Liberating women's history: Theoretical and critical essays*. Chicago: University of Chicago Press.

————. (1977). *The female experience: An American documentary*. Indianapolis, IN: Bobbs-Merrill.

Levin, M. (1977). Vs. Ms. In J. English (Ed.), *Sex equality*. Englewood Cliffs, NJ: Prentice-Hall.

Lewis, M., and R. Simon. (1986). A discourse not intended for her: Learning and teaching within patriarchy. *Harvard Educational Review, 56*(4), 457–472.

Lewis, R. (Ed.). (1981). *Men in difficult times: Masculinity today and tomorrow*. Englewood Cliffs, NJ: Prentice-Hall.

Lloyd, G. (1984). The man of reason: "Male" and "female" in Western philosophy. Minneapolis: University of Minnesota Press.

Lord, A. (1984). *Sister outsider*. Trumansburg, NY: The Crossing Press.

Lowe, M. (1982). Social bodies: The interaction of culture and women's biology. In R. Hubbard, M. S. Henifin, and B. Fried (Eds.), *Biological woman: The convenient myth*. Cambridge, MA: Schenkman Publishing.

Lucas, J. R. (1977). Against equality again. *Philosophy: The Journal of the Royal Institute of Philosophy, 52*(201), 255–280.

Lugones, M. (1989). Playfulness, world-travelling, and loving perception. *Hypatia, 2*(2), 3–19. Reprinted in Garry and Pearsall (1989).

————. (1991). On the logic of pluralist feminism. In C. Card (Ed.), *Feminist ethics*. Lawrence, KS: University of Kansas Press.

Lugones, M. C., and E. V. Spelman. ([1983] 1986). Have we got a theory for you! Feminist theory, cultural imperialism and the demand for the woman's voice. *Women's Studies International Forum 6*(6). Reprinted in *Women and values: Readings in recent feminist philosophy* (pp. 19–31). Belmont, CA: Wadsworth.

Luke, C., and J. Gore (Eds.). (1992). *Feminisms and critical pedagogy*. New York: Routledge.

Maccoby, E. (Ed.). (1966). Sex differences in intellectual functioning. *The development of sex differences* (pp. 25–55). Stanford: Stanford University Press.

MacDonald, M. (1980). Schooling and the reproduction of class and gender relations. In L. Barton, R. Meighan, and S. Walker (Eds.), *Schooling, ideology and the curriculum*. Sussex, Eng.: The Falmer Press.

MacKay, D. G. (1980a). Language, thought and social attitudes. In H. Giles, W. P. Robinson, and P. M. Smith (Eds.), *Language: Social psychological perspectives; selected papers from the first international conference on social psychology and language held at the University of Bristol, England* (pp. 89–96). Oxford, Eng.: Pergamon Press.

————. (1980b). Psychology, prescriptive grammar and the pronoun problem. *American Psychologist, 35*(5), 444–449.

————. (1983). Prescriptive grammar and the pronoun problem. In B. Thorne, C. Kramarae, and N. Henley (Eds.), *Language, gender, and society* (pp. 38–53). Rowley, MA: Newbury House.

MacKay, D. G., and D. C. Fulkerson. (1979). On the comprehension and production of pronouns. *Journal of Verbal Learning and Verbal Behavior, 18*(6), 661–673.

MacKinnon, C. (1982). Feminism, Marxism, method and the state: An agenda for theory. *Signs: Journal of Women in Culture and Society, 7*(3), 515–544.

————. (1987). Difference and dominance: On sex discrimination. *Feminism unmodified*. Cambridge, MA: Harvard University Press.

————. (1989). *Equality rights*. Ottawa, ON: Ontario Canadian Council on Social Development.

Mahoney, P. (1983). How Alice's chin really came to be pressed against her foot: Sexist processes of interaction in mixed-sex classrooms. *Women's Studies International Forum, 6*(1), 107–115.

———. (1985). *Schools for the boys? Co-education reassessed.* London, Eng.: Hutchinson Publishing Group.

Mahowald, M. (1983). *Philosophy of woman: An anthropology of classic and current concepts* (2nd ed.). Indianapolis, IN: Hackett Publishing.

Mahtani, M. (1994). Polarity versus plurality: Confessions of an ambivalent woman of colour. *Canadian Woman Studies: les cahiers de la femme, 14*(2), 14–18.

Mainardi, P. (1978). The politics of housework. In A. M. Jaggar and P. R. Struhl (Eds.), *Feminist frameworks: Alternative theoretical accounts of the relations between women and men.* New York: McGraw Hill.

Majaj, L. S. (1994). Boundaries, borders, horizons: Boundaries, Arab/American. In C. Camper (Ed.), *Miscegenation blues: Voices of mixed race women.* Toronto, ON: Sister Vision, Black Women and Women of Colour Press.

Martin, J. R. (1976). What should we do with a hidden curriculum when we find one? *Curriculum Inquiry, 6*(2), 149.

———. (1981a). Sophie and Emile: A case study of sex bias in the history of educational thought. *Harvard Educational Review, 51*(3), 357–372.

———. (1981b). The ideal of the educated person. Presidential Address at the Thirty-seventh Annual Meeting of the Philosophy of Education Society, April 1981, Houston, TX. Originally published in *Educational Theory, 31*(2) (1981), pp. 97–109, and in *Philosophy of Education 1981: Proceedings of the 37th Annual Meeting of the Philosophy of Education Society,* copyright 1982 by the Philosophy of Education Society. Reprinted in Martin (1994).

———. (1982a). Excluding women from the educational realm. *Harvard Educational Review, 52*(2), 133–148.

———. (1982b). Sex equality and education. In M. Vetterling-Braggin (Ed.), *"Femininity," "masculinity," and "androgyny."* Totowa, NJ: Littlefield, Adams.

———. (1984). Bringing women into educational thought. *Educational Theory, 34*(4), 341–355.

———. (1985a). Becoming educated: A journey of alienation or integration? *Journal of Education, 167*(3), 71–84.

———. (1985b). *Reclaiming a conversation: The ideal of the educated woman.* New Haven: Yale University Press.

———. (1986). Redefining the educated person: Rethinking the significance of gender. *Educational Researcher, 15.*

———. (1990). The contradiction and challenge of the educated woman. In J. Antler and S. K. Biklen (Eds.), *Changing education: Women as radicals and conservators.* Albany, NY: State University of New York Press.

———. (1992). *The schoolhome.* Cambridge, MA: Harvard University Press.

———. (1994). *Changing the educational landscape: Philosophy, women, and curriculum.* New York and London: Routledge.

Martin, M. (1976). Pedagogical arguments for the preferential hiring and tenuring of women teachers in the university. In C. Gould and M. Wartofsky (Eds.), *Women and philosophy: Toward a theory of liberation.* New York: Capricorn Books.

Martyna, W. (1978). Using and understanding the generic masculine: A social-psychological approach to language and the sexes. *Dissertation Abstracts International, 39*, 3050B.

———. (1983). Beyond the he/man approach: The case for nonsexist language. In B. Thorne, C. Kramarae, and N. Henley (Eds.), *Language, gender, and society* (pp. 25–37). Rowley, MA: Newbury House.

Mayle, P. ([1973] 1980). *Where do I come from?* 15th printing. Secaucus, NJ: Lyle Stuart.

McClung, N. ([1915] 1972). *In times like these.* Toronto, ON: University of Toronto Press.

McCormack, T. (1987). Feminism, women's studies and the new academic freedom. In J. Gaskell and A. McLaren (Eds.), *Women and education: A Canadian perspective.* Calgary, AB: Detselig Enterprises Ltd.

McIntosh, P. (1987). White privilege and male privilege: A personal account of coming to see correspondences through work in women's studies. In A. Minas (Ed.), *Gender basics: Feminist perspectives on women and men* (pp. 30–38). Belmont, CA: Wadsworth.

———. (1992). Feeling like a fraud. Parts I, II. *Working papers: The Stone Center.* Wellesley, MA: Wellesley College.

McLaren, P. (1989). *Life in schools: An introduction to critical pedagogy in the foundations of education.* New York and London, Eng.: Longman.

Mead, M. (1935). *Sex and temperament in three primitive societies.* New York: Morrow.

Mies, M., V. Bennholdt-Thomsen, and C. Von Werlhof. (1988). *Women: The last colony.* London, Eng.: Zed Books Ltd.

Mikkelson, M. D. (1979, Nov./Dec.). Co-ed gym—It's a whole new ballgame. *Journal of Physical Education and Recreation, 63.*

Milburn, G. (1977). Forms of curriculum: Theory and practice. In H. A. Stevenson and J. D. Wilson (Eds.), *Precepts, policy education* (pp. 191–212). London: Alexander, Blake.

Mill, J. S. (1970). The subjection of women. In A. S. Rossi (Ed.), *Essays in sex equality.* Chicago: University of Chicago Press.

———. (1972). *Utilitarianism, on liberty, and considerations on representative government: Selections from Auguste Comte and Positivism.* (Ed. H. B. Acton.) London, Eng.: J. M. Dent and Sons Ltd.

Miller, N. (1985). Mastery, identity and the politics of work. In M. Culley and C. Portuges (Eds.), *Gendered subjects: The dynamics of feminist teaching.* Boston: Routledge.

Millett, K. (1970). *Sexual politics.* Garden City, NY: Doubleday.

———. (1973). Sexual politics: A manifesto for revolution. In A. Koedt, E. Levine, and A. Rapone (Eds.), *Radical feminism.* New York: Quadrangle Books.

Minnich, E. K. (1990). *Transforming knowledge.* Philadelphia: Temple University Press.

Mohanty, C. T., A. Russo, and L. Torres (Eds.). (1991). *Third world women and the politics of feminism.* Bloomington, IN: Indiana University Press.

Money, J., and A. Ehrhardt. (1972). *Man & woman boy & girl.* Baltimore: Johns Hopkins University Press.

Money, J., and P. Tucker. (1975). *Sexual signatures: On being a man or a woman.* Toronto, ON: Little, Brown and Co.

Moraga, C., and G. Anzaldua (Eds.). (1981). *This bridge called my back: Writings by radical women of color.* New York: Kitchen Table Women of Color Press.

Morgan, K. P. (1974). Socialization, social models, and the open education movement: Some philosophical speculations. In D. Nyberg (Ed.), *The philosophy of open education* (pp. 278–314). New York: Routledge and Kegan Paul.

———. (1977). Socialization and the impossibility of human autonomy. Paper presented at the American Philosophical Association, Western Division.

———. (1978, January). Androgyny: Vision or mirage? A philosophical analysis. Paper presented to the Women's Research Colloquium, York and University of Ontario.

———. (1982). Androgyny: A conceptual analysis. *Social Theory and Practice, 8*(3), 245–283.

———. (1987a). The perils and paradoxes of feminist pedagogy. *Resources for Feminist Research/Documentation Sur La Recherche Feministe, Special Issue, 16*(3): Women and Philosophy/Femmes et Philosophie. Maureen Ford, Barbara Houston, Kathryn Morgan, Katherine Pepper-Smith (Eds.). Toronto, ON: Ontario Institute for Studies in Education (1987), pp. 44–52. The original article was reprinted in Debra Shogan (Ed.) (1992), *A Reader in Feminist Ethics.* Toronto, ON: Canadian Scholars Press.

———. (1987b). Women and moral madness. In M. Hanen, and K. Nielsen (Eds.), *Science, morality, and feminist theory.* Calgary, Alberta: University of Calgary Press. Reprinted in L. Code, S. Mullett, and C. Overall (Eds.) (1987), *Feminist perspectives: Philosophical essays in method and morals.* Toronto, ON: University of Toronto Press. And D. Shogan (Ed.) (1992), *A reader in feminist ethics.* Ontario: Canadian Scholars Press.

———. (1991). Gender-blind, gender-free, or gender-sensitive? Contemporary challenges and choices. Keynote Address. Conference: Education in the Nineties. Camasen College, Victoria, British Columbia.

Morgan, K. P., et al. (1996, forthcoming). *A path still not strewn with roses: The report of the Gender Issues Committee, University of Toronto.* Toronto, ON: School of Graduate Studies, University of Toronto.

Morris, J. K. (1993). Interacting oppressions: Teaching social work content on women of color. *Journal of Social Work Education, 29*(1), 99–110.

Morris, R. (1989). Safety problems and sexual harassment on campus. In C. Filteau (Ed.), *Proceedings of a conference on women in graduate studies in Ontario.* Toronto, ON: Ontario Council on Graduate Studies.

Morton, W. L. (1964). *The critical years.* Toronto, ON: McClelland and Stewart.

Moscarello, R., J. Katalin, J. Margittai, and M. Rossi. (1994). Differences in abuse reported by female and male Canadian medical students. *Canadian Medical Association Journal, 150*(3), 357–363.

Moulton, J., G. M. Robinson, and C. Elias. (1978). Psychology in action: Sex bias in language use: "Neutral" pronouns that aren't. *American Psychologist, 33*(11), 1032–1036.

Murdoch, I. (1970). *The sovereignty of good.* London, Eng.: Routledge and Kegan Paul.

Nell, O. (1976). How do we know when opportunities are equal? In C. Gould and M. Wartofsky (Eds.), *Women and philosophy: Toward a theory of liberation.* New York: G. P. Putnam's Sons.

Ng, R. (1989). Sexism, racism, nationalism. *Race, class, gender: Bonds and barriers. Socialist Studies Annual 5.* Toronto, ON: Between the Lines.

———. (1994). Sexism and racism in the university: Analyzing a personal experience. *Canadian Woman Studies: les cahiers de la femme, 14*(2), 41–46.

Nicholson, L. (1983). Affirmative action, education, and social class. *Proceedings of the Philosophy of Education Society.* Normal, IL: Philosophy of Education Society.

———. (1986). *Gender and history.* New York: Columbia University Press.

Nilsen, A. P. (1977). Sexism in children's books, classroom materials. In A. P. Nilsen, H. Bosmajian, H. S. Gershuny, and J. P. Stanley (Eds.), *Sexism and language.* Urbana, IL: National Council of Teachers of English.

Noddings, N. (1984). *Caring: A feminine approach to ethics and moral education.* Berkeley: University of California Press.

———. (1986). Fidelity in teaching, teacher education, and research for teaching. *Harvard Educational Review, 56*(4), 496–510.

———. (1992). *The challenge to care in schools.* New York: Teachers College Press.

Novak, E. R., G. S. Jones, and H. W. Jones. (1970). *Novak's textbook of gynecology.* Baltimore, MD: Williams and Wilkens.

Nunner-Winkler, G. (1984). Two moralities? A critical discussion of an ethic of care and responsibility versus an ethic of rights and justice. In W. Kartines and J. Gerwitz (Eds.), *Morality, moral behavior and moral development.* New York: John Wiley and Sons.

Nyad, D., and C. L. Hogan. (1981). *Basic training for women.* New York: Hogan and Hilltown Press.

O'Connor, A. (1992). Any woman can tell you: Special report. *The Reporter: The Magazine of the Ontario English Catholic Teachers' Association, 18*(2), 16–22.

Oglesby, C. A. (Ed.). (1978). *Women and sport: From myth to reality.* Philadelphia: Lea and Febiger.

Ontario Confederation of University Faculty Associations. (1992). Educational equity. *Canadian Women's Studies, 13*(2). Special title: *Gender equity and institutional change,* 99–102.

Ontario Teachers Federation. (1982). The science education of women in Canada—A statement of concern. *CSSE News, 9*(5), 8.

Orenstein, P. (1994). *Schoolgirls.* New York: Doubleday.

Osborne, M. L. (Ed.). (1979). *Woman in Western thought.* New York: Random House.

Pang, O. (1991). Teaching children about social issues. In C. E. Sleeter (Ed.), *Empowerment through multicultural education.* Albany, NY: State University of New York Press.

Park, R. J. (1974, May). Concerns for the physical education of the female sex from 1675 to 1800 in France, England and Spain. *Research Quarterly AAHPER,* 104–119.

———. (1978). "Embodied selves": The rise and development of concern for physical education, active games and recreation for American women, 1776–1865. *Journal of Sport History, 5*(2), 5–42.

Parrington, G. (1984, July). Radical feminism and the curriculum. *The Salisbury Review.*

Pearson, C., D. Shavlik, and J. Touchton (Eds.). (1989). *Educating the majority: Women challenge tradition in higher education.* New York: Macmillan.

Peirce, C. S. (1931–1958). *Collected papers of Charles Sanders Peirce.* Ed. C. Hartshorne, P. Weiss, and A. Burks. 8 vols. Cambridge, MA: Harvard University Press.

Pelham, A. (1981, October). Family Protection Act: Dear to new right, but unlikely to get out of committees. *Congressional Quarterly, Weekly Report, 39,* p. 1916.

Perkins, D. N. (1981). *The mind's best work.* Cambridge, MA: Harvard University Press.

Peters, R. S. (1965). Education as initiation. In R. D. Archambault (Ed.), *Philosophical analysis and education* (pp. 87–111). London, Eng.: Routledge and Kegan Paul.

———. (1972). Education and the educated man. In R. F. Dearden, P. H. Hirst, and R. S. Peters (Eds.), *A critique of current educational aims.* London, Eng.: Routledge and Kegan Paul.

Pierce, C. (1975). A review essay: Philosophy. *Signs: Journal of Women in Culture and Society, 1*(2), 497–498.

Piercy, M. (1973). *Small changes.* New York: Doubleday.

———. (1982). *Circles on the water: Selected poems of Marge Piercy.* New York: Knopf.

Pleck, J. H., and J. Sawyer (Eds.). (1981). *Men and masculinity.* Boston: MIT Press.

Pratt, M. B. (1984). Identity: Skin, blood, heart. In E. Bulkin, M. B. Pratt, and B. Smith. *Yours in struggle: Three feminist perspectives on anti-Semitism and racism.* Brooklyn, NY: Long Haul Press.

Pyke, S. W. (1991). Gender issues in graduate education. Trevor N. S. Lennam Memorial Lecture. Calgary, AB: University of Calgary.

Ramazanoglu, C. (1987). Sex and violence in academic life or you can keep a good woman down. In J. Hanmer and M. Maynard (Eds.), *Women, violence and social control.* London, Eng.: Macmillan.

Rich, A. (1978). *The dream of a common language: Poems 1974–1977.* New York: W. W. Norton.

———. (1979a). Taking women students seriously. *On lies, secrets, and silence: Selected prose, 1966–1978.* New York: W. W. Norton. Reprinted in M. Culley and C. Portuges (Eds.) (1985), *Gendered subjects: The dynamics of feminist teaching.* New York: Routledge and Kegan Paul.

———. (1979b). Toward a woman-centered university. *On lies, secrets, and silence: Selected prose, 1966–1978.* New York: Routledge and Kegan Paul.

———. (1980). Compulsory heterosexuality and lesbian existence. *Signs: Journal of Women in Culture and Society, 5*(4), 631–660.

———. (1985). Taking women students seriously. In M. Culley and C. Portuges, *Gendered subjects: The dynamics of feminist teaching.* Originally published in *On lies, secrets, and silence* (1979). New York: W. W. Norton.

———. (1986). *Blood, bread, and poetry.* New York: Norton.

Ringelheim, J. (1985). Women and the Holocaust: A reconsideration of research. *Signs: Journal of Women in Culture and Society, 10*(4), 741–761.

Robertson, J. J. (1990). *A capella: Report on Canadian adolescent girls.* Ottawa, ON: Canadian Teachers Federation.

Roe, A. (1952). *The making of a scientist.* New York: Dodd, Mead and Company.

———. (1956). *The psychology of occupations.* New York: John Wiley and Sons.

Rohrbaugh, J. (1979). *Women: Psychology's puzzle.* New York: Basic Books.

Rosaldo, M. Z., and L. Lamphere (Eds.). (1974). *Woman, culture, and society*. Stanford: Stanford University Press.

Rose, H. (1994). *Love, power, and knowledge*. Bloomington, IN: University of Indiana Press.

Rossi, A. (1964, Spring). Equality between the sexes: An immodest proposal. *Daedalus, 93*, 607–652.

———. (1972). Barriers to the career choice of engineering, medicine, or science among American women. In J. M. Bardwick (Ed.), *Readings in the psychology of women* (pp. 72–82). New York: Harper and Row.

Rotkin, K. (1976). The phallacy of our sexual norm. In A. G. Kaplan and J. Bean (Eds.), *Beyond sex-role stereotypes: Readings toward a psychology of androgyny*. Boston: Little, Brown and Co.

Rousseau, J. (1964). *His educational theories selected from Emile, Julie, and other writings*. In R. L. Archer. Woodbury, NY: Barron's Educational Series.

———. (1976). *Emile*. Trans. Barbara Foxley. New York: Dutton.

Rowe, M. P. (1981). Building mentorship frameworks as part of an effective equal opportunity ecology. In J. Farley (Ed.), *Sex discrimination in higher education: Strategies for equality*. Ithaca: New York State School of Industrial and Labor Relations.

Rubin, J., F. Provenzano, and Z. Luria. (1976). The eye of the beholder: Parents' views on sex of newborns. In A. Kaplan and J. Bean (Eds.), *Beyond sex role stereotypes: Readings toward a psychology of androgyny*. Boston: Little, Brown and Co.

Ruddick, S. (1983). Pacifying the forces: Drafting women in the interests of peace. *Signs: Journal of Women in Culture and Society, 8*(3) 471–489.

———. (1984a). Maternal thinking. In J. Treblicot (Ed.), *Mothering: Essays in feminist theory*. Totowa, NJ: Rowman and Allenheld. Originally published in *Feminist Studies, 6*(2), Summer 1980.

———. (1984b). New combinations: Learning from Virginia Woolf. In C. Ascher, L. DeSalvo, and S. Ruddick (Eds.), *Between women* (pp. 137–160). Boston: Beacon Press.

———. (1984c). Preservative love and military destruction: Some reflections on mothering and peace. In J. Treblicot (Ed.), *Mothering: Essays in feminist theory*. Totowa, NJ: Rowman and Allanheld.

———. (1989). *Maternal thinking: Toward a politics of peace*. Boston: Beacon Press.

Ruth, S. (1980). *Issues in feminism: A first course in women's studies*. Boston: Houghton Mifflin.

———. (1981). Methodocracy, misogyny and bad faith: The response of philosophy. In D. Spender. *Men's studies modified: The impact of feminism on the academic disciplines*. New York: Pergamon Press.

Saario, T., C. Jacklin, and J. C. Tittle. (1973). Sex role stereotyping in the public schools. *Harvard Educational Review, 43*(3), 386–416.

Sadker, M., and D. Sadker. (1980). Sexism in teacher education texts. *Harvard Educational Review, 50*(1), 36–45.

———. (1994). *How America's schools cheat girls*. New York: Charles Scribners.

Safilios-Rothschild, C. (1974). *Women and social policy*. Englewood Cliffs, NJ: Prentice-Hall.

Sapon-Shevin, M., and N. Schniedewind. (1991). Cooperative learning and empowering pedagogy. In C. E. Sleeter (Ed.), *Empowerment through multicultural education*. Albany, NY: State University of New York Press.

Sarah, E. (1980). Teachers and students in the classroom: An examination of classroom interaction. In D. Spender and E. Sarah (Eds.), *Learning to lose: Sexism in education*. London, Eng.: Women's Press.

Schafer, R. (1968). *Aspects of internalization*. New York: International Universities Press.

Schmidt, B. C., Jr. (1991). False harmony: The debate over freedom of expression on America's campuses. *Vital Speeches of the Day, 58*(2), 45–48.

Schneider, B. E. (1987). Graduate women, sexual harassment and university polity. *Journal of Higher Education, 58*(1), 46–65.

Schneider, J. W., and S. L. Hacker. (1973). Sex role imagery and the use of the generic "man" in introductory texts: A case study in the sociology of sociology. *American Sociologist, 8*, 12–18.

Schniedewind, N. (1983). Feminist values: Guidelines for teaching methodology in women's studies. In C. Bunch and S. Pollack (Eds.), *Learning our way: Essays in feminist education*. Trumansburg, NY: The Crossing Press.

Schweickart, P. (1990). Reading, teaching, and the ethic of care. In S. L. Gabriel and I. Smithson (Eds.), *Gender in the classroom: Power and pedagogy*. Urbana, IL: University of Illinois Press.

Scott, J. W. (1992). Reply to Joseph A. Shea, Jr.: Letters to the editor. *Change, 7*.

Scully, D. (1980). *Men who control women's health: The miseducation of obstetricians and gynecologists*. Boston: Houghton Mifflin.

Shakeshaft, C. (1987). *Women in educational administration*. Newbury Park/Beverly Hills, CA: Sage.

Shepelak, N. J., D. Ogden, and D. Tobin-Bennett. (1984). The influence of gender labels on the sex typing of imaginary occupations. *Sex roles, 11*(11–12), 983–996.

Sherman, J., and E. Beck. (1979). *The prison of sex: Essays in the sociology of knowledge*. Madison, WI: University of Wisconsin Press.

Shogan, D. (1992). *Feminist ethics*. Toronto, ON: Canadian Scholars Press.

Shulman, A. K. (1969, 1971, 1972). *Memoirs of an Ex-Prom Queen*. Reprinted by permission of Alfred A. Knopf, Inc., and Granada Publishing Limited.

Siedentop, D. (1972). *Physical education: Introductory analysis*. Dubuque, IA: Wm. C. Brown.

Silberman, M. (Ed.). (1971). *The experience of schooling*. New York: Holt, Rinehart and Winston.

Simeone, A. (1987). *Academic women: Working toward equality*. South Hadley, MA: Bergin and Garvey.

Singer, J. (1976). *Androgyny: Toward a new theory of sexuality*. Garden City, NY: Doubleday.

Sleeter, C. E. (Ed.). (1991). *Empowerment through multiculturalism*. Albany, NY: State University of New York Press.

Smith, D. (1978). A peculiar eclipsing: Women's exclusion from man's culture. *The everyday world as problematic: A feminist sociology*. Boston: Northeastern University Press.

———. (1987). An analysis of ideological structures and how women are excluded: Considerations for academic women. *Women and education: A Canadian perspective*. Calgary, AB: Detselig Enterprises Ltd.

————. (n.d.). *A future for women at the University of Toronto: The report of the Ad Hoc Committee on the Status of Women.* Occasional Paper #13. Toronto: Ontario Institute for Studies in Education.

Sniezek, J. A., and C. H. Jazwinski. (1986). Gender bias in English: In search of fair language. *Journal of Applied Social Psychology, 16*(7), 642–662.

Snodgrass, J. (Ed.). (1977). *For men against sexism.* Albion, CA: Times Change Press.

Snook, I. A. (1972a). *Indoctrination and education.* London, Eng.: Routledge and Kegan Paul.

————. (1972b). Indoctrination and moral responsibility. In I. A. Snook (Ed.), *Concepts of indoctrination: Philosophical essays.* London, Eng., and Boston: Routledge and Kegan Paul.

Sommers, C. (1991). The feminist revelation. In E. F. Paul, F. O. Miller Jr., and J. Paul (Eds.), *Ethics, politics, and human nature* (pp. 141–158). London: Basil Blackwell.

Spears, B. (1978). Prologue: The myth. In C. A. Oglesby (Ed.), *Women and sport: From myth to reality* (p. 11). Philadelphia: Lea and Febiger.

Spelman, E. V. (1988). *Inessential woman: Problems of exclusion in feminist thought.* Boston: Beacon Press.

Spender, D. (1980a). Constructing women's silence. *Man made language.* Boston: Routledge and Kegan Paul.

————. (1980b). Talking in class. In D. Spender and E. Sarah (Eds.), *Learning to lose: Sexism in education.* London, Eng.: Women's Press.

————. (1981). Education: The patriarchal paradigm and the response to feminism. In D. Spender (Ed.), *Men's studies modified.* New York: Pergamon Press.

————. (1982). *Invisible women: The schooling scandal.* London, Eng.: Writers and Readers Publishing Cooperative.

————. (1984). Sexism in teacher education. In S. Acker and D. W. Piper (Eds.), *Is higher education fair to women?* (pp. 132–142). Guildford, Surrey: SRHE and NFER-NELSON.

————. (1992). The entry of women to the education of men. In C. Kramarae and D. Spender, *The knowledge explosion* (pp. 235–253). New York and London, Eng.: Teachers College Press.

Spender, D., and E. Sarah (Eds.). (1980). *Learning to lose: Sexism in education.* London, Eng.: Women's Press.

Stacey, J., S. Bercaud, and J. Daniels. (Eds.). (1974). *And Jill came tumbling after: Sexism in American education.* New York: Dell.

Stanworth, M. (1983). *Gender and schooling: A study of sexual division in the classroom.* London, Eng.: Hutchinson.

Stoller, R. J. (1968). *Sex and gender, vol. I: On the development of masculinity and femininity.* London, Eng.: The Hogarth Press.

Sumner, W. (1987). Positive sexism. *Social Philosophy and Policy, 5*(1), 204–222.

Surrey, J. (1991). The self-in-relation: A theory of women's development. In J. Jordan, A. Kaplan, J. B. Miller, I. Stiver, and J. Surrey (Eds.), *Women's growth in connection: Writings from the Stone Center.* New York: The Gilford Press.

Switzer, J. Y. (1990). The impact of generic word choices: An empirical investigation of age- and sex-related differences. *Sex Roles, 22*(1 and 2), 69–82.

Tataka, S. R. (1991). Who is empowering whom? The social construction of empow-erment. In C. E. Sleeter (Ed.), *Empowerment through multicultural education*. Albany, NY: State University of New York Press.

Tatum, B. (1992). Talking about race, learning about racism: The application of racial identity development theory in the classroom. *Harvard Educational Review, 61*(1), 1–23.

Tavris, C. (1983, February). How would your life be different if you'd been a boy? *Redbook, 160*, p. 94.

Taylor, H. ([1851] 1970). The enfranchisement of women. In A. Rossi (Ed.), *Essays on sex equality*. Chicago: University of Chicago Press. Originally printed in *Westminster Review*, July 1851.

Tesfagioris, F. H. W. (1993). In search of a discourse and critique/s that center the art of black women artists. In S. M. James and A. P. A. Busia. *Theorizing black feminism: The visionary pragmatism of black women*. New York: Routledge.

Thiele, B. (1987). Vanishing acts in social and political thought: Tricks of the trade. In C. Pateman and E. Gross (Eds.), *Feminist challenges: Social and political theory*. Boston: Northeastern University Press.

Thompson, A. (1989). Friendship and moral character: Feminist implications for moral education. *Philosophy of Education 1989*. Normal, IL: Philosophy of Edu-cation Society.

Thompson, J. (1983). *Learning liberation: Women's response to men's education*. London, Eng.: Croom Helm.

Thorne, B., and N. Henley (Eds.). (1975). *Language and sex: Difference and domination*. Rowley, MA: Newbury House.

Tittle, C. K., K. McCarthy, and J. F. Steckler. (1974). *Women and literature and testing practices*. Princeton: Educational Testing Service in collaboration with the Asso-ciation for Measurement and Evaluation in Guidance.

Todd, J. (1988). *Feminist literary history*. New York: Routledge.

Treblicot, J. (1977). Sex roles: The argument from nature. In J. English. *Sex equality* (pp. 121–129). Englewood Cliffs, NJ: Prentice-Hall.

Trofimenkoff, S. M. (1989). A woman administrator looks at life and love in the grad-uate school. In C. Filteau (Ed.), *Women in graduate studies in Ontario* (p. 115). Toronto, ON: Ontario Council on Graduate Studies.

Trofimenkoff, S. M., and A. Prentice. (Eds.). (1977). *The neglected majority: Essays in Canadian women's history*. Toronto, ON: McClelland and Stewart.

United States Commission on Civil Rights. (1976). *A guide to federal laws and regula-tions prohibiting sex discrimination*. Washington, DC: U.S. Government Printing Office Clearinghouse Publication 46; Rev. 1976.

Vallance, E. (1973–1974). Hiding the hidden curriculum. *Curriculum Theory and Network, 4*(1).

Van de Wetering, J. E. (1991). Political correctness: The insult and the injury. *Vital Speeches of the Day, 58*(4), 100–103.

Varpolatti, A. (1986). Personal communication. London, ON: University of Western Ontario.

Vertinsky, P. (1979). Sexual equality and the legacy of Catherine Beecher. *Journal of Sport History, 6*(1), 38–49.

Walker, A. (1983). Saving the life that is your own: The importance of models in the artist's life. *In search of our mother's garden*. San Diego: Harcourt, Brace, Jovanovich.

Walker, G. L., L. Erickson, and L. Woolsey. (1985). Sexual harassment: Ethical research and clinical implications in the academic setting. *International Journal of Women's Studies 8*(4), 424–433.

Walker, J. (1983). In a different voice: Cryptoseparatist analysis of female moral development. *Social Research, 50,* 3.

Walkerdine, V. (1983). Progressive pedagogy and political struggle. *Screen, 27*(5), 54–60. Reprinted in Luke and Gore (1992).

Warren, M. W. (1980). *The nature of woman: An encyclopedia and guide to the literature.* Inverness, CA: Edgepress.

———. (1983). Justice and gender in school sports. In B. C. Postow (Ed.), *Women, philosophy, and sport: A collection of new essays* (chapter 1). Metuchen, NJ, and London, Eng.: Scarecrow Press.

Washington, M. H. (1985). How racial differences helped us discover our common ground. In M. Culley and C. Portuges (Eds.), *Gendered subjects: The dynamics of feminist teaching* (pp. 221–229). Boston: Routledge.

Wasserstrom, R. A. (1977). Racism, sexism, and preferential treatment: An approach to the topics. *UCLA Law Review,* 581–615. Reprinted in S. Bishop and M. Weinzweig (Eds.), *Philosophy and women.* Belmont, CA: Wadsworth.

———. (1979). Racism and sexism. In S. Bishop and M. Weinzweig (Eds.), *Philosophy and women* (pp. 5–20). Belmont, CA: Wadsworth Publishing Company.

Weedon, C. (1987). *Feminist practice and poststructuralist theory.* Oxford, Eng.: Blackwell.

Weil, S. (1951). Reflections of the right use of school studies with a view to the love of God. *Waiting for God.* New York: G. Putnam's.

Weiler, K. (1988). *Women teaching for change: Gender, class and power.* New York: Bergin and Garvey.

Weis, L. (1991). Disempowering white working class females: The role of the high school. In C. Sleeter (Ed.), *Empowerment through multicultural education* (pp. 95–121). Albany, NY: State University of New York Press.

Weitz, S. (1979). *Sex roles.* New York: Oxford University Press.

Weitzman, L. J. (1979). *Sex role socialization.* Palo Alto, CA: Mayfield.

West, A. G. (Ed.). (1973). *Report on sex bias in the public schools.* New York: Education Committee, NOW.

West, C. (1993). The dilemma of the black intellectual. *Keeping faith: Philosophy and race in America.* New York: Routledge.

Wiirtenberg, J., S. Klein, B. Richardson, and V. Thomas. (1981). Sex equity in American education. *Educational Leadership, 38*(4), 311–319.

Williams, B. (1985). *Ethics and the limits of philosophy.* Cambridge, MA: Harvard University Press.

Williams, P. J. (1991). The brass ring and the deep blue sea. *The alchemy of race and rights: Diary of a law professor.* Cambridge, MA: Harvard University Press.

Wilson, E., and S. H. Ng. (1988). Sex bias in visual images evoked by generics: A New Zealand study. *Sex Roles, 18*(3/4), 159–168.

Wilson, L. C. (1978). Teachers' inclusion of males and females in generic nouns. *Research in the Teaching of English: Official Bulletin of the National Council of Teachers of English, 12*(2), 155–161.

Wollstonecraft, M. ([1792] 1975/1988). *A vindication of the rights of women,* 2nd ed. New York: Norton.

Woolf, V. (1938). *Three guineas.* New York: Harcourt Brace.

Wylie, A., K. Okruhlik, S. Morton, and L. Thielen-Wilson. (1990). Philosophical feminism: A bibliographic guide to critiques of science. *Resources for Feminist Research: Documentation sur la Recherche Feministe, 19*(2). Toronto, ON: Ontario Institute for Studies in Education.

Young, I. (1980). Throwing like a girl: A phenomenology of feminine body comportment motility and spatiality. *Human Studies 3,* 137–156.

———. (1983). Is male gender identity the cause of male domination? In J. Treblicot (Ed.), *Mothering: Essays in feminist theory.* Totowa, NJ: Rowman and Allenheld.

Young, M. F. D. (Ed.). (1971). *Knowledge and control.* New York: Collier-Macmillan.

Young-Bruehl, E. (1987). The education of women as philosophers. *Signs: Journal of Women in Culture and Society, 12*(2), 207–221.

Zimmerman, D. H., and C. West. (1974). Sex roles, interruptions and silences in conversations. In B. Thorne and N. Henley (Eds.), *Language and sex: Difference and dominance.* Rowley, MA: Newbury House.

About the Book and Authors

In this innovative book, four prominent philosophers of education introduce readers to the central debates about the role of gender in educational practice, policymaking, and theory. More a record of a continuing conversation than a statement of a fixed point of view, *The Gender Question in Education* enables students and practicing teachers to think through to their own conclusions and to add their own voices to the conversation.

Throughout, the authors emphasize the value of a gender-sensitive perspective on educational issues and the relevance of an ethics of care for educational practice. Among the topics discussed are feminist pedagogy, gender freedom in public education, androgyny, sex education, multiculturalism, the inclusive curriculum, and the educational significance of an ethics of care.

The multiauthor, dialogic structure of this book provides unusual breadth and cohesiveness as well as a forum for the exchange of ideas, making it both an ideal introduction to gender analysis in education and a model for more advanced students of gender issues.

Ann Diller and **Barbara Houston** are professors of education at the University of New Hampshire. **Kathryn Pauly Morgan** is professor of philosophy, women's studies, and bioethics at the University of Toronto. **Maryann Ayim** is professor of education at the University of Western Ontario.

Index

Affirmative action, 206
Agonito, R., 110
Aisenberg, N., 109, 126, 127, 131–132
Alcoff, L., 80, 83, 84(n4)
Allen, J., 103(n2), 104(n6)
American Association of University
    Women, x
Androcentric solipsism, 114–116,
    121(n7)
Androgyny, 3, 67–73
    assessment tool, 70–71
    defined, 67–68
Anzaldua, G., 106, 109, 120(n2), 128
Aquinas, T., 125
Aristotle, 33, 104(n11), 125
Ashenden, R., W., 59–60
Attentive love, 163
Atwood, M., 146–147
Auerbach, J., 103(n2)
Axelrod, R., 162
Axes of privilege, 4, 105–107, 120(n2)
Ayim, M., xiii, 2, 5–6, 9, 32, 43, 53, 81,
    83, 85(n9), 110, 199, 211–216

Backhouse, C., 111, 118
Baier, A. 93, 104(n4)
Baker, R., 171
Banks, J., 134
Bardwick, J.M., 67, 73
Barker-Benfield, G. J., 175
Bartky, S., 146
Barton, L., 133(n6)
Bazin, N. T., 67, 69, 74(n9)
Bean, J., 198(n23)
Beardsley, E., 74(n10)
Beauvoir, S. d., 111, 113, 127
Belenky, M. F., 138
Bem, S. L., 43, 71, 74(n9)
Bem Sex-Role Inventory (BSRI), 71
Benhabib, S., 103(n3), 133(n8)

Bennett, W., 114, 121(n4)
Bennholdt-Thomsen, V., 111
Bercaud, S., 52, 197(n18)
Berlin, P., 196(n9)
Bernstein, B., 108, 126, 129, 133(n6)
Bishop, S., 296(n7)
Black, N., 114
Black studies courses, 204
Block, J. H., 68
Bloom, A., 114, 121(n4), 203–205, 207,
    209, 210–218
Blum, L., 103(n2), 104(nn6, 7)
Bourdieu, P., 108, 126, 129, 133(n6)
Bowles, S., 108
Boxill, B., 62(n3), 196(n6), 197(n16)
Brammer, R., 173
Brant, B., 117
Brewer, R. M., 128
Briskin, L., 132(n1)
Bronowski, J., 109
Broughton, J., 85(n4), 104(n5)
Broverman, D. M., 73(n7)
Broverman, I. K., 73(n7)
Brown, C., 30
Burbules, N., 126
Butler, J., 81, 82, 85(n7), 134
Byrne, E. M., 10

Cammaert, L., 118
Camper, C., 134
Campus speech codes, 5–6
Canada
    antidiscrimination legislation, 29(n5)
    sexism, 30(n11)
    University of Toronto, 118–119
Cannon, L. W., 105
Caplan, P., 130
Card, C., 85(n4), 103(n2), 104(n6)
Caring, ethics of care, 89–94
Caring apprenticeships, 99

Carmichael, C., 9
Carty, L., 109, 113, 134
Chamberlin, M., 129, 134
Chesler, P., 67
Chodorow, N., 85(n8), 128, 151, 152
Clark, J., 118
Clark, M., x
Clarke, C., 134
Clarkson, P. S., 73(n7)
Clausen, J., 129
Cline, S., 207, 213
Clitoridectomy, 176, 212
Cobb, R., 197(n17)
Cochrane, J., 182
Coeducation
   myth, 116–117
   physical education, 181–184, 197(n16)
Co-enjoyment, pluralism of, 166–167
Coexistence, pluralism of, 161–163
Co-exploring, pluralism of, 163–166
Cole, S. G., 133(n7)
Collins, P. H., 109, 113, 128
Colonization, girls and women in
   education, 112–113
Communication, speech patterns, 52–54,
   56, 112
Communities of inquiry, 141
Community of support, 141
Consequences analysis, sexism, 16–18, 44
Constantinople, A., 43, 71
Content analysis, sexism, 10–12
Cook, R., 30
Cooperation, pluralism of, 161–163
Core gender identity, 81, 83
Cornell, D., 83, 84, 85(n8)
Courtenay-Hall, P., 130
Criteria analysis, sexism, 18
Critical nurturance, paradox, 123,
   127–129, 135–143
Culley, M., 128, 132(n1), 133(n2), 146,
   147, 148
Cultural values
   and androgyny, 69
   gender roles necessary for replication,
   37–39
Curriculum, universities, 209–213

Dagg, A. I., 118
Daly, M., 74(n9), 104(n6)
Daniels, J., 52, 197(n18)
Danziger, K., 133(n4)
Darwin, C., 125
David, D., 173
Davies, B., 75–80, 81, 82, 84(nn1, 3),
   85(nn6, 10)
Davis, D. L., 15, 16
Day, D., 118
Deconstruction, defined, 84–85(n4)
Deconstructionist approach, 75–84
Dehli, K., 113
Delamont, S., 9–10
Delpit, L. C., 163, 164–165
Dewey, J., 167
Diller, A., xii, 52, 56, 63, 89, 104(nn9,
   12), 135, 158, 179
Dinnerstein, D., 128
Discrimination, U.S. Civil Rights
   Commission definition, 13
Dittmar, L., 155
Diversity, pluralism, 161–168
Domain ethic, ethics of care, 94–96
Double standard, 121(n6), 122(n8), 172
Douvan, E., 67
Dowsett, G. W., 59–60
Draper, R., 211
Dress code, 66
D'souza, D., 200–213
Dulberg, L., 57, 197(n14)
Dziech, B. W., 118

Easlea, B., 109, 110
Eberhart, O. M. Y., 210
Education
   androcentric solipsism, 114–116,
   121(n7)
   androgynous, 67–73
   ethics of care, 98–102
   feminist, 146
   gender-free, 32, 34–48
   gender-sensitive, 32, 60–62
   myths, 113–120
   pluralism, 5, 161–168
   power in, 108–109
   single sex classrooms, 57, 60

See also Sexism in education;
Universities
Educational equity, 120(n1)
Educational power, 108–109
Ehrenreich, B., 175
Ehrhardt, A., 81, 194
Eichler, M., 62(n1), 84(n2), 106, 109,
114, 120(n1), 121(n6), 128, 196(n3),
198(n23)
Eisenhart, M. A., 112
Eitzen, S. D., 62(n5), 196(n3)
Elgin, S. D., 138
Eliade, M., 74(n9)
Elias, C., 210
Ellsworth, E., 128
English, E., 175
English, J., 49(n9), 191, 196(n4)
Engrossment, 161, 163
ethics of care, 91
Equal educational opportunities, 52,
117–120
Esland, G. M., 108, 126
Ethics of care, 3–4, 89–92, 102–103
criticisms, 94–98
as domain ethic, 94–96
in education, 98–102
engrossment, 91
feminist perspective, 96–98
motivational displacement, 92–93
primacy of the particular, 92
rational ontology, 90–91

Factual solipsism, 114
Falk, W. D., 19
Family Protection Act, 34, 37, 198(n20)
Farrel, W., 173
Fasteau, M., 173
Feinberg, W., 168(n2)
Felshin, J., 196(n9), 197(n16)
Feminine ethics. *See* Ethics of care
Feminist perspective
critical nurturance, 4, 123, 124–132,
135–143
deconstructionist approach, 75–84
education, 146
ethics of care, 96–98
gender-free education, 32, 41–48

gender-sensitive education, 32,
50–62
role model paradox, 123, 144–158
sexuality as phallocentric, 170–178
sexual politics, 49(n6)
Feminist teachers, 146
Finn, J., 57, 111, 197(n14)
Fiol-Matta, L., 128, 134
Fischel, A., 62(n5), 196(n3)
Fisher, B., 147, 153, 155–158
Fitzgerald, L. F., 118
Ford, M., 132
Foucault, M., 106, 126, 133(n6)
Fowlkes, D., 128
Franzosa, S., 169(n3)
Frazier, N., 10, 52, 65, 67, 73(nn4, 7),
197(n18)
Freedom of speech, liberal position,
201–209
Freeman, A., 6,7 69, 74(n9)
Freeman, B. C., 197(n18)
Freire, P., 111, 121(n5)
French, J., 207
French, P., 207
Friedman, S. S., 132(n1)
Frieze, I., 198(n23)
Frye, M., 11, 29, 48–49(n3), 49(n8),
73(n2), 101, 102, 103(n2), 104(n6),
163
Fulkerson, D. C., 210

Gaskell, J., 109, 114, 116, 117
Gender
as access barrier, 41–48, 116–117
communication patterns, 52–54, 56
core gender identity, 81, 83
deconstructionist approach, 75–84
defined, 62(n1), 77, 84(n2)
ethics of caring, 100–101, 102
institutionalized, 43–49
nominalism, 80
as structuring process, 59, 75
Gender bias, 51–54
gender valuation, 59–60
perceived value, 54, 55–56
See also Sexism; Sexism in education
Gender blindness, 48(n1), 62(n2)

Gender freedom
    as cure for sexism, 45–46
    differentiated from gender sensitivity,
        60–61
    meaning of term, 50
Gender-free education
    feminist perspective for, 32, 41–48
    traditional perspective against, 32,
        34–40
Gender roles, 194
    patriarchal society, 42–43
    traditional perspective, 33–40
Gender-sensitive education, 32, 60–62
Gender-sensitive perspective, 48, 60–61
Gender valuation, 59–60
Genitals, sex education, 170–178
Gerber, E., 196(n9), 197(n16)
Gilligan, C., 3, 78–80, 89, 103, 103(n2),
    125, 163, 168(n1)
Gilman, C. P., 49(n6), 126, 133(n5)
Gintis, H., 108
Giovanni, N., 167
Giroux, H., 131
Glasser, W., 137, 143(n1)
Gold, Y., 118
Goldberg, S., 33, 35, 38, 39
Gore, J., 121(n3), 126
Gornick, V., 25, 197(n18)
Gould, C., 196(n7)
Gould, L., 41
Graham, A., 210
Greene, M., 141
Griffin, P. S., 52, 183, 191–192, 197(n13)
Grimshaw, J., 103(n2)
Gross, B., 196(n7)
Gutmann, A., 124

Hacker, S. L., 210
Hall, R. M., x, 111, 118
Halley, A., 133
Hamilton, M. C., 210
Harassment, 118–119, 122(n9)
Harrington, M., 109, 126, 127, 131–132
Harris, R., 111, 118
Harrison, L., 210
Hartman, J., 128
Harvard Educational Review

Heald, S., 113
Hegel, G., 125
Heide, W. S., 190
Heilbrun, C. G., 74(n9)
Held, V., 95–96, 103(n2), 126
Henley, N., 49(n4), 192
Henley, N. M., 53, 210
Hentoff, N., 200, 213
Heterosexuality, as norm, 176–177
Hidden curriculum, 66–67
    physical education, 186–194, 197(n19)
Hill, S., 74(n12)
Hoagland, S. L., 103(n2), 104(n6), 163
Hoffman, A., 182
Holland, D. C., 112
Homosexuality, 176–177
hooks, b., 108, 109, 113, 126, 129–130,
    131
Hosken, F., 176
Houston, B., xii, 2, 4–5, 9, 43, 50, 52, 56,
    75, 81, 83, 85(nn4, 9), 86(n10),
    103(n2), 104(nn6, 12), 132, 143(n3),
    144, 169(n3), 179, 208
Howard, J. A., 210
Hrdy, C. B., 110
Hudson, J., 196(n11)
Hull, G. T., 113
Hurston, Z. N., 153
Hyde, J. S., 210

Industrial arts classes, sexism, 24, 26–27
Intellectual curiosity, gender bias,
    111–112
Intentional analysis, sexism, 10–12, 43,
    44
Irvine, J., 175

Jacklin, C., 62(n5), 196(n3)
Jackson, P., 66
Jaggar, A., 49(nn5, 9), 196(n5)
James, S. M., 126, 128, 133(n5)
James, W., 141, 161–162, 166
Jazwinski, C. H., 210
Jeffcoate, T., 172
Johnson, E. P., 117
Johnson, P., 126
Jointly constituted community, 141–142

Jones, G. S., 172
Jones, H. W., 172
Jordan, J., 144–146, 205
Julty, S., 173

Kagan, J., 85(n9), 150, 151
Kant, I., 104(n11), 125
Kaplan, A. G., 74(n9), 198(n23)
Katalin, J., 118
Kelly, L., 119
Kennard, J., A., 179, 180
Kenway, J., 111
Kessler, D. J., 59–60, 84(n3)
Ketchum, S. A., 47
Key, M. R., 53
Kimberly-Clark pamphlet, 170–172,
    174–176
Kincaid, P., 182
Kittay, E., 104(n3)
Kohlberg, L., 78, 104(n5)
Kolenda, K., 211
Koveski, J., 30
Kramarae, C., 128, 146
Kramer, H., 110
Kristeva, J., 78–79, 80, 83, 85(nn6, 8)

Lamphere, L., 69
Larkin, J., 118
Lather, P., 124
Laurence, M. K., 131, 154, 158
Laviqueur, J., 57
Leach, M., 75, 76
Lepley, P., 197(n17)
Lerner, G., 29–227
Levin, M., 40(n2)
Levine, C., 104(n5)
Lewis, M., 112
Lewis, R., 173
Lewontin, R., 110
Libby, W., 109
Liberal education, 209
Literature, gender bias, 115
Lloyd G., 110
Lowe, M., 110
Lucas, J. R., 33, 39
Lugones, M., 106, 109, 120(n2), 141,
    161, 164, 166

Luke, C., 120(n3)
Luria, Z., 196(n10)

Maccoby, E., 67, 194
MacDonald, M., 112
MacKay, D. G., 210
MacKinnon, C., 106, 114, 120(n1)
MacNeil, R., 200, 201–202, 206, 208,
    211
Mahoney, P., 52, 118
Mahowald, M., 110
Mahtani, M., 117
Mainardi, P., 17
Majaj, L. S., 106, 117, 120(n2)
Male supremacy, myth, 112–113,
    113–116
Margittai, J., 118
Martin, J. R., x, 1–2, 48(n1), 51, 60, 61,
    62(n7), 63(n4), 100, 104(n9), 109,
    111, 114, 121(n4), 134, 143(n3),
    169(n3), 184–
185, 190, 197(n19), 208
Martin, M., 130
Martyna, W., 210
Masturbation, 175
Mayle, P., 173, 175
McCarthy, K., 210
McClung, N., 126, 133(n5)
McClure, C., 128
McCormack, T., 122(n10)
McIntosh, P., 109, 117
McKenna, K., 84(n3), 113
McLaren, A., 109, 114, 116, 117, 126
Mead, M., 69
Messer-Davidow, E., 128
Meyers, D., 104(n3)
Michell, G., 63, 111, 118
Mies, M., 111
Mikkelson, M. D., 183
Milburn, G., 209
Mill, John Stuart, 46, 49(n6), 73(n8),
    121(nn6, 8), 203–204, 214(n1)
Miller, N., 147
Millett, K., 23, 42, 197(n18)
Minnich, E. K., 109, 114, 128
Modra, H., 111
Mohanty, C. T., 128

Money, J., 36, 81, 194
Moraga, C., 106, 120(n2)
Morality, ethics of care, 89–103
Moral politics, sex education, 170–178
Moran, B., 197(n18), 23
Morgan, K. P., xii, 3, 4, 5, 41, 49(n7), 64,
    105, 121(n6), 124, 130, 132,
    133(nn3, 4), 135–136, 139, 140,
    143(n3), 146, 148–
149, 150, 152, 153, 157, 170
Morris, J. K., 118, 134
Morton, W. L., 30
Moscarello, R., 118
Motivational displacement, ethics of
    care, 92–93
Moulton, J., 210
Multiculturalism
    pluralism, 161–168
    role models, 133(n8)
    university curriculum, 211–212
Murdoch, I., 163
Myths, 4, 113
    coeducation myth, 116–117
    equal opportunity myth, 117–120
    universality myth, 113–116, 121(n5)

Nelson, B., 143(n3), 169(n3)
Ng, R., 109
Ng, S. H., 210
Nicholson, L., 43, 85(n8), 108
Nilsen, A. P., 66, 73(nn5, 6)
Noddings, N., 3, 90–103, 103(nn1, 2),
    104(nn8, 10, 12), 125, 161,
    163–165, 168(n1)
Nominalism, 80
Non-traditional classes, sexism, 24,
    26–27
Normative solipsism, 121(n7), 114
Novak, E. R., 172
Novogrodsky, M., 109, 114, 116, 117
Nunner-Winkler, G., 104(n5)
Nurturance. *See* Critical nurturance

O'Connor, A., 202
Ogden, D., 210
Oglesby, C. A., 196(n11)
Orenstein, P., x

Ormerod, M., 118
Osborne, M. L., 49(n8)
Overgenderization, 104(n9)

Pang, O., 130
Paradoxes, feminist teachers, 127–132,
    135–143, 144–158
Park, R. J., 195(n1)
Parrington, G., 63
Passero, R. N., 210
Patriarchical society, 42–43
    myths, 113–120
Pearson, C. S., 109, 114
Peirce, C. S., 214
Pelham, A., 34, 198(n20)
Pepper-Smith, K., 132
Perceived value, gender bias, 54, 55–56
Perkins, D. N., 165
Peters, R. S., 30, 121(n4), 212–213
Philosophy, gender bias, 110–111
Physical education
    gender-free strategy, 51–52
    gender issues, 5, 40, 51–52
    gender-sensitive perspective,
        179–198
    hidden curriculum, 186–194, 197(n19)
    sex-integrated, pro and con, 181–184,
        197(n16)
    team sports, 24, 25–26, 27–28, 52, 57
Physical sciences, gender bias, 109–110
Piercy, M., 112, 156–157, 192–193
Plato, ix, 104(n11), 211
Platonic universalism, 115–116
Pleck, J. H., 173
Pluralism, 5, 161–168
Political correctness, 5–6, 199–214
Politics of identity, 84, 86(n12)
Portuges, C., 128
Pottker, S. J., 62(n5), 196(n3)
Power, educational power, 108–109,
    126–132
Pratt, M. B., 134
Prentice, A., 24, 29
Primacy of the particular, ethics of care,
    92
Provenzano, F., 196(n10)
Public education. *See* Education

Racism, "color-blindness," 206028
Racist language, 200
Radden, J., 132(n3), 169(n3)
Ramazanoglu, C., 119
Rational ontology, ethics of care, 90–91
Reis, J., 57, 197(n14)
Rich, A., 86(n12), 116, 117, 127, 168, 176, 178(n5), 198(n22)
Ringelheim, 85(nn4, 5), 103(n2), 104(n6)
Robinson, G. M., 210
Roe, A., 211
Rohrbaugh, J., 197(n15)
Role models, 4–5, 133
  multiculturalism, 133(n8)
  paradox, 123
Rosaldo, M. Z., 69
Rose, H., 123
Rosencrantz, P. S., 73(n7)
Rossi, A., 73, 74(n9)
Rossi, M., 118
Rotkin, K., 173, 178(n2)
Rousseau, J., 33, 64, 149
Rowe, M. P., 130
Rubin, J., 196(n10)
Ruddick, S., 85(n6), 103, 103(n2), 126, 133(n5), 149–154, 163, 168(n1)
Rule, J., 133(n7)
Russo, A., 128
Ruth, S., 12, 22–23, 111

Saario, T., 62(n5), 196(n3)
Sadker, D., 109, 118
Sadker, M., 10–11, 52, 65, 67, 73(nn4, 7), 109, 118, 197(n18)
Safilios-Rothschild, C., 73(nn1, 3)
Sandler, B. R., x, 111, 118
Sarah, E., x, 52, 53, 55
Sawyer, J., 173
Schafer, R., 150
Schmidt, B. D., Jr., 205, 208
Schneider, J. W, 210
Schniedewind, N., 124
School administrators, 66–67, 109
Schwieckart, P., 128
Scott, J. W., 206
Scott, P. B., 113

Scully, D., 175
Self-image, perceived value, 54, 55–56
Sex, defined, 62(n1), 77, 84(n2)
Sex education, 5, 170–178
Sex equity
  abolition of gender to ensure, 82
  physical education, 180
Sex integrated physical education, arguments, 181–184
Sexism, 2, 4, 5
  analysis, 9–10, 18–23, 73(n2)
  androgyny as cure for, 67–73
  as axis of privilege, 105–107, 113
  feminist perspective, 42–44
  freedom of speech and political correctness, 199–214
  gender-free society as cure for, 45–46
  See also Gender bias
Sexism in education, 40
  androcentric solipsism, 114–116, 121(n7)
  classroom recognition, 44
  colonization of girls and women, 112–113
  communication patterns, 52–54, 56, 112
  curriculum, 109
  double standard, 121(n6), 122(n8)
  dress code, 66
  gender of teachers and principals, 66–67
  harassment, 118–119, 122(n9)
  institutionalized, 64–67
  intellectual curiosity, 111–112
  literature study, 115
  myths, 113–120
  non-traditional courses, 24, 26–27
  philosophy, 110–111
  physical education, 5, 40, 51–52
  physical sciences, 109–110
  prohibitory messages, 67
  punishment, 24, 26
  rational objective knowledge valued over subjective intuitive knowledge, 44, 109–110, 115–116
  sex education, 170–178

stereotyped teaching materials, 24–25, 65–66
student-student interactions, 52–54
teacher interaction with students, 44, 52, 55, 56, 67
teachers' behavior, 55, 56–57
team sports, 24, 25–26, 27–28, 52, 57
textbooks, 24–25, 65–66, 109
Sexist language, 200
Sex segregation, 57, 60, 181
  physical education, 183
Sexuality
  anatomical description, 173–174
  arousal, 172
  clitoridectomy, 176, 212
  homosexuality, 176–177
  intercourse, 172, 174–175
  male initiation, 171
  mutuality, 172
Sexual politics, feminism, 49(n6)
Shakeshaft, C., 211
Shavlik, D., 109, 114
Shepelak, N. J., 210
Shogan, D., 132, 169(n3)
Shulman, A. K., 186–188
Siedentop, D., 196(n2), 197(n17)
Silberman, M., 66
Simon, R., 112
Singer, J., 74(n9)
Single sex classrooms, 57, 60
Smith, J. F., 143(n3), 169(n3)
Smith, B., 113
Smith, D., 111, 114, 119, 126–235
Sniezek, J. A., 210
Snodgrass, J., 73
Snook, I. A., 10, 17
Socialization, 133(nn4, 6), 198(n23)
Solipsism, 114–116
Sommers, C., 203
Spears, B., 179
Speech
  political correctness, 199–214
  racist and sexist language, 200
Speech codes, 5–6, 202
Speech patterns, 52–54, 56, 112
Spelman, E. V., 106, 10, 120(n2), 141, 162, 164, 166, 167

Spender, D., x, 49(n4), 52–57, 109, 128, 146, 207, 213
Sports. *See* Physical education
Sprenger, J., 110
Stacey, J., 52, 197(n18)
Stanton, E. C., 197(n12)
Stanworth, M., 52, 55, 56
Steckler, J. F., 210
Stereotypes, in education, 24, 25
Stoller, R. J., 81
Structuring process, gender, 59
Sumner, W., 130
Surrey, J., 110
Switzer, J. Y., 210

Tatum, B., 134
Tavris, C., 54
Taylor, H., 27
Teachers
  behavior, 55, 56–57, 67
  criteria, 67
  feminist teachers, 125–132, 146
  interaction with students, 44, 52, 55, 56
  paradox of critical nurturance, 123, 127–129, 135–143
  paradox of role models, 123, 129–132, 144–158
  textbooks for, 30(n10)
Team sports, 24, 25–26, 27–28, 52, 57
  See also Physical education
Textbooks
  gynecology, 172
  history, 24
  mathematics, 65
  reading, 24
  sex education, 170–178
  sexist, 24–25, 64–66
  spelling, 65–66
  stereotyped, 24–25, 64–66, 109
  for teachers, 30(n10)
Thiele, B., 114
Thompson, A., 143(n3), 169(n3)
Thompson, J., 116
Thompson, P., 118
Thorne, B., 49(n4), 53
Thurschwell, A., 83, 84, 85(n8)

Tittle, C. K., 62(n5), 196(n3), 210
Tobin-Bennett, D., 210
Todd, J., 80–81
Torres, L., 128
Touchton, J., 109, 114
Treblicot, J., 39, 49(n9)
Treichler, P., 146
Trofimenkoff, S. M., 24, 29, 120
Tucker, P., 36, 81

Universalism, Platonic, 115–116
Universality, myth, 113–116
Universities
  curriculum, 209–213
  gender bias, 109–120
  as meritocracies, 205–207
  race neutrality, 204–205

Vallance, E., 197(n19)
Van de Wetering, J. E., 200–201, 208, 213
Varpolatti, A., 138–139
Vertinsky, P., 195(n1)
Vogel, S. R., 73(n7)
Von Werlhof, C., 111

Walker, A., 115, 153
Walker, J., 85(n4)
Walkerdine, V., 124
Walters, R. H., 129

Warren, M. A., 9, 196(n8)
Wartofsky, M., 196(n7)
Washington, M. H., 154–155
Wasserstrom, R. A., 35, 42, 62(nn2, 3), 130, 196(n6), 208
Weedon, C., 85(n8)
Weil, S., 166
Weiler, K., 112, 125
Weiner, L., 118
Weinzweig, M., 196(n7)
Weis, L., 130
Weitz, S., 198(n23)
Weitzman, L. J., 198(n23)
Weitzman, L. M., 118
West, C., 65, 109
Williams, B., 93
Williams, P. J., 117
Wilmore, J., 181
Wilson, E., 210
Wilson, L. C., 210
Wollstonecraft, M., 127
Women's studies, 30(n12)
Woolf, V., 116, 149–150, 151, 152, 154, 158
Wylie, A., 111, 118
Wyrick, W., 196(n9)

Young-Bruehl, E., 152
Young, I., 85(n8), 193
Young, M. F. D., 109, 129, 133(n6)